Early Modern Women's Life-Writing and English Law

Edinburgh Critical Studies in Renaissance Culture

Series Editors: Lorna Hutson, Katherine Ibbett, Joe Moshenska and Kathryn Murphy

Selected titles available in the series

Legal Reform in English Renaissance Literature
Virginia Lee Strain

The Origins of English Revenge Tragedy
George Oppitz-Trotman

Crime and Consequence in Early Modern Literature and Law
Judith Hudson

Shakespeare's Golden Ages: Resisting Nostalgia in Elizabethan Drama
Kristine Johanson

Refusing to Behave in Early Modern Literature
Laura Seymour

Shakespeare's Virtuous Theatre: Power, Capacity and the Good
Kent Lehnhof, Julia Reinhard Lupton and Carolyn Sale

Writing Europe in Renaissance France: Travels in Reality and Imagination
Niall Oddy

Epistolary Courtiership and Dramatic Letters: Thomas Overbury and the Jacobean Playhouse
Jackie Watson

Writing Doubt in Montaigne's Essais*: Thinking Relationally with Seneca and Plutarch*
Luke O'Sullivan

The Ecology of Dress in Shakespeare and his Contemporaries
Sophie Chiari and Anne-Marie Miller-Blaise

Shakespeare High and Low: Character, Audience, Career
Jeffrey Knapp

Shakespeare, the Sea and the Stage
Peter Womack

The English Baroque in Early Modern Literature
Robert Hudson Vincent

Early Modern Women's Life-Writing and English Law
Lotte Fikkers

For a full list of titles in the series, visit the Edinburgh Critical Studies in Renaissance Culture website at www.edinburghuniversitypress.com/series/ECSRC

Early Modern Women's Life-Writing and English Law

Lotte Fikkers

EDINBURGH
University Press

Edinburgh University Press is one of the leading university presses in the UK. We publish academic books and journals in our selected subject areas across the humanities and social sciences, combining cutting-edge scholarship with high editorial and production values to produce academic works of lasting importance. For more information visit our website: edinburghuniversitypress.com

Edinburgh University Press Ltd
13 Infirmary Street
Edinburgh EH1 1LT

First published in hardback by Edinburgh University Press 2025

Typeset in 10.5/13 Adobe Sabon by
IDSUK (DataConnection) Ltd, and
printed and bound by CPI Group (UK) Ltd,
Croydon, CR0 4YY

A CIP record for this book is available from the British Library

ISBN 978-1-3995-3813-8 (hardback)
ISBN 978-1-3995-3814-5 (paperback)
ISBN 978-1-3995-3815-2 (webready PDF)
ISBN 978-1-3995-3816-9 (epub)

European Research Council
Established by the European Commission

This project has received funding from the European Research Council (ERC) under the European Union's Horizon 2020 research and innovation programme (grant agreement No. 864635 – FEATHERS).

MIX
Paper | Supporting responsible forestry
FSC www.fsc.org FSC® C013604

Contents

Acknowledgements

In writing this book, I have had the support of many wonderful people and have consequently incurred many debts along the way. Ruth Ahnert has been an incredibly supportive mentor from the very beginning of this project and her time, energy, advice and attention to detail have been invaluable. Joad Raymond, too, has read and offered useful comments on early drafts, for which I am grateful. I am also grateful to the lovely community at Queen Mary. I wish to thank in particular Alexandra Effe, Lucy Gwynn, Nydia Pineda and Melissa Schuh: they have made my time in London feel like home away from home.

I am equally grateful to my current colleagues at Leiden, especially those in the English department. A huge thanks to LUCAS, for support in various forms, including offering funds for digitisation, travel and image rights. Being part of the FEATHERS team is an ungoing privilege: thanks to Clodagh Murphy, Jonathan Powell and Holly Riach for many stimulating workshops (and borrels). Pete Langman, unofficial FEATHERS team member and official word wizard, has made this book much better than it would have been without his keen eye. Special thanks go to Nadine Akkerman, friend, mentor and manuscript detective extraordinaire: your support means more than I can put into words here. Many thanks, too, to Hanna de Lange.

This book would not have come into the world if it wasn't for their guidance and belief in it: EUP editors Emily Sharp and Elizabeth Frazer and the series editors, particularly Lorna Hutson, who has shown support for this project from its very beginning. I also wish to thank all anonymous readers: their suggestions have improved this book in many ways. Thanks, too, to the many archivists and reading room personnel who have helped me over the years. An earlier version of part of Chapter 1 was published as 'Early Modern Women in the English Courts of Law', *Literature Compass*, September 2018 (doi: 10.1111/lic3.12499). Some material from Chapter 4 is used in 'The Self-Portrayal of Widows in the

Early Modern English Courts of Law', in *The Oxford Handbook of Early Modern Women's Writing in English*, edited by Elizabeth Scott-Baumann, Danielle Clarke and Sarah Ross (2022), pp. 305–18.

Finally, the biggest thank you is owed to Hein, for enduring love and support: you simply make everything better.

Series Editors' Preface

Edinburgh Critical Studies in Renaissance Culture may, as a series title, provoke some surprise. On the one hand, the choice of the word 'culture' (rather than, say, 'literature') suggests that writers in this series subscribe to the now widespread assumption that the 'literary' is not isolable, as a mode of signifying, from other signifying practices that make up what we call 'culture'. On the other hand, most of the critical work in English literary studies of the period 1500–1700 which endorses this idea has rejected the older identification of the period as 'the Renaissance', with its implicit homage to the myth of essential and universal Man coming to stand (in all his sovereign individuality) at the centre of a new world picture. In other words, the term 'culture' in the place of 'literature' leads us to expect the words 'early modern' in the place of 'Renaissance'. Why, then, 'Edinburgh Critical Studies in *Renaissance Culture*'?

The answer to that question lies at the heart of what distinguishes this critical series and defines its parameters. As Terence Cave has argued, the term 'early modern', though admirably egalitarian in conception, has had the unfortunate effect of essentialising the modern, that is, of positing 'the advent of a once-and-for-all modernity' which is the deictic 'here and now' from which we look back.[1] The phrase 'early modern', that is to say, forecloses the possibility of other modernities, other futures that might have arisen, narrowing the scope of what we may learn from the past by construing it as a narrative leading inevitably to Western modernity, to 'us'. *Edinburgh Critical Studies in Renaissance Culture* aims rather to shift the emphasis from a story of progress – early modern to modern – to a series of critical encounters and conversations with the past, which may reveal to us some surprising alternatives buried within texts familiarly construed as episodes on the way to certain identifying features of our endlessly fascinating modernity. In keeping with one aspect of the etymology of 'Renaissance' or 'Rinascimento' as 'rebirth', moreover, this series features books that explore and interpret anew elements of the critical encounter between writers of the period 1500–1700 and texts of Greco-Roman literature, rhetoric, politics, law, oeconomics, *eros* and friendship.

The term 'culture', then, indicates a licence to study and scrutinise objects other than literary ones, and to be more inclusive about both the forms and the material and political stakes of making meaning both in the past and in the present. 'Culture' permits a realisation of the benefits to be reaped after two decades of interdisciplinary enrichment in the arts. No longer are historians naïve about textual criticism, about rhetoric, literary theory or about readerships; likewise, literary critics trained in close reading now also turn easily to court archives, to legal texts, and to the historians' debates about the languages of political and religious thought. Social historians look at printed pamphlets with an eye for narrative structure; literary critics look at court records with awareness of the problems of authority, mediation and institutional procedure. Within these developments, modes of research that became unfashionable and discredited in the 1980s – for example, studies in classical or vernacular 'source texts', or studies of literary 'influence' across linguistic, confessional and geographical boundaries – have acquired a new critical edge and relevance as the convergence of the disciplines enables the unfolding of new cultural histories (that is to say, what was once studied merely as 'literary influence' may now be studied as a fraught cultural encounter). The term 'Renaissance' thus retains the relevance of the idea of consciousness and critique within these textual engagements of past and present, and, while it foregrounds the Western European experience, is intended to provoke comparativist study of wider global perspectives rather than to promote the 'universality' of a local, if far-reaching, historical phenomenon. Finally, as traditional pedagogic boundaries between 'Medieval' and 'Renaissance' are being called into question by cross-disciplinary work emphasising the 'reformation' of social and cultural forms, so this series, while foregrounding the encounter with the classical past, is self-conscious about the ways in which that past is assimilated to the projects of Reformation and Counter-Reformation, spiritual, political and domestic, that finally transformed Christendom into Europe.

Individual books in this series vary in methodology and approach, sometimes blending the sensitivity of close literary analysis with incisive, informed and urgent theoretical argument, at other times offering critiques of grand narratives of the period by their work in manuscript transmission, or in the archives of legal, social and architectural history, or by social histories of gender and childhood. What all these books have in common, however, is the capacity to offer compelling, well-documented and lucidly written critical accounts of how writers and thinkers in the period 1500–1700 reshaped, transformed and critiqued the texts and practices of their world, prompting new perspectives on what we think we have learned from them.

Lorna Hutson, Katherine Ibbett, Joe Moshenska and Kathryn Murphy

Note

1. Terence Cave, 'Locating the Early Modern', *Paragraph*, 29:1 (2006) 12–26, 14.

Notes and Conventions

Spelling and punctuation of original documents, whether in manuscript or print, have been modernised, except for titles of texts. Names of litigants have not been modernised, to do justice to the way these complainants, defendants and witnesses recorded their own names (or let them be recorded). To create narrative consistency, however, all documents by one person, such as Mary Cheeke, are discussed under one name, regardless of whether they are signed by Mary Chicke, Cheke or Cheeke. References to the cases maintain their original spelling: church courts used the Latin *contra* (*plaintiff c defendant*); English bill courts chose *versus* (*plaintiff v defendant*).

References to Shakespeare's plays are taken from John Jowett, William Montgomery, Gary Taylor and Stanley Wells (eds), *The Oxford Shakespeare: The Complete Works*, 2nd ed. (Oxford University Press, 2005); those to the Bible from the *Authorized King James Version with Apocrypha* (Oxford University Press, 2008).

Introduction: Tracing Early Modern Women's Lives

In 1613, Elinor Kilby is alleged to have told her neighbour Elizabeth Chatfield that 'I do not get my living as thou (. . .) doest by laying thy legs abroad'. We know this because Chatfield, presumably horrified at such a scurrilous accusation, promptly sued Kilby for slander. If Chatfield's intention had been to bridle her neighbour's tongue and thus prevent Kilby from causing her reputation further damage, she was to be sorely disappointed. Even if Kilby's public slander could be disproved, the means of disproof made the slander still more public – after all, witness statements had to be gathered and made public to allow for the court to pass judgement. In the hurly-burly of the courtroom, all manner of secrets might tumble forth from the now unbridled tongue of the slanderer. Indeed, according to a witness, Kilby told Chatfield that she was 'an honester woman than thou', and that she 'would be ashamed to give entertainment to so many men as thou doest in that base and lewd fashion'.[1] In court, Kilby and Chatfield found themselves shaping their own lives in direct opposition to one another, Kilby denigrating the target of her (alleged) slander to present herself as honest and believable, while Chatfield sought to show herself as free from taint by showing Kilby to be untrustworthy.

In a time when the majority of the English population was illiterate, being embroiled in lawsuits may have been the only opportunity many people had of leaving traces of their lives. Even if people could write, there was no fixed format in which to do so: although the wish to record personal achievements and daily events in a life may be ancient, the genre conventions of conventional forms like the diary or autobiography that could help give shape to such an urge were not fully developed until the mid-seventeenth century.[2] The established scholarly narrative would suggest that, before the mid-sixteenth century, life-writing occurred merely incidentally, but by the end of the seventeenth century the practice of writing about oneself was well established. While the

Figure 0.1 Elizabeth Chatfield's mark below her deposition (London Metropolitan Archives, DL/C/221, f. 1231r). Courtesy of the Bishop of London and the London Diocesan Fund.

early modern period thus appears to have borne witness to an explosion in the production of life-writing, the casual reader would be forgiven for assuming that this was a primarily, if not exclusively, male phenomenon.

It is, indeed, difficult to reconstruct a picture of everyday female experience from the extant corpus of life-writing, and this may well be because the most immediately recognisable forms of life-writing, autobiographies and diaries, are largely penned by men.[3] Those few that have come down to us from female pens include Anne Clifford's *Diaries* (1616–19) and Anne Halkett's 'True accountt' (*c.*1677/8). Important as these are, they are not representative of women's experiences in general, as there are hardly any equivalent texts written by women below the level of the middle ranks.[4] The same holds true for men.[5] Recent scholarship, however, has demonstrated that early modern life-writers experimented heavily with form. According to Michelle M. Dowd and Julie A. Eckerle, generic literary conventions were seen as 'flexible guidelines', rather than 'fixed entities', which allowed, and even encouraged, life-writers 'to experiment with various combinations of different forms', as the conventions of life-writing itself were being formulated.[6] This understanding has led scholars to seek to trace the lives of early modern men and women in texts outside of the genres of autobiography and diary. Adam Smyth, for example, has traced the lives of early modern men and women in unorthodox types of texts such as account books and parish registers. Even following the embracing of these sources as examples of early modern life-writing, those illuminating the lives of men still outnumber those of women. Yet women's lives can also be found in more unorthodox sources, and thousands of such lives lie hidden in the legal archives. That legal archives are rich source materials is without doubt – after all, it has been speculated that the late Elizabethan England population of roughly 4 million people was involved in 1,102,000 legal actions every year.[7] What is becoming increasingly clear, however, is that they contain rich source materials from which we can hope to reconstruct much of the everyday lives of ordinary people. Furthermore, as much of the text preserved in court records concerns people's statements about themselves, they become a rich source of life-writing, and one more open to women than more obvious, self-defining acts of life-writing such as autobiographies and diaries. Indeed, the early modern law courts were sites of cultural production that provided opportunities for women's voices to be heard, and the nature of legal proceedings enabled even the illiterate to leave a perpetual record in manuscript of their lives.

Women were articulating their experiences before the generic conventions of life-writing became more fixed and rigid in such a way as to mostly exclude them. This can be seen if we place legal records from 1558 to 1649 alongside those more recognisable forms of self-expression that emerged in the mid-seventeenth and early eighteenth centuries. By reading legal records (including bills, answers and depositions) alongside these diaries and autobiographies, such as Anne Halkett's 'True accountt', we can trace the similarities between the narrative strategies and tropes employed by women in the courtroom and the literary strategies adopted by later female life-writers. Legal records can be fruitfully explored as forms of life-writing, offering opportunities to gain access to the narratives early modern women told about their lives, themselves and their experiences, and their motives for doing so.

Early Modern Life-Writing and Gender

The autobiographical *Book of Margery Kempe* (*c*.1438) is often cited as the first example of life-writing in English, and not only are other examples from this period rare, but the incidence of similar texts did not accelerate until the middle of the sixteenth century, when writing about oneself began to become increasingly popular.[8] By the end of the seventeenth century, however, the practice of autobiographical writing was well established. One of the many factors that helped stimulate the desire to write about oneself was the changing religious landscape of the sixteenth and seventeenth centuries.[9] The arrival of the Reformation in England and the subsequent rise of the Anglican church put an end to the Sacrament of Penance – the act of confession practised by Catholics. As a response to this loss, spiritual self-examination was encouraged.[10]

In 1656 John Beadle published a guide that was aimed at helping Christians to put this idea into practice. In his preface to Beadle's manual, John Fuller describes the usefulness of such a form of diary-keeping:

> We have our State Journals, relating the National affairs. Tradesmen keep their shop books. Lawyers have their books of presidents. Physicians their Experiments. Some wary husbands have kept a Diary of daily disbursements. Travellers a Journal of all they have seen, and hath befallen them in their way. A Christian that would be exact hath more need, and may reap much more good by such a Journal as this. We are all but Stewards, Factors here, and must give a strict account in that great day to the high Lord of all our ways, and of all his ways towards us.[11]

Fuller's words signal that spiritual self-reflection could be a helpful practice in avoiding damnation and is a rehearsal for when the day of judgement comes. It is thus a useful and recommended practice in establishing a person's righteousness.

Fuller's gendered language is no coincidence, as the shape that autobiographical writing began to take in the seventeenth century was distinctly male.[12] This was primarily because writing was deemed to be a man's prerogative.[13] Decorum already insisted that a woman's place was a quiet place, with Aristotle's recommendation that women remain silent sitting alongside St Paul's arguments against women preaching or even speaking in church and repeated in contemporary works such as Giovanni Michele Bruto's *The Necessarie, Fit, and Convenient Education of a Young Gentlewoman* and Thomas Wilson's *Arte of Rhetorique*.[14] If speaking was discouraged, the act of writing was considered more than unseemly for a woman. In her poem 'The Introduction', Anne Finch (1661–1720) observed the stigma she was fighting against by writing: 'Alas! A woman that attempts the pen / Such an intruder on the rights of men / Such a presumptuous Creature, is esteem'd / The fault, can by no virtue be redeem'd'.[15] Although Finch obviously did not let herself be deterred from writing, it is clear that women had fewer options than men: the norms of acceptable feminine behaviour constrained and discouraged them from writing.[16] Moreover, not all women who may have had autobiographical inclinations were able to indulge them. Some enlightened and elite families provided their female children with education, such as Lucy Hutchinson who enjoyed 'att one time 8 tutors in severall quallities, languages, musick, dancing, writing and needlework'.[17] But such examples were few and far between: although many girls were taught to read, only an elite minority also learned to write.[18] According to David Cressy's calculations, only 10 per cent of all seventeenth-century women were literate (compared to roughly 50 per cent of men) based on the number of women able to sign their names, with slightly higher proportions among the elite and in the London area.[19] Although scholars now agree that the percentage given by Cressy is likely to be the absolute minimum, it seems clear that most women were not able to write fluent prose, even if they could read and/or sign their names or initials.[20] As such, many early modern women were simply incapable of writing down the details of their lives. Those few pieces of women's life-writing from this period that are immediately recognisable as such come from the pens of a very select group, those with the luxury of writing practice.

It is, therefore, no surprise that, when scholars started to turn their eyes to autobiography in the 1950s, they focused primarily on those texts produced by men: after all, they were greatly in the majority. In his influential 1956 essay on the form and function of autobiographical writing, Georges Gusdorf, for instance, sees the genre as entirely dominated by male writers: its history can be traced 'in a series of masterpieces' written by men such as Aristotle and Rousseau, and autobiography, according to him, 'expresses a concern peculiar to Western man'.[21] The autobiographical texts of these men are characterised, as Gusdorf sees it, by their coherence and comprehensiveness, and by having as their focus the individual life and exceptional achievements of their subjects. Gusdorf's ideas have long been the standard in the study of autobiography. As a result, studies of autobiography have for a long time focused primarily on men's texts, and this was still the case as recently as 1980, when Stephen Greenblatt published his *Renaissance Self-Fashioning*, which considers only early modern male, canonical writers.[22]

Since the 1980s, however, feminist scholarship has started to challenge Gusdorf's theories, which exclude women (and other groups), as relevant examples of autobiographers, and has pointed out that autobiography is not the only available form of writing about the self. Shari Benstock, for instance, finds that Gusdorf's criteria for autobiography do not map unto women's self-writings: '[t]he self that would reside at the center of the text is decentered – and often is absent altogether – in women's autobiographical texts'.[23] Moreover, opposed to man's attempts to produce a 'complete and coherent expression of his entire destiny' stand the 'internal cracks and disjunctures, rifts and ruptures' that characterise women's autobiography.[24] Susan Stanford Friedman concurs with Benstock that Gusdorf's theories are inapplicable to the autobiographical impulses of women, as well as those of other minorities: 'the individualistic concept of the autobiographical self that pervades Gusdorf's work raises serious theoretical problems for critics who recognize that the self, self-creation, and self-consciousness are profoundly different for women, minorities, and many non-Western people'.[25] Gender, in the words of Dowd and

Eckerle, 'fundamentally affects the way in which we read autobiography and the "self" it purportedly creates'.[26] To understand women's autobiography, then, these scholars have suggested we need to overhaul existing ways of reading and evaluating these texts, something that becomes apparent when we consider 'autobiography' as but one sub-genre contained within the more all-encompassing field of 'life-writing'.

Indeed, a re-appraisal of autobiography requires a rethinking of its terminology. Meredith Anne Skura has recognised the need to separate our modern-day perceptions of the autobiography from the actual sixteenth-century practice of life-writing, and Adam Smyth has convincingly argued that 'the difficulty we have now in attributing generic or bibliographic labels to these texts signals the looser, more permeable, tentative, mixed approach to textual classification that pertained in early modern England'.[27] Indeed, '[t]he exploration and exploitation of a variety of forms, rather than adherence to a recognized format for articulating the self, is the crucial characteristic of self-writing, and in particular of women's self-writing, of the period'.[28] In the recognition that writing about the self comes in a wide variety of forms, especially in the early modern period, the term 'autobiography' is exposed as being too limited to encompass the entire practice, and is but one of myriad forms. The result of this is that the term 'life-writing' is now widely used to embrace the manifold ways in which individuals can write about their own and other people's lives.[29] The capaciousness of the concept of life-writing makes it the perfect way of thinking about the function of women's legal records, because it shows us that there are alternative ways of recording a life than in the conventional formats of the diary and (auto)biography.[30]

In order to properly include women in the history of life-writing, it is thus necessary to rethink the ways in which early modern men and women created and kept records of their lives.[31] Smith and Watson consider all life-writing as relational, as its subject characterises itself in relation to others, an opinion shared by Natalie Zemon Davis, who explains that '[v]irtually all the occasions for talking or writing about the self involved a relationship: with God or God and one's confessor, with a patron, with a friend or a lover, or especially with one's family and lineage'.[32] Mary Mason has demonstrated that this is particularly true of the female life-writer, who was more likely to write about her husband, pass on wisdom to her children or to produce spiritual texts than write directly about herself. Moreover, women were so acutely sensitive to the expectations of their potential readers that they had to carefully balance 'anticipated reader expectations and responsive authorial maneuvers'.[33] The conventional formats of life-writing thus do not fit the often dialogical and relational self-expressions of early modern women. Rather than make themselves the subject of their writing, women could, it seems, use their relationship with others as a way of writing about themselves without losing their sense of decorum.[34]

Indeed, there is evidence that many more women recorded details of their lives than is suggested by the records. Funeral sermons for women reveal that many women kept diaries and other personal records which are no longer extant, though whether this is because they were destroyed or censored by family members or executors, and if so whether this had been requested of them by the deceased, is not clear.[35] What is plain is that women were far more prolific life-writers than the quantity of surviving texts suggests. While Cynthia S. Pomerleau has estimated that 10 per cent of all seventeenth-century autobiographies we know of were written by women, the possibility of high rates of loss suggests many more early modern women may have produced accounts of their lives.[36] This lack of surviving examples of recognisably autobiographical writing by women leaves today's scholars with too little material to form a balanced perspective of the early modern world, and of women's experiences in that world in particular. This makes the need to examine alternative sources all the more pressing.

One of the forms in which early modern people were able to leave records of their lives was in the texts created for and during legal proceedings. These records are a rich and as-yet barely tapped source of life-writing, especially that of women.[37] Courtrooms gave women a place in which they chose, were invited or were forced to write about themselves, and to do so within specific parameters. The adversarial nature of the courtroom, which places one legal party in opposition with another, makes legal records echo the relational tendencies noted in women's life-writing, as it creates an occasion for a woman to shape her account in relation to her legal opponent.

Anne Clifford and the Conflation of Law and Life-Writing

Early modern life-writing is now recognised as inhering in many different forms, including testimony.[38] The official legal records that derive from a person bearing witness, including bills of complaint, personal answers and depositions, however, are often not yet given the same status. Smith and Watson's list of 'Sixty Genres of Life Narrative' does not include court records, for instance.[39] Yet these sources, too, are plainly types of life-writing, and types which, furthermore, allowed women to write themselves into the record.

The ostensible opposition between the discourses of the legal and literary worlds may be why legal records are not generally embraced under the term of life-writing. Often legal and literary discourses are treated as binary opposites, in which the legal discourse is characterised by its supposed rational and factual nature, and the literary discourse is characterised as fictional and subjective.[40] Despite their status, legal pleadings and depositions are hardly ever factual, objective texts. The literal truth of any statement made to the court is perhaps of less importance than its form – its primary goal is not to present fact but to shape opinion. Both the information shared and the presentation of this information must be arranged in such a way as to convince. This shape would be determined by the litigant and by their lawyer or the court officers involved in taking down these statements. The authors of pleadings would thus make use of rhetoric in the widest sense. According to Edward Muir and Guido Ruggiero:

> [i]t could well be argued that every judicial document in a case is a tissue of lies: defendants reconstructing their past to make it as innocent sounding as possible; accusers recasting events to make the accused seem as guilty as possible; investigators working to fit individuals and events into preconceived notions of crime; witnesses shaping their testimony because of animosities, friendships, the desire to please the powerful, or the need to thwart them.[41]

As such, many legal records are at least partly fictionalised. Some bills of complaint may even be complete fabrications, judging from the number of vexatious litigation claims in the early modern period. To take the statements we find in the legal records as the unvarnished truth is as naïve as to consider an autobiography to be, as Brodzki and Schenk suggest is the case for uncritical eyes, 'as untroubled a reflection of identity as the surface of a mirror can provide'.[42] Autobiographies, in common with other forms of life-writing, never offer the absolutely unmediated experience of the author, who functions as both writer and editor of their own work.[43] Legal records, mediated and manipulated as they (invariably) are, are in no way to be set as in opposition to life-writing. In fact, law and literature were entwined to such a degree in early modern England that the categories rather bleed into one another. The activities of Anne Clifford are a case in point, as her legal activities pervade her life-writing.

Much of the course of Clifford's life was shaped by her father's will, in which he left the Clifford estates to his brother rather than to his daughter.[44] Following in her mother's footsteps, who diligently laboured to secure her daughter's inheritance for her, Clifford spent much of her time tracing documentary evidence that would prove she was rightful heir to the estate and thus overturn her father's will. Her various suits aimed at recovering her family's land proved fruitless, however, as the so-called King's Award of 1617 settled the dispute mostly along the lines of George Clifford's will. When her uncle died in 1643 without leaving direct male heirs, Clifford finally inherited the property. This did not end Clifford's legal proclivity, though, as she continued to find herself at law trying to consolidate and even expand her newfound property and her status as landowner.[45]

Clifford's legal activities pervade her life-writing. They may even have spurred it: as Megan Matchinske has pointed out, it is likely that 'Clifford begins the Knole account to vindicate her own precarious position as litigant and obstructer'.[46] Even after recovering her inheritance, however, legal issues remained present in Clifford's writings and her activities as a writer are dominated by her legal actions.[47] In her analysis of Clifford's *Great Books of Records*, Jessica L. Malay identifies the important role of legal records in Clifford's attempt at writing the history of her ancestors. The inclusion of the legal records relating to her own life in the section about herself in the *Great Books* is one of Clifford's autobiographical strategies.[48] The account of her life is thus filled with encounters with the law and at the same time legal records also tell part of that life. As such, Clifford's life-writing indicates how intricately connected the spheres of law and literature could be in the period. Clifford is not the only writer for whom this was the case: there are many more women whose legal records contain narratives of the self, and these stories do not need to be told in diaries or autobiographies in order to count as life-writing.

Recovering Women from the Law

Tracing women's lives in the legal archives comes with a particular set of interpretative problems, however. Archives are never neutral places of information and knowledge storage, but instead reflect existing hierarchies and power (im)balances.[49] This is particularly the case for archives of courts of law. Those entering the doors of the courts as litigants or witnesses were subject to the court's rules and procedures, and so were the documents created for these courts. Rather than being able to shape these records freely to their will, then, these legal parties formed the weaker, dependent party in an unequal power relationship. The successive compilation of these records into an archive thus excludes and obscures much of the lives these litigants lived. Nonetheless, although these archives were never formed to provide access to women's life stories, by reading against the archival grain, focusing both on what these records do and do not include, it becomes possible to recover traces of women's lives.[50] Reading against the grain allows us to view the responses of minority groups to the inherently hierarchical conditions they lived in and were subjected to in the courts of law.

This is necessary not only because legal records are created under very hierarchical conditions, but also because scholarship itself is subject to ideology and ingrained assumptions about, amongst other things, the role of women in history. In order to ensure a more inclusive kind of scholarship that pays due attention to minority groups, Rebecca Olson advocates 'responsible speculation'. The method 'rejects assumptions that bind unknown variables to stable givens in favor of more complex and multivariate structures of logic',[51] with the intention of 'expos[ing] the biases inherent in more dominant methodologies'.[52] What the method may mean for women's studies becomes clear from Valerie Wayne's recent *Women's Labour and the History of the Book in Early Modern England*. The edition draws heavily on responsible speculation in a bid to 'move beyond assumptions of women's irrelevance and the limitations of the archives'.[53] The approach allows the collection's contributors to highlight the important role women played in the production of books. By encouraging scholars 'to imagine equally plausible alternatives' to those suggested by more dominant critical assumptions, responsible speculation challenges the underlying assumptions at work in scholars' methods, and questions the 'stable givens'.[54] This makes the method highly useful for tracing women's narratives in the legal records.

This is particularly the case because women formed a minority of those entering the courts of law, institutions in which only men were allowed to work and which upheld man-made laws. In their 1994 collection *Women, Crime and the Courts in Early Modern England*, Jenny Kermode and Garthine Walker demonstrate that the role of women in legal proceedings in early modern England had been much neglected by social historians until the late 1990s. One of the reasons for this neglect is the quantitative methodology favoured by many social historians. Throughout the centuries women have always been 'a minority of those officially prosecuted' and with quantification of sources this has led to 'women being duly counted and then discounted'.[55] Although men did dominate the world of legal proceedings in the early modern period, women's role was far from marginal, which has been demonstrated by, amongst others, scholars studying the church courts.[56] Frances E. Dolan, Laura Gowing and Eleanor Hubbard, for instance, have successfully traced women's role in the ecclesiastical courts.[57] Maria Cioni has done the same for the Court of Chancery.[58] Tim Stretton's study of female litigants in the Court of Requests has further explored women's involvement in early modern equity proceedings.[59] These pioneering scholars have put the role of women in various early modern legal proceedings firmly on the map. Their research has been primarily historical in its approach, but the law can also be viewed from a literary perspective. Genelle Gertz has analysed early modern women's heresy trial narratives, produced outside of the courts, showing that this genre was able 'to authorize women's resistant voices'.[60] Subha Mukherji, Lorna Hutson, Bradin Cormack, Quentin Skinner and Penelope Geng have made a huge contribution to the intersecting fields of law and literature, by exploring how law was represented on the early modern stage.[61] This present study is less interested in dramatic representations of the law, but instead analyses legal records within a literary framework to provide a window onto the lives of early modern women, focusing on the stories that these women allowed to become part of the public record, and the narrative and rhetorical strategies they used to tell that story.

Carolyn Sale has turned to legal records in her belief that 'the legal archives would hold, in one form or another, a narrative of female agency'.[62] Indeed, Sale argues,

> [w]hen we make it a priority to focus on how women write – in the sense of using certain modes of writing to assert their own agency – we create opportunities to tell narratives important to literary history that might not get told if we focused only on literary representations of the ways in which early modern women were inscribed or superscribed by various cultural discourses.[63]

The agency early modern women could exert, and that Sale is interested in, is of course limited. Like everyone else at the time, women had to adapt themselves to the power structures that ensnared them. Even those women who had a form of agency acted within the patriarchal system, or their 'capacity for agency is in fact produced by a feature of the patriarchal structure itself', but this did not prevent women from acting at the very top of the patriarchal system, although very few ever did.[64] Unearthing these acts makes it possible, or perhaps even compels us, to challenge our own cultural discourses about early modern women's writing, writing practices and agency.[65] This is equally important when it comes to texts whose authorship is difficult to ascertain, as Sale demonstrates in her discussion of the Star Chamber case of *Hole v White*, in which local constable John Hole singles out Thomasine White as creator of a libel designed to humiliate him. According to Sale:

> Despite the fact that she leaves behind her no tell-tale 'hand,' and no text with her signature, Thomasine White suggests that women may have played an authoritative role in theatrical practices in the period. The scrawl with which

> she signed her deposition serves as the metonymic mark for the other women involved in provincial theatrics in early modern England whose history we could not begin to write if we relied solely on conventional literary texts.[66]

Here, Sale engages in responsible speculation to show that women, too, could play a significant part in (often highly theatrical) libel performances.[67] Even if they were illiterate, women could be part of a network of publication of libels, helping to disseminate libellous verses and breathing life into them by engaging in street theatre. Court records thus give insight into the agency held and wielded by otherwise powerless individuals. In a very real way, legal pleadings also made the illiterate literate, and gave power to the powerless by including their stories on the record. Turning to less conventional literary sources can provide us with a fuller perspective on women's agency and their self-portrayals. In line with Sale, this book reads legal records for evidence of women's (textual) authority and does so in order to make early modern literary history more poly-vocal by drawing attention to narratives of women whose life stories would otherwise be missing from it.

In its aim to recover women's life stories from legal sources, this present study is necessarily highly interdisciplinary in nature. Bringing together the fields of history, law and literature enables the mining of legal records to trace the narratives of early modern women, but in straddling these different domains, there is a risk of not doing justice to each of the individual elements. It is therefore important to stress that this book uses parts of these different domains to further our knowledge of early modern women's lives and the ways they chose to talk about this. To do so, it deals with examples and case studies in order to illustrate larger patterns, and thus favours a qualitative approach over a quantitative one. By examining legal records in such a way, we can trace the lives of women otherwise unrepresented in history. While some of these traces are exactly that, the merest glimpse of a life, others can furnish us with far greater insight, culminating in what Paul Griffiths has called a biography 'from the cradle to the court'.[68] We can also gain a new perspective on women we thought we already knew, such as Anne Halkett.

In the following chapters, the rhetoric employed in more canonical texts of life-writing is compared to that used in legal pleadings from a variety of courts of law. The records of these courts are kept throughout England, but here, the focus lies on the records found in archives in and around London. This does not mean that the sources are geographically limited to the capital. Litigants from all over the country travelled to the various London-based courts to deal with local matters. In total, some 1,100 records from various jurisdictions and diverse types of law and custom have been consulted; those containing exemplary strategies used, too, by female life-writers – mostly from church and equity court records – have found their way into this book. *Early Modern Women's Life-Writing and English Law* thus takes a broadstroke approach to these sources, intending to show that women's presence in the legal archives is ubiquitous. In locating these sources, I am heavily indebted to the scholars who have paved the way: these are in particular Gowing and Hubbard, who have demonstrated that London's consistory court records and the Bridewell Court Books are full of cases by and about women; Stretton, whose work on women in the Court of Requests has pointed the way to this important court and its female litigants; and Adam Fox, whose work on oral and literate culture has highlighted the many slander and libel cases to be found in the Court of Star Chamber. This book draws on the sources made accessible by these (social) historians, available in great quantities, and puts them in conversation with more traditional, but only scantily available examples of women's life-writing. This relative paucity of female-authored literary texts can be supplemented with many more documents if we are willing to accept that authorship was often a collaborative act in the early modern period.

Early Modern Women's Life-Writing and English Law aims to break new ground by opening up areas of women's literary history through the reading of texts not normally seen as literary. By comparing the rhetoric used in legal pleadings from the variety of courts of law described previously to that used in more canonical texts of life-writing, the everyday experiences (by which I mean 'the routine and quotidian experience of ordinary people in particular times, places and circumstances'[69]) of women from diverse walks of life can be retrieved. A typical early modern English woman went through three stages in her life, from maid, to wife, to widow. This book is structured around events such a typical woman might well have encountered in her life and that may have necessitated her entry into the legal arena. As the common law considered a woman's legal persona to be covered by that of her husband upon marriage, the institute formed a crucial, transitional moment in a woman's life, determining her legal status before, during and after marriage – and so it is treated here. Something as vital to an average woman's life-cycle as motherhood had no direct bearing on her legal status and, by extension, is not granted a separate chapter here, but mothers' stories are scattered throughout the various chapters.

The opening chapter views the creation of legal pleadings as a collaborative enterprise in which lawyer and litigant work together, showing that the mediation to which legal testimony is subjected is a characteristic of early modern literary production, rather than a barrier to treating these sources as types of life-writing. In the four chapters that follow this opening chapter, legal pleadings from a variety of courts are close-read

Figure 0.2 Woodcut showing women sitting around a table, A widow, wife and maid (The British Library, C.117.b.52, title page).

alongside the more recognisable life-writing of early modern women. Chapter 2 focuses on the way women constructed images of themselves in courtship and marriage cases, and chapter 3 addresses women and their attempts to safeguard their sexual reputation, as this could have an impact on women's chances on the marriage market and the success of their marriage. The various ways widows presented themselves in the courtroom are discussed in chapter 4. Finally, chapter 5 explores two case studies in which the female defendants' legal records are no longer extant. By turning to more obviously literary texts, the chapter draws attention to the fictional nature of all life-writing, including those texts produced at the instigation of the courts of law. Together, these chapters show how women articulated their own experiences and mediated the social, cultural and legal restrictions placed upon them.

Notes

1. *Elizabeth Chatfield c Elinor Kilby* (1613), witness statement of William Davye, LMA, DL/C/221, ff. 1301v-2v, at 1302r. The case is also discussed in Laura Gowing, 'Gender and the Language of Insult in Early Modern London', *History Workshop*, 35 (1993): 1–21, at 9.

2. Adam Smyth, *Autobiography in Early Modern England* (Cambridge University Press, 2010), p. 2.
3. William Matthews' bibliography of British diaries lists 361 diaries for the period 1442–1699, of which only 15 are penned by women (43 diaries are listed as anonymous) (Matthews, *British Diaries: An Annotated Bibliography of British Diaries Written between 1442 and 1942* (Cambridge University Press, 1950)). Sara Heller Mendelson adds six more female diarists to that list ('Stuart Women's Diaries and Occasional Memoirs', in Mary Prior (ed.), *Women in English Society 1500–1800* (Routledge, 1985), pp. 181–210, at 202–4).
4. Heller Mendelson, 'Stuart Women's Diaries', p. 183. Ramona Wray has identified three texts by women below the upper strata of society: the life-writing of Barbara Blaugdone, Barbara Scaife and Anne Herring (Wray, 'Autobiography', in Laura Lunger Knoppers (ed.), *The Cambridge Companion to Early Modern Women's Writing* (Cambridge University Press, 2009), pp. 194–207).
5. Alan Macfarlane, *The Family Life of Ralph Josselin, a Seventeenth-Century Clergyman* (Cambridge University Press, 1970), p. 4.
6. Michelle M. Dowd and Julie A. Eckerle, 'Introduction', in Michelle M. Dowd and Julie A. Eckerle (eds), *Genre and Women's Life Writing in Early Modern England* (Ashgate, 2007), pp. 1–13, at 4.
7. B. J. Sokol and Mary Sokol, *Shakespeare, Law, and Marriage* (Cambridge University Press, 2003), pp. 2–3; Tim Stretton, 'Women, Property and Law', in Anita Pacheco (ed.), *Early Modern Women's Writing* (Blackwell, 2002), pp. 40–57, at 53. Indeed, various scholars have argued that the early moderns were 'law-minded', see: C. W. Brooks, *Pettyfoggers and Vipers of the Commonwealth: The 'Lower Branch' of the Legal Profession in Early Modern England* (Cambridge University Press, 1986); James Sharpe, 'The People and the Law', in Barry Reay (ed.), *Popular Culture in Seventeenth-Century England* (Croon Helm, 1985), pp. 244–70, at 245–6; Steve Hindle, *The State and Social Change in Early Modern England, 1550–1640* (Palgrave Macmillan, 2000), pp. 14; 91; Dominic Birch, 'Legal Pluralism in Early Modern England and Colonial Virginia', *Journal of Institutional Studies*, 5(2) (2019): 717–46, at 734; John Walter, '"Law-Mindedness": Crowds, Courts and Popular Knowledge of the Law in Early Modern England', in Michael Lobban, Joanne Begatio and Adrian Green (eds), *Law, Lawyers and Litigants in Early Modern England: Essays in Memory of Christopher W. Brooks* (Cambridge University Press, 2019), pp. 164–84.
8. See, for instance, Paul Delany's *British Autobiography in the Seventeenth Century* (Routledge, 1969) and Brigitte Glaser's *The Creation of the Self in Autobiographical Forms of Writing in Seventeenth-Century England: Subjectivity and Self-Fashioning in Memoirs, Diaries, and Letters* (C. Winter, 2001). Barry Windeatt suggests that medieval English life-writing is 'only exceptionally expressed through any extended narrative'; instead, it is more 'subsumed and implicit' ('Medieval Life-Writing: Types, Encomia, Exemplars, Patterns', in Adam Smyth (ed.), *A History of English Autobiography* (Cambridge University Press, 2016), pp. 13–26, at 13).

9. Alan Stewart, *The Oxford History of Life-Writing*, Vol. 2 Early Modern (Oxford University Press, 2018), p. 5. Miriam Nandi offers an overview of various other factors that account for the early moderns' increased interest in life-writing (*Reading the Early Modern English Diary* (Palgrave Macmillan, 2021), pp. 36–41).
10. T. C. Price Zimmermann, 'Confession and Autobiography in the Early Renaissance', in Anthony Molho and John A. Tedeschi (eds), *Renaissance Studies in Honor of Hans Baron* (Northern Illinois University Press, 1971), pp. 119–40, at 122; Julie A. Eckerle, *Romancing the Self in Early Modern Englishwomen's Life Writing* (Ashgate, 2013), p. 12.
11. John Beadle, *The Journal or Diary of a Thankful Christian* (London, 1656), sig. b1v, archive.org/details/journalor00bead. Accessed 18 March 2024.
12. See Bella Brodzki, 'Gender and Life Writing', in Margaretta Jolly (ed.), *Encyclopedia of Life Writing: Autobiographical and Biographical Forms*, Vol. 1 (Fitzroy Dearborn Publishers, 2001), p. 870; Bella Brodzki and Celeste Schenck, 'Introduction', in Bella Brodzki and Celeste Schenck (eds), *Life/Lines: Theorizing Women's Autobiography* (Cornell University Press, 1988), pp. 1–15, at 1–2.
13. Patricia Crawford, 'Women's Published Writings 1600–1700', in Prior (ed.), *Women in English Society*, pp. 211–82, at 214.
14. Bella Mirabella, 'Feminist Self-Fashioning: Christine de Pizan and *The Treasure of the City of Ladies*', *The European Journal of Women's Studies*, 6 (1999): 9–20, at 10; Giovanni Michele Bruto, *The Necessarie, Fit, and Convenient Education of a Young Gentlewoman* (London: 1598), STC 3947, p. 74; Thomas Wilson, *Arte of Rhetorique*, ed. by Thomas J. Derrick (Garland Publishing, 1982), pp. 400–1.
15. Anne Finch, 'The Introduction', *The Poems of Anne Finch, Countess of Winchelsea*, ed. by Myra Reynolds (University of Chicago Press, 1903), p. 4.
16. Wendy Wall, *The Imprint of Gender: Authorship and Publication in the English Renaissance* (Cornell University Press, 1993), p. 280.
17. Lucy Hutchinson, 'Life of Mrs. Hutchinson', in Lucy Hutchinson, *Memoirs of the Life of Colonel Hutchinson, Written by his Widow Lucy*, ed. by Harold Child (Kegan Paul Trench Trubner, 1904), p. 33.
18. Mendelson, 'Stuart Women's Diaries', p. 182.
19. David Cressy, *Literacy and the Social Order: Reading and Writing in Tudor and Stuart England* (Cambridge University Press, 1980), pp. 41; 107; 113.
20. See, for instance, Heidi Brayman Hackel, *Reading Material in Early Modern England: Print, Gender, and Literacy* (Cambridge University Press, 2005) and Heidi Brayman Hackel and Catherine E. Kelly, 'Introduction', in Brayman Hackel and Kelly (eds), *Literacy, Authorship, and Culture in the Atlantic World, 1500–1800* (University of Pennsylvania Press, 2008). Eleanor Hubbard has shown that women who could sign their initials should be included in the literacy figures, as having this ability indicates reading skills, if not writing skills (Hubbard, 'Reading, Writing, and Initialing: Female Literacy in Early Modern London', *Journal of British Studies*, 54 (2015):

553–77). Margaret W. Ferguson and Mihoko Suzuki argue for a new 'historically contextualized investigation of literacy' in order to establish more accurate literacy rates, see: Ferguson and Suzuki, 'Women's Literacies and Social Hierarchy in Early Modern England', *Literature Compass*, 12(11), (2015): 575–90.

21. The original text is 'Conditions et limites de l'autobiographie', published in Günter Reichenkron and Erich Haase (eds), *Formen der Selbstdarstellung: Analekten zu einer Geschichte des literarischen Selbtsportraits*. Festgabe für Fritz Neubert (Duncker and Humblot, 1956). All references here are taken from James Olney's translation of the same piece: Georges Gusdorf, 'Conditions and Limits of Autobiography', translated by James Olney, in James Olney (ed.), *Autobiography: Essays Theoretical and Critical* (Princeton University Press, 1980), pp. 28–48, at 28; 29.
22. Stephen Greenblatt, *Renaissance Self-Fashioning: From More to Shakespeare* (University of Chicago Press, 1980).
23. Shari Benstock, 'Authorizing the Autobiographical', in Shari Benstock (ed.), *The Private Self: Theory and Practice of Women's Autobiographical Writings* (Routledge, 1988), pp. 10–33, at 20.
24. Gusdorf, p. 35; Benstock, p. 20.
25. Susan Stanford Friedman, 'Women's Autobiographical Selves: Theory and Practice', in Sidonie Smith and Julia Watson (eds), *Women, Autobiography, Theory: a Reader* (University of Wisconsin Press, 1998), pp. 72–82, at 72 in particular.
26. Dowd and Eckerle, 'Introduction', p. 3.
27. Meredith Anne Skura, *Tudor Autobiography: Listening for Inwardness* (University of Chicago Press, 2008); Smyth, *Autobiography*, p. 214.
28. Elspeth Graham, 'Women's Writing and the Self', in Helen Wilcox (ed.), *Women and Literature in Britain 1500–1700* (Cambridge University Press, 1996), pp. 209–33, at 213.
29. It is embraced, for example, in Sidonie Smith and Julia Watson's *Reading Autobiography: A Guide for Interpreting Life Narratives*, 2nd ed. (University of Minnesota Press, 2010).
30. See, for instance, Zachary Leader's edition *On Life-Writing* (Oxford University Press, 2015) and particularly Patrick Hayes' essay on digital life-writing (Patrick Hayes, 'Human 2.0? Life-Writing in the Digital Age', in Leader (ed.), *Life-Writing*, pp. 233–56).
31. For an overview of work on (women's) life-writing, see Michelle M. Dowd and Julie A. Eckerlie, 'Recent Studies in Early Modern English Life Writing', *English Literary Renaissance*, 40(1) (2010): 132–62. Section B deals with women's life-writing specifically.
32. Smith and Watson, *Reading Autobiography*, p. 278; Natalie Zemon Davis, 'Boundaries and the Sense of Self in Sixteenth-Century France', in Thomas C. Heller, Morton Sosna, and David E. Wellbery (eds), *Reconstructing Individualism: Autonomy, Individuality, and the Self in Western Thought* (Stanford University Press, 1986), pp. 53–63, at 53.

33. Sidonie Smith, *A Poetics of Women's Autobiography: Marginality and the Fictions of Self-Representation* (Indiana University Press, 1987), p. 49.
34. Mary G. Mason, 'The Other Voice: Autobiographies of Women Writers', in Brodzki and Schenk (eds), *Life/Lines*, pp. 19–44, at 22. See also: Wray, 'Autobiography', p. 203; Stanford Friedman, 'Women's Autobiographical Selves', pp. 72–82, at 72; 75–6 in particular; Philippa Kelly, Lloyd Davis and Ronald Bedford, 'Introduction', in Ronald Bedford, Lloyd Davis and Philippa Kelly (eds), *Early Modern Autobiography: Theories, Genres, Practices* (University of Michigan Press, 2006), pp. 1–16, at 14; Felicity A. Nussbaum, *The Autobiographical Subject: Gender and Ideology in Eighteenth-Century England* (Johns Hopkins University Press, 1989), p. 137. Elspeth Graham, Hilary Hinds, Elaine Hobby and Helen Wilcox, on the other hand, emphasise that it is impossible to make general claims about whether women define the self as relational more than men, see: 'Introduction', in Elspeth Graham, Hilary Hinds, Elaine Hobby and Helen Wilcox (eds), *Her Own Life: Autobiographical Writings by Seventeenth-Century Englishwomen* (1989; Routledge, 2005), pp. 1–25, at 19.
35. Effie Botonaki, 'Seventeenth-Century Englishwomen's Spiritual Diaries: Self-Examination, Covenanting, and Account Keeping', *The Sixteenth-Century Journal*, 30(1) (1999): 3–21, at 3.
36. Cynthia S. Pomerleau, 'The Emergence of Women's Autobiography in England', in Estelle Jelinek (ed.), *Women's Autobiography: Essays in Criticism* (Indiana University Press, 1980), pp. 21–38, at 21. See also: Effie Botonaki, *Seventeenth-Century English Women's Autobiographical Writings, Disclosing Enclosures* (Edwin Mellen Press, 2004), p. 1.
37. Recent exceptions include Suzannah Lipscomb, *The Voices of Nîmes: Women, Sex, and Marriage in Reformation Languedoc* (Oxford University Press, 2019); Teresa Phipps and Deborah Youngs (eds), *Litigating Women: Gender and Justice in Europe, c. 1300–c. 1800* (Routledge, 2021); and especially Mary Chadwick, Daniel Patterson and Jessica Malay's 'Autobiographical Acts in Seventeenth-Century English Petitioning', *Journal for Early Modern Cultural Studies*, 22(1) (2022): 84–106, which convincingly treats Quarter Sessions' petitions as 'sources of autobiographical acts', enabling 'petitioners to narrativize their pasts in order to effect change in the present or future' (pp. 85; 91). Imogen Peck's work has revealed that the law and the process of petitioning encouraged other minority groups to fashion specific identities for themselves, too; in the case of the petitioning orphans Peck discusses as victims of war deserving of relief (Peck, '"For the dead Fathers sake"? Orphans, Petitions and the British Civil Wars, 1647–1679', in Brodie Waddell and Jason Peacey (eds), *The Power of Petitioning in Early Modern Britain* (UCL Press, 2024), pp. 143–68).
38. See Bella Brodzki, 'Testimony', in Margaretta Jolly (ed.), *Encyclopedia of Life Writing: Autobiographical and Biographical Forms*, Vol. 2 (Fitzroy Dearborn Publishers, 2001), pp. 870–1; Smith and Watson, '*Testimonio*', in *Reading Autobiography*, p. 282.
39. See Appendix A to Smith and Watson's *Reading Autobiography*.

40. Susan Sage Heinzelman and Zipporah Batshaw Wiseman, 'Preface', in Susan Sage Heinzelman and Zipporah Batshaw Wiseman (eds), *Representing Women: Law, Literature, and Feminism* (Duke University Press, 1994), pp. vii–ix, at viii. For the changing relationship between fact and fiction in the early modern period, see Barbara J. Shapiro, *A Culture of Fact: England, 1550–1720* (Cornell University Press, 2000), pp. 59–62; 197–207.
41. Edward Muir and Guido Ruggiero, 'Afterword: Crime and the Writing of History', in Edward Muir and Guido Ruggiero (eds), *History from Crime*, trans. by Corrada Biazzo Curry, Margaret A. Gallucci and Mary M. Gallucci (Johns Hopkins University Press, 1994), pp. 226–36, at 230.
42. Brodzki and Schenk, 'Introduction', in Brodzki and Schenck (eds), *Life/Lines*, pp. 1–15, at 1.
43. Dan Doll and Jessica Munns, 'Introduction', in Dan Doll and Jessica Munns (eds), *Recording and Reordering: Essays on the Seventeenth- and Eighteenth-Century Diary and Journal* (Rosemont Publishing & Printing Corp., 2006), pp. 9–21, at 10.
44. See the ODNB entry for a detailed account of Clifford's life: Richard T. Spence, 'Clifford, Anne [*known as* Lady Anne Clifford], countess of Pembroke, Dorset, and Montgomery (1590–1676), noblewoman and diarist', *Oxford Dictionary of National Biography* (25 September 2014). Accessed 18 March 2024.
45. These endeavours have been documented in detail in Richard T. Spence's *Lady Anne Clifford, Countess of Pembroke, Dorset and Montgomery (1590–1676)* (Sutton Publishing, 1997), see chapters 7 and 8 in particular.
46. Megan Matchinske, 'Serial Identity: History, Gender, and Form in the Diary Writing of Lady Anne Clifford', in Dowd and Eckerle (eds), *Genre and Women's Life Writing*, pp. 65–80, at 67. Jessica Malay has argued that Clifford's *Great Books of Record*, too, served (amongst other things) as vindication of her legal activities, see: Jessica L. Malay, 'Constructing a Narrative of Time and Place: Anne Clifford's *Great Books of Record*', *The Review of English Studies*, 66(277) (2015): 859–75, at 871.
47. Jessica L. Malay, 'Introduction', in Anne Clifford, *Anne Clifford's Autobiographical Writing, 1590–1676*, ed. by Jessica L. Malay (Manchester University Press, 2018), pp. 1–14, at 3.
48. Ibid., p. 9.
49. This has been noted in, amongst others, Alexandra Walsham, 'The Social History of the Archive: Record-Keeping in Early Modern Europe', *Past & Present*, Supplement 11 (2016): 9–48; Ann Stoler, *Along the Archival Grain: Epistemic Anxieties and Colonial Common Sense* (Princeton University Press, 2008); and Arlette Farge, *The Allure of the Archives*, trans. by Thomas Scott-Railton (Yale University Press, 2013).
50. See Walsham, 'The Social History', 44, for examples of studies that 'read against the grain'. See also Lindsay R. Moore, *Women before the Court: Law and Patriarchy in the Anglo-American World, 1600–1800* (Manchester University Press, 2019), pp. 11–12 on reading legal records against the grain.

51. Rebecca Olson, 'The Continuing Adventures of Blanchardyn and Eglantine: Responsible Speculation about Early Modern Fan Fiction', *PMLA*, 134(2) (2019): 298–315, at 298.
52. Ibid., 299.
53. Valerie Wayne, 'Introduction', in Valerie Wayne (ed.), *Women's Labour and the History of the Book in Early Modern England* (The Arden Shakespeare, 2020), pp. 1–26, at 19.
54. Olson, 'The Continuing Adventures', 311; 299.
55. Jenny Kermode and Garthine Walker, 'Introduction', in Kermode and Walker (eds), *Women, Crime and the Courts in Early Modern England* (UCL Press, 1994), pp. 1–15, at 4.
56. This holds true for other early modern countries and jurisdictions as well. The registers of Languedoc's Reformed churches that Suzannah Lipscomb has studied testify to early modern French women's initiative before the consistories and contain testimonies by women, as well as about them, for example. See Lipscomb, *The Voices of Nîmes*. Emma Hawkes has demonstrated that not only early modern women had knowledge of the law, but late medieval gentlewomen did too (Hawkes, '"[S]he wil . . . protect and defend her rights boldly by law and reason . . .": Women's Knowledge of Common Law and Equity Courts in Late-Medieval England', in Noël James Menuge (ed.), *Medieval Women and the Law* (Boydell Press, 2000), pp. 145–61). Mihoko Suzuki has shown that many seventeenth-century English women held legal expertise, which they gained through self-education, from legal experiences or from reading and watching literary representations of trials (Suzuki, 'Daughters of Coke: Women's Legal Discourse in England, 1642–1689', in Sigrun Haude and Melinda S. Zook (eds), *Challenging Orthodoxies: The Social and Cultural Worlds of Early Modern Women* (Ashgate, 2014), pp. 165–92).
57. Frances E. Dolan, *Dangerous Familiars: Representations of Domestic Crime in England, 1550–1700* (Cornell University Press, 1994); Laura Gowing, *Domestic Dangers: Women, Words, and Sex in Early Modern London* (Oxford University Press, 1996); Eleanor Hubbard, *City Women: Money, Sex, and the Social Order in Early Modern London* (Oxford University Press, 2012).
58. Maria L. Cioni, *Women and Law in Elizabethan England, With Particular Reference to the Court of Chancery* (Garland Publishing, 1985).
59. Tim Stretton, *Women Waging Law in Elizabethan England* (Cambridge University Press, 1998).
60. Genelle Gertz, *Heresy Trials and English Women Writers, 1400–1670* (Cambridge University Press, 2012), p. 2.
61. Subha Mukherji, *Law and Representation in Early Modern Drama* (Cambridge University Press, 2006); Lorna Hutson, *The Invention of Suspicion: Law and Mimesis in Shakespeare and Renaissance Drama* (Oxford University Press, 2007); Bradin Cormack, *A Power to do Justice: Jurisdiction, English Literature, and the Rise of Common Law, 1509–1625*

(Chicago University Press, 2007); Quentin Skinner, *Forensic Shakespeare* (Oxford University Press, 2014); Penelope Geng, *Communal Justice in Shakespeare's England: Drama, Law, and Emotion* (University of Toronto Press, 2021).

62. Carolyn Sale, 'The "Roman Hand": Women, Writing and the Law in the *Att.-Gen. V. Chatterton* and the Letters of the Lady Arbella Stuart', *English Literary History*, 70(4) (2003): 929–61, at 957.
63. Ibid., 957.
64. Martha Howell, 'The Problem of Women's Agency in Medieval and Early Modern Europe', in Sarah Joan Moran and Amanda Pipkin (eds), *Women and Gender in the Early Modern Low Countries* (Brill, 2019), pp. 21–31, at 22.
65. Sale, 'The "Roman Hand"', 957; 928–30.
66. Carolyn Sale, 'Contested Acts: Legal Performances and Literary Authority in Early Modern England', unpublished PhD dissertation (Stanford University, 2002), p. 256.
67. Clare Egan has further explored women's role in libel performances, from engineering them to being part of their audiences, in her article 'Women and the Performance of Libel in Early-Modern Devon', *Medieval English Theatre*, 38 (2017): 145–62.
68. Paul Griffiths, *Lost Londons: Change, Crime, and Control in the Capital City, 1550–1660* (Cambridge University Press, 2008), p. 181.
69. Angela McShane and Garthine Walker, 'Introduction: The Extraordinary and the Everyday in Early Modern England', in Angela McShane and Garthine Walker (eds), *The Extraordinary and the Everyday in Early Modern England: Essays in Celebration of the Work of Bernard Capp* (Palgrave Macmillan, 2010), pp. 1–5, at 4.

Chapter 1

Constraints of the Courtroom and its Records

Different courts had different legal procedures and spheres of speciality, and therefore gave rise to different kinds of records. In order to be able to understand these sources, it is necessary to put them into context. As with all texts, court records are formed through the intersection of a number of different, and sometimes conflicting, forces. Because the early modern law was not only disparate but split between various jurisdictions, each one of the many different available courts had its own procedure and its own sphere of influence. The narratives that we find in the archives must, therefore, be approached with caution, as they were forged in the red-hot spaces that coalesced between the litigant's story and the court's modus operandi.[1] This is, however, no different for more obviously literary texts: these, too, must be read in light of generic markers and literary conventions.

The Early Modern Courts of Law and Their Records[2]

Women could find themselves in court for a variety of reasons. As plaintiffs, they could take others to court, for example to enforce marriage contracts, claim an inheritance or collect debts. Naturally, they could also be sued or tried as defendants. Resolving legal issues between complainants and defendants required proof, which could be provided in the form of witness statements. Women could thus also find themselves in court as witnesses, in which case they would have to offer answers in the form of a deposition made in response to a list of questions, the interrogatory.

When they sought out the courts of law as plaintiffs, women had a variety of courts to choose from. What we now refer to as the early modern legal system was in fact made up of several bodies of law scattered throughout England, each with its own jurisdiction, procedure and set of rules.[3] The law primarily fell into one of four areas: common law, equity law, ecclesiastical law or the law of custom. Each dealt with its own, distinct area, even if these areas did sometimes overlap. The litigant that initiated legal proceedings also selected the law court in which proceedings would take place. Often there was no real choice, as jurisdiction determined that a case of a certain nature ought to be heard by a particular court. Disputes over wardship, for instance, would naturally be debated in the prerogative Court of Wards and Liveries. In cases where jurisdictions overlapped, however, the plaintiff had a choice of forum. In order to collect outstanding debts, litigants could try their luck in the Court of Common Pleas, the King's Bench or the courts of equity. Relatively small debts could also be considered by the customary courts. Forum choice was an important weapon, as the litigant would take their suit to the court that they thought would be most amenable to their case. Alternatively, they brought their suit to the court that offered the best remedy.[4] Victims of slander may have preferred the monetary damages offered by Star Chamber over the public penance meted out by the ecclesiastical courts, for example. This does not necessarily mean that defendants were tied to the forum chosen by their legal opponents: when they were sued, litigants could start alternative proceedings in another court that they felt might view their predicament more favourably. As a result, the same suit could be pursued in more than one tribunal at the same time.[5] The various chapters in Brodie Waddell and Jason Peacey's recent edition on petitioning reveal that supplicants had enough legal and political knowledge to select a suitable forum for their petition and that, as Hannah Worthen puts it, 'moving between different jurisdictions was a commonplace part of petitionary practice'.[6] Savvy women could thus use the legal system to their advantage, even if they were more limited in their choices than men.[7]

At the same time, this wealth of choice could make the legal system difficult to navigate, and matching a suit to the most appropriate forum – the one most likely to provide redress – was not always a straightforward task. A newly widowed woman could encounter all four jurisdictions in her attempts at securing what was rightfully hers after the passing away of her husband, for instance.[8] If her late husband had owned real property, a widow was entitled to a third of it for her lifetime, her so-called dower. She needed to turn to the common law if there were any problems in enforcing her rights. The common law differentiated between those women who were married and those who were not. Its principle of *coverture* meant that some of the rights of married women (referred to as *femes coverts*) became subsumed by those of her husband, as the law viewed husband and wife as one – and, naturally, the husband was the mouthpiece of this union: a wife could not start legal proceedings without her husband's permission or presence, own or control property, or enter into contract.[9] Obviously, this prevented a woman from suing her husband under common law. Although married women may have lacked agency under the common law, single women and widows (called *femes soles*) were not faced with the same kind of restrictions, as the rules of *coverture* did not apply to them.

Common law was exercised in the central London courts (such as King's Bench, Common Pleas and the Court of Exchequer) and in the provinces (the Assizes and Quarter Sessions).[10] The records left by these courts can be particularly difficult to work with when trying to reconstruct the lives and narratives of early modern women, as the surviving records are often formulaic and written in (abbreviated) Latin.[11] Litigants did not produce their own bills and were dependent on attorneys or the local Justice of the Peace to note down their accounts. Although these Justices of the Peace generally seem to have executed their functions most diligently, the execution of their tasks did not require legal training, and they were under no obligation to create and preserve formal records of most of their legal dealings beyond recording objective details, such as names of the people involved and jury decisions. Even when they did leave any records behind, they vary greatly in detail. Nevertheless, Jonathan Powell's work on the plea rolls of the central common law courts shows that in such sources, too, the everyday experiences of women can be located, if one is able to navigate the source material.[12]

If the widow in our example and her husband had created a marriage settlement prior to their marriage and issues arose over this following his death, she would have to turn to equity to find redress. This second legal jurisdiction originated in the fifteenth century in order to moderate the common law's harshness.[13] Their alleged flexibility made the equity courts attractive to litigants and distinguished them from the common law courts.[14] Equity did rule on the basis of precedent, but it could, and did, take the particular circumstances of individual litigants into account. The poor, the vulnerable and the ignorant in law were especially likely to find their way to the courts of equity in the hope of a sympathetic ear. By focusing not only on the conflicting points of law presented in a case, but also on the individual circumstances of the litigants, the Masters of Chancery could use discretion in a manner not available to the judges ruling under common law. A story entrusted to the courts of equity would not be a simple recapitulation of the pertinent facts, however, as the very nature of the court encouraged these stories to be substantial not only in detail, but also in supporting colour.

Unsurprisingly, therefore, women flocked to the equitable courts in London (the Court of Requests, the Court of Chancery and the equity side of the Court of Exchequer), as well as the Palatinates of Lancaster, Chester and Durham.

Equity procedure ensured that the individual details of a litigant's story can be detected. The equitable courts followed chancery procedure, in which English was the main language (although Latin appears in administrative records on occasion): a case would be initiated by the plaintiff, who would petition for equitable justice from the king, council or Lord Chancellor in his or her bill or petition.[15] Defendants rebutted the claims made in the bill in their answer. These pleadings were drawn up outside court by lawyers, who were instructed by their litigants. Local commissioners dealt with the taking of depositions in the countryside and were meant to read back the depositions to the deponents, in order for them to check that the written testimony reflected the orally given statements. Pleadings addressed to the equitable courts usually followed a standard structure, as did the answers to such bills.[16] The litigant's personal narrative was woven around these formulaic features.

If the husband of our widow had left any moveable goods, or if there were problems with his will, the widow had to turn to ecclesiastical law to stake out her claims. This third jurisdiction was overseen by the church courts, which not only dealt with cases concerning last wills and testaments, but also busied themselves with all things matrimonial, moral, defamatory and heretical. Various studies have shown that women's participation in these courts, both as litigants and witnesses, was considerable.[17] The nature of the jurisdiction may well have been the cause of this: matrimonial issues naturally involved husband and wife as litigants; issues of morality, which were all too often concerned with different kinds of extramarital sex, also usually implicated defendants of both genders; and defamation has long been recognised as a typically female crime.[18] Unlike common law, ecclesiastical law allowed a woman to sue without her husband's permission or presence, which must also have been a contributing factor in drawing women into litigation. In the church courts, procedures could be initiated in one of two ways: by an individual litigant seeking redress from one or more fellow citizens (known as instance causes), or by church court officials, who could instigate proceedings based on disciplinary prosecution where they deemed morality was at stake (known as office causes). In practice, the distinction between the two was often blurred. The libels, articles and personal answers produced in these courts provide excellent insights into the lives of its litigants – at least, as they chose to present them.

If our widow's husband had held land from a manor, the widow would be entitled to at least a third of it, her so-called 'freebench'. To stake out her claims in this area she would have to turn to customary law. This fourth jurisdiction was constituted by the manorial and borough courts, local courts that were usually limited by their geographical range. These courts occupied themselves with minor offences worth up to a set amount of money (the amount depending on the offence in question), and local transfers and inheritances of land. Customs differed greatly between manors and were delivered orally from one generation to another. Since customary law was essentially unwritten, memory was particularly important in customary lawsuits. As such, custom was fluid, uncertain and especially vulnerable to popular feeling, even though it is recognised as the first kind of precedent. The procedures of customary law, too, could differ greatly between one village and the next. The quality of records differs between court as well: some records were conscientiously prepared and compiled, others simply summarise the main facts. Many of these records have not survived.

Although all these different jurisdictions offered women various possibilities and placed different restrictions on them, the early modern legal system as a whole placed no general disqualification on women. In theory, a woman's gender was not considered an impediment to find access to the courts of law. Her marital status, however, could prevent her from suing on her own behalf. Women were also generally viewed as less reliable witnesses than men. A witness's credibility was tied to his or her social status; the testimony of a man of property was thus accorded more weight than that of a woman of the lower echelons of society.[19] Nevertheless, women still gained access to the legal system, and their testimony was heard, even if it was regarded as less reliable than that of male witnesses.

The evidence of women's voices, and the manner in which they actively wrote and rewrote their life stories through their interaction with, and manipulation of, the legal system in early modern England is to be found in the textual byproducts of the legal process. Because of the richness of the sources and the opportunities they offered to female litigants to present their side of the matter, the pleadings addressed to so-called English bill courts, whose proceedings were almost entirely conducted through manuscript submission, are particularly fruitful for reading women's narratives.[20] These bill courts include the Court of Chancery, the Court of Requests, the equity side of the Court of Exchequer and the Court of Star Chamber. In common with church courts, whose records, too, provide good access to such traces as women left of their lives, these courts derived their procedure from civil law. The textual byproducts peculiar to these courts include bills, answers, interrogatories and depositions.[21] There are also other 'witnesses' to the legal process available, such as ballads, printed or manuscript slanders, biographies, autobiographies, diaries and pamphlets. Such sources can be particularly useful in cases when there is no access to legal records, for example because they are no longer extant. Like legal records, such sources are, of course, partial and not necessarily accurate.

Interpreting Legal Records

Although texts are seldom straightforward, difficulty of interpretation is something that scholars foreground particularly in their analysis of legal records. In the wake of the linguistic turn, historians have turned to the language and rhetoric used by litigants to see how their experiences are represented. Using legal records to learn more about the everyday lives of early modern men and women is complicated by the nature of these records, however: these sources are mediated through the use of a lawyer, commissioner or court clerk, which makes it difficult to distinguish the litigant's voice from that of the mediator. There is thus tension between the desire to work with sources that might provide a unique window into the lives of hitherto marginalised voices and the anxiety that it may be impossible to attribute the voice in legal records solely to the litigant or deponent.[22]

This problem comes to the fore particularly in depositions, the sworn testimony of witnesses. These texts were produced outside of the courtroom, when deponents answered pre-recorded questions ('interrogatories') to court clerks, who jotted these answers down. Stretton has convincingly argued that it is likely that it was the scribe who provided the exact wording in a deposition, 'with an eye to the legal purposes of the court', as interrogatories and depositions were often separated in legal proceedings.[23] Certainly, comparisons between the questions put to witnesses and the answers to such questions in witness depositions often reveal striking similarities in choice of words and word order. The linguist Bridget Cusack, on the other hand, has demonstrated that it is possible to untangle the two levels of language, the scribe's and the deponent's, present in depositions.[24] She offers an example from the deposition of Mary Gashe: 'and beinge asked whether the soldier that she formerly named did not lie with her, she sayth that neither he nor any other had to do with her but only the said Slan'. Here, the court offers Mary the phrase *lie with*, but Mary chooses the less direct *have to do with*.[25] Such disentanglement can be aided by information about the composition of depositions, as is the case for Anne Lion's eyewitness report as written down by Sir Henry Wotton:

> she was so far from disguising or reserving any circumstance, that she prevented all my inquisitiveness in some questions which I had prepared, making a clear, a free, and a noble report of all that had passed, which she did dictate unto me, as I wrote in her window, in her own words, without any enforcement or interruption, as followeth: '[. . .]'.[26]

These examples show that the voices of the individual deponents can sometimes be read in depositions, even when those texts were written by scribes. In the majority of cases, however, it seems impossible to separate the voices of the deponent and his scribe, but that is not to say that the voices did not merge.

While we may not be able to easily untangle voices, we can assign some authority to litigants and deponents over the stories they told. An early modern debate on the problems of transcription reveals that, while clerks and commissioners were not necessarily trained to accurately record the words of a deponent, their intent was to convey as best as they could the deponent's meaning.[27] Although perhaps not always succeeding in perfectly reflecting a deponent's authentic voice, generally clerks did their best to at least try and achieve accuracy, if not literal precision.[28] There is also evidence to suggest that deponents supported the content of the legal records they helped forge into being, even if their exact words got lost in the process. This evidence is found in the signatures present on legal records and the fact that such records were sent on to the courts. Deponents were asked to sign the depositions they had given after the depositions had been read back to them, allowing them to correct and alter any errors or inaccuracies.[29] This was important for, as Cordelia Beattie has shown, the claims made by an individual in their pleading or deposition, their 'subject position', needed to match whatever that person was willing to testify to should the case require court appearance.[30] What is more, as Lloyd Bowen has shown, this testimony needed not only 'to be believable but *verifiable*'.[31] While individual voices may not be found in the legal archives in pristine form, we can still look for individuals' narratives or stories.[32]

Moreover, invisible or hard-to-detect entanglements of voice do not necessarily detract from the status of words as 'life-writing', as these can also be found in some autobiographies. This is most noticeable where the person whose life is recorded is not the one wielding the pen. While we may well know that at least one of the amanuenses who physically wrote Margery Kempe's *Book* was not averse to adjusting what he

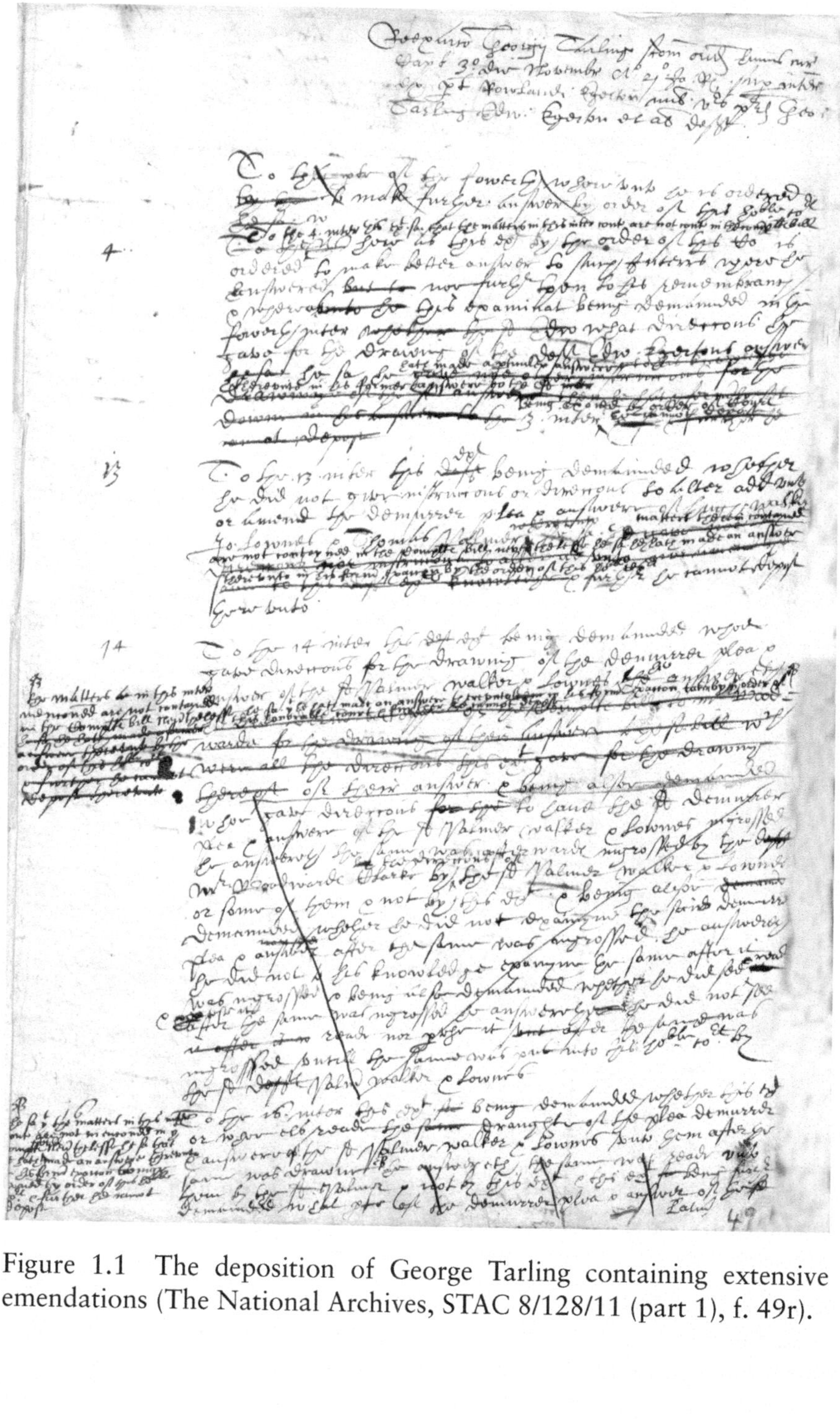

Figure 1.1 The deposition of George Tarling containing extensive emendations (The National Archives, STAC 8/128/11 (part 1), f. 49r).

Figure 1.2 The deposition of Alice Grace with some minor emendations, including to her age (The National Archives, REQ 2/395/36, f. 7r).

heard dictated to him to better suit his own tastes, we have no difficulty in identifying Kempe as the ultimate 'author' of the work.[33] This view is not affected by the fact that Kempe describes herself, or lets herself be described by her amanuenses, in the third person, much as any litigant's pleading or deposition would be presented to the court.[34] In the case of both an amanuensis and their employer, and a litigant and their lawyer, there is at least some level of collaboration, and the relationship between speaker and writer is, to an extent, symbiotic.

This collaboration is also typical for the production of texts in early modern England. The category of 'author' was far from fixed in the sixteenth century, and it certainly did not carry with it modern notions of a single and stable authorial intent. Instead we should consider authorship in this period to be a product of collaboration.[35] Several forms of collaborative authorship are recognisable in this period, such as social authorship, in which one person is responsible for the main text, but others are involved in transcribing, editing and circulating it. Another form of collaborative writing is that of composite authorship, a term usually used to describe texts in which one author finishes the work of a (often dead) colleague.[36] While Diane Purkiss reminds us that '*[a]ny text* produced by an early modern woman was prone to male intervention, in the process of composition as well as at the point of transcription or printing', it was not only women's texts that were products of collaboration with or intervention by others.[37] Helen Smith has deftly traced the influences women had on men's texts, showing that textual collaboration, in all its various forms, was the norm, for not only women's literary productions, but also men's.[38] Indeed, even Shakespeare sought out collaborators (or was sought out by them): the current scholarly consensus holds that he worked with a variety of co-authors on at least eight of his plays.[39] Accepted forms of life-writing, such as is to be found in the diaries of Sarah Cowper, are no exception to this. In one of her books Cowper reflects on her life-writing by considering that 'if other mens sentences were left out, the pages would be void'.[40] Cowper thus borrows other people's words to create her own, highly personal account of her life.

Even though literary scholars have embraced the concept of social authorship, it still poses problems. Anne Askew's (1521–46) *The Examinations* is an example of this. While we know that the basic account of her sufferings and persecutions was penned by Askew herself, the printed forms in which it has been passed down to us were subject to significant annotations, commentary and editing by John Bale and, later, John Foxe. It is difficult, of course, to ascertain the precise level of editorial interference that these men indulged themselves in without the original manuscripts. Bale and Foxe certainly had reason to appropriate Askew's narrative of suffering for her Protestant beliefs: the hagiographical text turned Askew into a martyr and an example for fellow Protestants. Nevertheless, the general scholarly consensus seems to be that Askew can be considered the author of her own text, despite Bale's and Foxe's editorial interventions.[41] Rather than treating *The Examinations* as a form of composite authorship, however, some critics appear to attempt to recuperate a single, authoritative voice to show that Bale imposed his voice upon Askew's text. For them, Askew's text is in many ways a text of conflict, in which her 'authentic narrative' has been sullied by Bale's imposition of his insensitive and misogynistic agenda.[42] It is perhaps more helpful, and certainly more accurate in light of the way pre-modern texts were constructed, to see Askew's text 'as an exemplary instance of (. . .) collaborative coauthorship'.[43] This is not just the case for Askew's text, as Genelle Gertz has demonstrated that the male editors of accounts of medieval and early modern women's heresy trials can be seen as 'agents in the production of women's texts', regardless of their editing practices.[44] This notion is also helpful for our understanding of early modern women's writings more broadly.[45]

The combined efforts of lawyers and litigants need to be treated as a form of collaborative authorship, too, in line with Frances E. Dolan's recent call to 'recast mediation as collaboration, a collaboration that facilitated women's expression as much as or rather than occluding it' when it comes to depositions.[46] Dolan's arguments for the use of the term 'collaboration', rather than 'mediation' are persuasive. She points her readers' attention to letters sent by women.[47] At first glance, it may be thought that women had more control over the letters they wrote than over their depositions. However, just as in court a woman's words would be mediated by a court clerk or lawyer, many women employed scribes and secretaries to pen their instructions, and it is usually difficult to disaggregate the different influences on the letter, or tell whose hand it was written in, just as is the case for women's 'petitioning words'.[48] Just as a woman's employment of a scribe or secretary does not lead scholars to reject letters composed in such a way as not 'fitting' to be included under the heading 'life-writing', neither should it lead them to ignore legal records. It is the conflation of mediator and collaborator which allows, nay demands, that legal records including (but certainly not limited to) depositions should be treated as forms of life-writing. Indeed, mediation does not necessarily cause the loss of authority; instead, texts can derive authority from the fact that they have been mediated.[49] The depositions drawn up for criminal trials show that, while examinates may 'lose' authority over their own witness statements through the interference of examiners or justices of the peace, at the same time these witnesses give their statements an increased authority through their willingness to swear to their accuracy.[50] While a deposition contains two layers, as it exists of a memorial reconstruction of a past event by the witness, as well as a recording of this reconstruction by the examiner, neither layer is necessarily more authoritative than the other, just differently so. By applying the literary concept of collaborative authorship to the historical texts that are legal records, then, we can perhaps still not hear the unmediated, authentic voices of litigants, but it does make it possible to view those litigants as (co-) authors of their own texts, and to recognise the 'textual co-presence' of litigants and lawyers, and deponents and court clerks, in those texts.[51]

That collaboration is not necessarily limited to just a litigant and a single lawyer, moreover. The term 'lawyer' obscures the various forms in which aid was available to individuals seeking legal help. As officers of the Court of Star Chamber, to name one example, attorneys could help litigants navigate the legal process. The communication between litigant and attorney could be mediated by a solicitor, while counsellors were needed to sign bills of complaint and argue in court. Scriveners and scribes were available to pen legal instruments upon request. How pleadings were produced and who, exactly, was involved in their production remains unclear, despite a handful of attempts made at unraveling the way pleadings were written.[52] Indeed, as Gwilym Dodd has noted, pleadings 'almost never displayed authorial markings, and indirect evidence for authorship is unfortunately extremely scarce'.[53] We may not know precisely, then, how pleadings came into being, but we do know they were the product of a collaboration between a litigant and one or more people with at least some legal knowledge.

Bowen has recently made a similar case for recognising petitions as collaborative texts and suggests that to do so 'helps in understanding petitions as multi-authored texts which nonetheless script individual lives and over which petitioners had a critical degree of control and agency'.[54] It is nevertheless easy to assume that pleadings owe more to the lawyer (or lawyers) than to the client, not least when confronted by the abundance of plainly formulaic language contained within bills of complaint and personal answers.[55] These formulae, however, actually make it easier to isolate the stories of individual litigants – if formulae were limited to individual lawyers rather than more generally adhered to then lawyer and client would melt into one as the pleadings were put into writing. Lawyer and client's words would sound as well as look as if they were written in the same ink. In order to find the individual story of the litigant one must focus on what remains after the formulaic language is put aside.[56] Bills of complaint addressed to the Court of Requests, for example, use 'formulaic markers', but the rest of the narrative contained in a bill is 'far more personalized'.[57] It is that personalised account that can contain traces of women's lives.

It is in formulae, too, that we learn to differentiate between literary genres. But just as to make assumptions that the literary conventions behind the sonnet form would stifle creativity in the poet would be to commit an error of some magnitude, so would making the assumption that the same is true in court pleadings. Generic markers and conventions may set down laws of engagement, but at the same time these laws allow authors to express themselves.[58] Moreover, as Adam Smyth reminds us, pre-modern autobiographies tend to rely 'on the overt redeployment of existing scripts': it is in the alignment with other, older life stories that texts can 'produce a sense of self'.[59] The formulaic nature of legal records, I would argue, can be seen as such a script or generic convention. So while it may be tempting to view the use of formulaic markers as a problem specific to legal documents, this may not be very helpful in an analysis of those records. Instead, viewing these records through a literary lens can highlight issues such as the influence of generic conventions, as well as narrative perspective, elisions in storytelling, and the role of the perceived audience.[60]

Those gaps that are inevitable in legal records must be considered as generic markers, also – what is left out is easy to misread. Because they were produced with a very specific purpose in mind, and bound by their individual generic conventions, legal records exclude much more information than they contain. As Paul Strohm has noted, if one worked exclusively with documentary evidence, such as legal records, one would never know that Chaucer was a poet.[61] In working with such records, one therefore has to accept that many questions will remain unanswered. Indeed, alongside focusing on what *is* present in a legal record, one must thus also assess what *is not* there. This is particularly important for legal records whose legal context is otherwise lacking. Documents relating to the same suit were not always filed together in the archives, which can make it difficult to trace the paper trail of such a case. A single document can be all that is left of such a case. Moreover, cases were not always seen through from beginning to end. Often, cases were stopped before judgement was given, for reasons as various as lack of funds, the start of alternative proceedings regarding the same topic in a different court or because mediation out of court had resolved the issue.[62] As a result, there are many cases in which court records do not include a court's verdict.[63] In such cases, substantial context in which individual records can be placed is missing. What remains, however, is an individual's attempt to write their life in opposition to the view created by their legal opponent – even if that opposing view is no longer present in the legal archive.

While it is plain that legal records can, indeed must, contain elements of a life, there remains the question of intent – no litigant sought out the courts of law solely to engage in a little life-writing. In *The Oxford History of*

Life-Writing, Alan Stewart distinguishes between those texts that only 'accidentally bear autobiographical traces' and the ones in which their authors 'deliberately set out to *write lives*, whether their own or others'.[64] Legal records, his volume suggests, belong in the former category.[65] Certainly, not every litigant would turn to the courts of law in order to leave a trace of their lives. They did so in an attempt to defend their rights or stake out their claims. Nevertheless, it is the fact that litigants wrote their lives, no matter how small a part of it, in opposition to the lives that were being imposed upon them by their antagonists or their particular situation, that makes them life-writers. In this respect, whether they did so deliberately or not is of little import. The simple fact of the matter is that legal records by their very nature contain glimpses of what early modern people found important in their lives – and the fact that they were fighting over these traces, no matter how small, indicates their importance.

Moreover, *all* life-writing is, in one way or another, elicited by external forces, and in that sense purposeful, even if it appears to be accidental. An individual may not go to court because they want to assert their life story, but once they are there, they will assert it as hard and as cunningly as they can. All life-writers are provoked into writing their lives, whether by God, an event or an experience.[66] In this sense, court is merely another provocation. That legal testimony is usually elicited or even demanded does not deny it the status as life-writing, it rather asserts it as such. Autobiographies, in their deliberate attempts to assert objectivity, attempt to hide their confrontational nature. They, too, are responses to an external stimulus that causes a recognition of the self and potential loss of control thereof. Autobiographies, therefore, are more like court records than one might like to think – it is just that the court has different rules.

As the following chapters show in detail, women shaped their legal records in complex ways that are closely related to more obviously 'literary products' of the traditional sub-genres of life-writing such as autobiography and diaries. These texts are consciously constructed as narratives with the intent of shaping the response of both the court and, by implication, posterity. That they are written with a certain purpose in mind perhaps reinforces the old adage that 'history is written by the victors', but it certainly challenges the idea still beloved of many that 'history is a matter of fact'. The word 'fact' had a very specific forensic meaning in this period, and we do well to remember this when considering the pleadings left by women in the courts of early modern England: in the legal context, a 'fact' was an alleged past event or human deed or action whose occurrence was to be proved by evidence such as testimony.[67] Life-writing, whether done in traditional autobiographies or legal records such as pleadings, was an attempt at establishing a narrative of 'facts' in that very specific legal sense of the word. These texts were designed to persuade members of the court and contemporaries of the accuracy of these 'facts' and the strategies women used to do this make it plain that they were attempting to control how they, and their lives, were seen by others.

Notes

1. Cordelia Beattie, 'Your Oratrice: Women's Petitions to the Late Medieval Court of Chancery', in Bronach Kane and Fiona Williamson (eds), *Women, Agency and the Law, 1300–1700* (Pickering & Chatto, 2013), pp. 17–30, at 20; Beattie, 'Single Women, Work, and Family: The Chancery Dispute of Jane Wynde and Margaret Clerk', in Michael Goodich (ed.), *Voices From the Bench: The Narratives of Lesser Folk in Medieval Trials* (Palgrave Macmillan, 2006), pp. 177–202, at 178.
2. The following section has appeared in an earlier version as Lotte Fikkers, 'Early Modern Women in the English Courts of Law', *Literature Compass*, 15(12) (2018): doi.org/10.1111/lic3.12499.
3. The seventeenth-century jurist Sir Edward Coke counted fifteen separate jurisdictions, but his list does not include those courts operating under the law of equity, for example, while the Courts of Chivalry and Admiralty are grouped together. 'Lex & consuetudo Parliamenti', on the other hand, is distinguished from 'Statute Law' (Sir Edward Coke, *The First Part of the Institutes of the Lawes of England* (1628; London, 1629), STC (2nd ed.) / 15785), f. 11v.
4. Cordelia Beattie offers an insightful overview of various reasons why women petitioned the late medieval Court of Chancery: 'Choosing Chancery? Women's Petitions to the Late Medieval Court of Chancery', in Teresa Phipps and Deborah Youngs (eds), *Litigating Women: Gender and Justice in Europe, c.1300–c.1800* (Routledge, 2021), pp. 99–115.
5. C. W. Brooks, *Pettyfoggers and Vipers of the Commonwealth: The 'Lower' Branch of the Legal Profession in Early Modern England* (Cambridge University Press, 1986), p. 12.
6. Brodie Waddell and Jason Peacey (eds), *The Power of Petitioning in Early Modern Britain* (UCL Press, 2024); Worthen, 'The Process and Practice of Petitioning in Early Modern England', in Waddell and Peacey (eds), *The Power of Petitioning*, pp. 61–82, at 77.
7. Tim Stretton, *Women Waging Law in Elizabethan England* (Cambridge University Press, 1998), p. 33.
8. For a detailed discussion of the rules of inheritance, see Eileen Spring, *Law, Land, & Family: Aristocratic Inheritance in England, 1300 to 1800* (University of North Carolina Press, 1993); Ralph Houlbrooke, *The English Family 1450–1700* (Longman, 1984); Amy Louise Erickson, *Women*

and Property in Early Modern England (Routledge, 1993), particularly chapter 2; Stretton, *Women Waging Law*.

9. Maria L. Cioni, *Women and Law in Elizabethan England with Particular Reference to the Court of Chancery* (Garland Publishing, 1985), p. 27. This is not to say that married women did not actually do any of these things, as the rules of coverture were not applied rigidly in everyday life (Tim Stretton and Krista J. Kesselring, 'Introduction: Coverture and Continuity', in Tim Stretton and Krista J. Kesselring (eds), *Married Women and the Law: Coverture in England and the Common Law World* (McGill-Queen's University Press, 2013), pp. 3–23, at 8).
10. J. S. Cockburn offers a comprehensive overview of the Assizes' procedure and intricacies in *A History of English Assizes, 1558–1714* (Cambridge University Press, 1972).
11. Henry French, 'Legal and Judicial Sources', in Laura Sangha and Jonathan Willis (eds), *Understanding Early Modern Primary Sources* (Routledge, 2016), pp. 35–57, at 43. For an overview of sources commenting on the records' sparseness, see Jonathan Powell, '"Scarce expressible in English": Theatre and the Common Law, *c.*1597–1624', unpublished PhD dissertation (King's College London, 2022), pp. 73–4.
12. Powell, '"Scarce expressible in English"'. I regret to say that I am not, hence these sources are absent from this study.
13. Erickson, *Women and Property*, p. 5.
14. Cioni, *Women and Law*, p. 5.
15. For a detailed study of the proceedings of the Court of Chancery, see W. J. Jones, *The Elizabethan Court of Chancery* (Clarendon Press, 1967).
16. Models were available; see, for instance, William West, *Of Symboleography the Second Part* (London, 1597), STC (2nd ed.) / 25277, which contains sample Chancery pleadings.
17. See, for instance, Laura Gowing, *Domestic Dangers: Women, Words, and Sex in Early Modern London* (Oxford University Press, 1996) and Eleanor Hubbard, *City Women: Money, Sex, and the Social Order in Early Modern London* (Oxford University Press, 2012).
18. Gowing, *Domestic Dangers*, p. 61.
19. William Holdsworth, *A History of English Law*, Vol. IX (Methuen & Company, 1976), pp. 187–8; Steven Shapin, *A Social History of Truth: Civility and Science in Seventeenth-Century England* (University of Chicago Press, 1994), pp. 87–91; Steven Shapin and Simon Schaffer, *Leviathan and the Air-Pump: Hobbes, Boyle, and the Experimental Life* (Princeton University Press, 1985), pp. 65–9; Garthine Walker, *Crime, Gender and Social Order in Early Modern England* (Cambridge University Press, 2003), p. 128; Michael R. T. Macnair, *The Law of Proof in Early Modern Equity* (Duncker und Humblot, 1999), p. 201.
20. Beal, 'Courts of Law', *Dictionary*, pp. 98–101.
21. Case papers or pleadings are part of the larger category of legal records, which also includes, for example, last wills and testaments and petitions.

For studies on early modern women's last wills and testaments, see Susan E. James, *Women's Voices in Tudor Wills, 1485–1603* (Routledge, 2016); Vicki Kay Price, '"Twoo Muche Vayne and Idle Chardge": The Precision of Inheritance in the 1601 Will of Bess of Hardwick', *Law & Literature*, (2021): doi.org/10.1080/1535685X.2021.1902639. For wills as forms of life-writing in earlier periods, see Katherine J. Lewis, 'Women, Testamentary Discourse and Life-Writing in Later Medieval England', in Noël James Menuge (ed.), (The Boydell Press, 2000), pp. 57–76; Elisabeth Salter, 'Women's Last Wills and Testaments in Hull, England (*c.*1450–1550)', *Early Modern Women*, 12(2) (2018): 33–53. For women's petitions, see James Daybell, *Women Letter-Writers in Tudor England* (Oxford University Press, 2006).

22. This has been noted and extensively discussed, see: Malcolm Gaskill, 'Reporting Murder: Fiction in the Archives in Early Modern England', *Social History* 23.1 (1998), pp. 1–30; Adam Fox, *Oral and Literate Culture in England, 1500–1700* (Clarendon Press, 2000), p. 83; Joanne Bailey, 'Voices in Court: Lawyers' or Litigants'?', *Historical Research*, 74 (2001): 392–408; John H. Arnold, *Inquisition and Power: Catharism and the Confessing Subject in Medieval Languedoc* (University of Pennsylvania Press, 2001), pp. 7; 229; Alexandra Shepard, *Meanings of Manhood in Early Modern England* (Oxford University Press, 2003), p. 12; Garthine Walker, 'Just Stories: Telling Tales of Infant Death in Early Modern England', in Margaret Mikesell and Adele Seeff (eds), *Culture and Change: Attending to Early Modern Women* (Associated University Presses, 2003), pp. 98–115, at 112; Lamar M. Hill, '"Extreame Detriment": Failed Credit and the Narration of Indebtedness in the Jacobean Court of Requests', in Buchanan Sharp and Mark Charles Fissel (eds), *Law and Authority in Early Modern England. Essays presented to Thomas Garden Barnes* (University of Delaware Press, 2007), pp. 136–56, at 139; Jeremy Goldberg, 'Echoes, Whispers, Ventriloquisms', in Bronach Kane and Fiona Williamson (eds), *Women, Agency and the Law, 1300–1700* (Pickering & Chatto, 2013), pp. 31–41, at 31; Holger Schott Syme, *Theatre and Testimony in Shakespeare's England* (Cambridge University Press, 2012), p. 49; Frances E. Dolan, *True Relations: Reading, Literature, and Evidence in Seventeenth-Century England* (University of Pennsylvania Press, 2013), chapter 4; Tim Stretton, 'Women, Legal Records, and the Problem of the Lawyer's Hand', *Journal of British Studies*, 58 (2019): 684–700.
23. Stretton, 'The Problem of the Lawyer's Hand', 692.
24. Cusack, *Everyday English*, p. 95.
25. Ibid., p. 96.
26. Logan Pearsall Smith (ed.), *The Life and Letters of Sir Henry Wotton*, Vol. 2 (Clarendon Press, 1907), p. 292.
27. Syme, *Theatre and Testimony*, pp. 56–7.
28. Ibid.
29. Hilary Jenkinson, however, suggests that it was quite common for clerks to forge a deponent's signature on their deposition to give it 'an air of

verisimilitude' ('Elizabethan Handwritings: A Preliminary Sketch', *The Library*, 3(1) (1922): 1–50, at 31).

30. Beattie, 'Your Oratrice', p. 22.
31. Bowen, 'Genre, Authorship and Authenticity in the Petitions of Civil War Veterans and Widows from North Wales and the Marches', in Waddell and Peacey (eds), *The Power of Petitioning*, pp. 33–60, at 54.
32. The two terms, 'narrative' and 'story', will be used interchangeably throughout this text. I use both words to mean an account of something that is given in a particular order. Mieke Bal defines 'story' as the content of a narrative text (Bal, *Narratology: An Introduction to the Theory of Narrative*, fourth edition (1985; University of Toronto Press, 2017), p. 5).
33. Liz Herbert McAvoy, '"Wonderfully Turnyng & Wrestyng hir Body": Agonies, Ecstasies, and Gendered Performances in *The Book of Margery Kempe*', in Margery Kempe, *The Book of Margery Kempe: An Abridged Translation*, ed. by Liz Herbert McAvoy (D.S. Brewer, 2003), p. 105; Charity Scott Stokes, 'Last Years, Re-drafting of Liber I, Writing of Liber II', *Mystics Quarterly*, 25 (1999) (online).
34. Barry Windeatt, 'Medieval Life-Writing: Types, Encomia, Exemplars, Patterns', in Adam Smyth (ed.), *A History of English Autobiography* (Cambridge University Press, 2016), pp. 13–26, at 21; Mary G. Mason, 'The Other Voice: Autobiographies of Women Writers', in James Olney (ed.), *Autobiography: Essays Theoretical and Critical* (Princeton University Press, 1980), pp. 207–35, at 211.
35. Victoria E. Burke, 'Manuscript Miscellanies', in Laura Knoppers (ed.), *Cambridge Companion to Early Modern Women's Writing* (Cambridge University Press, 2009), pp. 54–67, at 55; Margaret J. M. Ezell, '"To Be Your Daughter in Your Pen": The Social Functions of Literature in the Writings of Lady Elizabeth Brackley and Lady Jane Cavendish', *Huntington Library Quarterly*, 51(4) (1988): 281–96; Ezell, *Social Authorship and the Advent of Print* (Johns Hopkins University Press, 1999).
36. For more on posthumous publication in the early modern period, see Margaret J. M. Ezell, 'The Posthumous Publication of Women's Manuscripts and the History of Authorship', in George L. Justice and Nathan Tinker (eds), *Women's Writing and the Circulation of Ideas: Manuscript Publication in England, 1550–1800* (Cambridge University Press, 2002), pp. 121–36.
37. Diane Purkiss, *The Witch in History: Early Modern and Twentieth-Century Representations* (Routledge, 1996), p. 93.
38. Helen Smith, *'Grossly Material Things': Women and Book Production in Early Modern England* (Oxford University Press, 2012).
39. H. R. Woudhuysen, 'Shakespeare's Writing: From Manuscript to Print', in Margreta de Grazia and Stanley Wells (eds), *The New Cambridge Companion to Shakespeare* (Cambridge University Press, 2011), pp. 31–44, at 34.
40. Sarah Cowper, *Diary*, Vol. 4, p. 3.
41. Jennifer Richards, 'The Voice of Anne Askew', *Journal of the Northern Renaissance*, 9 (2017), paragraph 26.

42. Thomas S. Freeman and Sarah Elizabeth Wall, 'Racking the Body, Shaping the Text: The Account of Anne Askew in Foxe's "Book of Martyrs"', *Renaissance Quarterly*, 54(4) (2001): 1,165–96, at 1,166. Elaine V. Beilin emphasises Askew's 'deauthorization', arguing that '[h]er text is absorbed or overwritten in narratives with generic requirements different from the polemic in which she was engaged' (Beilin, 'A Woman of All Seasons: The Reinvention of Anne Askew', in Pamela Joseph Benson and Victoria Kirkham (eds), *Strong Voices, Weak History: Early Women Writers and Canons in England, France, and Italy* (University of Michigan Press, 2005), pp. 341–64; at 347; 351). Rudolph P. Almasy, too, perceives antagonism between author and editors (Almasy, 'Anne Askew Constructing Her Text, Constructing Her Self', *Reformation*, 10(1) (2005): 1–20, at 8–9). See also Clare Costley King'oo, who concurs that recent scholarship on Askew iterates 'a marked antagonism between the female martyr and her early male editors' ('Authenticity and Excess in The Examinations of Anne Askew', *Reformation*, 19(1) (2014): 21–39, at 25).
43. Patricia Pender, 'Reading Bale Reading Anne Askew: Contested Collaboration in The Examinations', *Huntington Library Quarterly*, 73(3) (2010): 507–22; at 520. See also Richards, who argues that 'Beilin's hankering for the "real" voice of Askew now seems anachronistic because of recent developments in material book history, which emphasize the collaborative nature of a printed book's production' ('The Voice of Anne Askew', paragraph 9).
44. Genelle Gertz, *Heresy Trials and English Women's Writers, 1400–1670* (Cambridge University Press, 2012), p. 5.
45. Danielle Clarke and Suzanne Trill have convincingly demonstrated that the work of Mary Sidney Herbert, for instance, too, can be considered a form of collaborative authorship. See Clarke, 'Producing Gender: Mary Sidney Herbert and Her Early Editors', in Sarah C. E. Ross and Paul Salzman (eds), *Editing Early Modern Women* (Cambridge University Press, 2016), pp. 40–59; Trill, '"We Thy Sydnean Psalmes Shall Celebrate": Collaborative Authorship, Sidney's Sister and the English Devotional Lyric', in Susan Wiseman (ed.), *Early Modern Women and the Poem* (Manchester University Press, 2013), pp. 97–116.
46. Dolan, *True Relations*, p. 118.
47. Ibid., p. 117.
48. Alison Truelove, 'Commanding Communications: The Fifteenth-Century Letters of the Stonor Women', in James Daybell (ed.), *Early Modern Women's Letter Writing, 1450–1700* (Palgrave, 2001), pp. 42–58, at 45; Laura Gowing, *Ingenious Trade: Women and Work in Seventeenth-Century London* (Cambridge University Press, 2021), p. 219.
49. Syme, *Theatre and Testimony*, p. 14.
50. Ibid., p. 53.
51. The phrase is used by Helen Smith to refer to the manifold ways in which collaboration can manifest itself in a text (*Grossly Material Things*, p. 52).

52. Gwilym Dodd offers a list of secondary sources that have engaged with this problem (Dodd, 'Writing Wrongs: The Drafting of Supplications to the Crown in Later Fourteenth-Century England', *Medium Aevum*, 80(2) (2011): 217–46, fn. 96). To that list can be added Margaret Elizabeth Avery, 'Proceedings in the Court of Chancery up to *c.*1460' (University of London, 1958), pp. 134–41; Wilfrid P. Prest, *The Rise of the Barristers: A Social History of the English Bar 1590–1640* (Clarendon Press, 1986), p. 16; R. M. Ball, 'The King's Remembrancer's Office in the Eighteenth Century', *Journal of Legal History*, 11 (1990): 90–113, at 102; R. H. Helmholz, *The Profession of Ecclesiastical Lawyers: An Historical Introduction* (Cambridge University Press, 2019), pp. 54–6.
53. Dodd, 'Writing Wrongs', 217.
54. Bowen, 'Genre, Authorship and Authenticity', p. 46.
55. See Stretton, *Women Waging Law*, p. 13.
56. See also Beattie, 'Your Oratrice', p. 22; and Powell, '"Scarce expressible in English"', p. 115.
57. Liam J. Meyer, '"Humblewise": Deference and Complaint in the Court of Requests', *Journal of Early Modern Studies*, 4 (2015): 261–85, at 268. Similarly, Gwilym Dodd argues that, while pleadings subscribed to a linguistic framework, there was still room for stylistic individualism ('Writing Wrongs: The Drafting of Supplications to the Crown in Later Fourteenth-Century England', *Medium Aevum*, 80(2) (2011): 217–46.
58. Helen Wilcox, '"Free and Easy as Ones Discourse"?: Genre and Self-Expression in the Poems and Letters of Early Modern Englishwomen', in Michelle M. Dowd and Julie A. Eckerle (eds), *Genre and Women's Life Writing in Early Modern England* (Ashgate, 2007), pp. 15–32, at 17.
59. Adam Smyth, 'Introduction: The Range, Limits, and Potentials of the Form', in Smyth (ed.), *A History of English Autobiography*, pp. 1–10, at 2.
60. Catherine Richardson, for instance, suggests reading legal records as part of a wider web of (literary) texts, in which one can look for shared 'familiar and meaningful *tropes*' (Richardson, *Domestic Life and Domestic Tragedy in Early Modern England: The Material Life of the Household* (Manchester University Press, 2006), p. 30).
61. Paul Strohm, *The Poet's Tale: Chaucer and the Year that Made the Canterbury Tales* (Profile Books, 2014), p. 7.
62. Stretton, 'The Problem of the Lawyer's Hand', p. 695.
63. Dolan, *True Relations*, p. 114.
64. Stewart, *The Oxford History of Life-Writing*, p. 5.
65. Arlette Farge seems to agree with Stewart, as she suggests that those who ended up in court 'never wanted to leave any written record, much less the one they ended up leaving' (Farge, *The Allure of the Archives*, translated by Thomas Scott-Railton (Yale University Press, 2013), p. 9).
66. Sidonie Smith and Julia Watson, *Reading Autobiography: A Guide for Interpreting Life Narratives*, second edition (Minneapolis and London:

University of Minnesota Press, 2010), p. 64; Philippa Kelly, Lloyd Davis and Ronald Bedford, 'Introduction', in Ronald Bedford, Lloyd Davis and Philippa Kelly (eds), *Early Modern Autobiography: Theory, Genres, Practices* (University of Michigan Press, 2006), pp. 1–16, at 4.

67. Barbara J. Shapiro, *A Culture of Fact: England, 1550–1720* (Cornell University Press, 2000), pp. 8–33.

Chapter 2

Courtship and Marriage

On the first pages of her *Meditations,* Elizabeth Delaval (1649–1717) provides a list of 'those resolution's I have made against the evill's of my life'.[1] At the top of this litany of 'many, many' sins is that of

> lament[ing] the loss of what is not a real but an imagenary good. No more shall my tear's be shed for the severity of my aunt who might without difuculty have setled me in the world according to my wish's, nor for the falcenesse of a lover who has been alltogether unwhorthy of my heart since the threat's of a coveitous father had power to change his, and poorly make him aske me to release the mulltitude of his vow's, which are all broke or will be soon, for I am told his father will force him to mary a daughter of the Earl of Rutlands whom he has yet never seen, which some time or other I am sure he will smart for[.][2]

The travails of courtship and the search for a suitable marriage partner appear to have been of the utmost importance in Delaval's life, as it was here that lay the primary cause of her sin. Although she had just been spurned by her suitor, the young woman was determined to hide her resentment: 'And this I do not say out of revenge but in true grief for sure I am that so it must be: that honest true love I have had for him is still so deeply rooted that I find no pleasure in the thought's of him being punish'd'.[3] It may be that this was merely a reflection of her character and maturity, but it could also be an indication of her awareness of the genre in which she was writing, the occasional meditation. The occasional meditation was a distinctively Protestant genre, in which the various meditations 'form a proof of the individual's spiritual service'.[4] Delaval's *Meditations*, however, defies easy categorisation, as her spiritual meditations are combined with descriptions of the everyday events taking place in her life, of which her romantic pursuits are the most important.[5]

It is also likely that Delaval understood how 'wrong' behaviour either during or following a failed courtship could harm a woman's reputation, and she was therefore eager to appear forgiving. As she was the only daughter of Sir James Livingston (1621/2–70), Delaval's match did not simply determine the course of her own life, it also had repercussions for the family name. This may be one of the reasons why her aunt devoted so much of her time to finding Delaval an eligible partner of good prospects. The young girl's head, however, was filled with ideas about romance and true love, ideas she picked up from reading the prose romances that her servant enabled her to read.[6] The conflicting motivations behind marrying for love or to safeguard the family honour form a key theme in the *Meditations*. The question of whom she should marry was an important source of the conflict that raged between Delaval and her aunt. On more than one occasion, Delaval described having disputes with her aunt over the choice of suitor: 'but becauce I once disobey'd my aunt in not giving my selfe to a young man that she had chose for me [. . .], she crosses me now out of revenge for my disobeydience to her'.[7]

The concern shown by Elizabeth Delaval and her aunt over finding an appropriate match in marriage was certainly not uncommon in early modern England. Although remaining a spinster was an option, marriage was considered the ideal. Indeed, according to legal guides regarding women's rights, such as *The Lawes Resolutions of Womens Rights* (1632), women were understood as either 'married or to be married'.[8] The process of finding a suitor and getting married was therefore of paramount importance in any woman's life, not just in Elizabeth Delaval's. Since a woman's social standing and financial security depended on finding a suitable match, it is no surprise that the court archives are bursting with accounts of allegedly broken marriage promises and disputes over the validity of marriages. Although the larger part of early modern English marital litigation focuses on the problems that could arise around the formation of marriages, marital disharmony and breakdown of marriages were by no means alien to early modern English culture. This chapter considers the way in which women present their cases as litigants of suits concerning both the formation and the dissolution of marriage. The narrative strategies they use, such as character assassination, resemble in important ways the literary tropes and narrative mechanisms we find in traditionally accepted genres of life-writing such as autobiography. Women engaged in these cases in starkly different ways and these engagements were dependent on whether the cases revolved around courtship or marriage. While a woman involved in a courtship case would invoke subtle techniques to discredit her male opponent while defending her own reputation (after all, this courtship may have come to naught, but the possibility of a future match must always be accounted for), a wife who sought escape from a bad or abusive husband was free to attack his reputation with rather more virulence.

The Law on Courtship and Marriage

Rather more of Elizabeth Delaval's *Meditations* is preoccupied with the search for a suitable match than with her subsequent marriage.[9] This emphasis on courtship over marriage is echoed in contemporary legal suits. Issues surrounding courtship outnumber cases concerning marital problems by a ratio of at least three to one.[10] That there are so many cases regarding courtship and marriage has to do with the ambiguity surrounding what constituted a valid marriage and how to prove such a marriage had been contracted. The law was relatively clear. Children could be betrothed from the moment they reached the age of seven, but the minimum age the law required for the formation of an actual marriage was twelve for girls and fourteen for boys.[11] The canons of 1604 introduced an age bump, as it required the consent of parents or guardians when anyone under the age of twenty-one wanted to contract themselves or get married.[12] Importantly, though, these same canons did not declare marriage without consent void, which meant that even those marriages contracted without consent were legally valid, even if they were frowned upon by the church.

Problems arose when determining what constituted a valid marriage. A simple exchange of consent formulated in the present tense was in theory enough to create a legally valid and binding marriage. According to the editor of *The Lawes Resolution*, 'the full contract of matrimony, is when it is made by words, *de praesenti*, in a lawful consent, and thus two be made man and wife existing without lying together'.[13] In practice, the church courts propagated solemnisation of the marriage and the publication of banns. But even if a marriage was not solemnised in church, it could still be considered as valid by the church courts. The requirements under the letter of the law thus deviated from the actual practices. The result was considerable uncertainty as to what could be asserted as a valid marriage. Those who wanted to be in no doubt were well advised to take the traditional path as laid down by the church: via the publication of banns, solemnisation via a church ceremony attended by witnesses and the exchanging of vows and rings, followed by consummation of the marriage. On the other hand, the special position of clandestine marriage allowed some leeway for those trying to wriggle out from under their promises of marriage – both in the future tense (*de futuro*, or betrothal) and the present tense (*de praesenti*, or spousals) – in the case of regret.

That concerns regarding the formation of marriage contracts made their way into contemporary drama shows how important the issue was. Indeed, Subha Mukherji reads the proliferation of people whose marital status is uncertain in early modern drama as a reflection of the real-life situation at the time.[14] Shakespeare's *Measure for Measure*, for instance, centres on the status of two marriage contracts: between Claudio and Juliet on the one hand, and Angelo and Mariana on the other. Claudio is imprisoned for impregnating Juliet, whom he considers to be his wife:

> Thus stands it with me. Upon a true contract,
> I got possession of Julietta's bed.
> You know the lady; she is fast my wife,
> Save that we do the denunciation lack
> Of outward order. This we came not to
> Only for propagation of a dower
> Remaining in the coffer of her friends,
> From whom we thought it meet to hide our love
> Till time had made them for us. But it chances
> The stealth of our most mutual entertainment
> With character too gross is writ on Juliet. (1.2.133–43)

According to Claudio, 'a true contract' had been made between Juliet and himself. Because the couple wanted to wait for Juliet's family's blessing, and the accompanying dower, the marriage had not yet been legitimised. Juliet's pregnancy, however, made keeping their relationship secret an impossibility and so Claudio found himself facing the death penalty for fornication, despite his explanation and Juliet's corroboration of his story. It remains uncertain what kind of contract has been agreed upon, and scholarly opinion is still divided.[15] Even if the couple had made spousals, the uncertain nature of the law meant that their future child could be termed illegitimate.[16] Even when two lovers agreed to be married, then, their mutual consent was not necessarily enough to avoid getting in trouble with the law.

The contract between Claudio and Juliet, who are expecting a child, is contrasted with that between Angelo and Mariana, who are not. Although Angelo admits 'there was some speech of marriage', he claims the negotiations were broken off because the 'promisèd proportions / Came short of composition' and Mariana's 'reputation was disvalued / In levity' (5.1.215–20).[17] After he has been tricked into sleeping with Mariana, Angelo is forced by the Duke to accept Mariana as his wife and he finally admits that he had been contracted to Mariana previously. Although the exact nature of the contract (*de futuro* or *de praesenti*) is never explicitly mentioned, the fact that consummation is seen to transform the relationship between Angelo and Mariana into a valid marriage suggests the couple had exchanged vows *de futuro*. This would explain the different treatment the two couples receive: while the child that Juliet is expecting will be born out of a non-solemnised marriage, and can therefore be seen as illegitimate, Mariana and Angelo's children, should they have any, will be born in wedlock. Conversely, in *The Duchess of Malfi*, John Webster makes the status of his title character's marriage contract clear: the Duchess and Antonio have exchanged vows *de praesenti.*[18] Because the marriage has not been solemnised, the couple's children are deemed illegitimate, both in the eyes of the law and the Duchess's brother Ferdinand.[19]

The underlying anxieties in both *Measure for Measure* and *The Duchess of Malfi* thus seem to centre around the question of whether a child conceived or born outside of a solemnised marriage could or should be considered legitimate: the question, as ever, boiled down to money (and inheritance). Both on the stage and in real life, the anxiety surrounding clandestine marriage was less the result of moral or religious scruples than concerns over legality.[20] The absence of evidence that a marriage had taken place could lead to a range of accusations against men and women alike. Another common accusation, bigamy, was also difficult to prove or dispel if no official ceremony had taken place and there was no church official who could confirm or deny a previous contract had been made. The choice of whether or not to start legal proceedings, then, was a complicated one.

This was particulary the case in matters concerning broken promises in the courtship phase. If a woman was jilted by her suitor, taking matters before a court of justice could make her look scorned and disobedient, two qualities that were condemned in contemporary literature on the 'proper' feminine traits, such as in Barnabe Rich's *The Excellency of Good Women*.[21] Since the courtship had not led to the desired result (marriage), the woman in question would have to start from scratch and find a new suitor. Seeing a predecessor dragged before the courts for having changed his mind while wooing a lady might well put off any potential beau, of course. Moreover, taking someone to court in order to force them to wed a woman they no longer desired might be considered an unfortunate way to begin a marriage. Conversely, failing to invoke legal proceedings following a broken contract might also harm a woman's reputation, as it could indicate there was a valid reason for the suitor to break off the courtship or engagement. Some women, however, did not have a choice. This was the case when women became pregnant before marriage. As if the scandal and damage to a woman's reputations were not enough, the church courts could also penalise women who bore illegitimate children.[22] Persuading the father of the child to marry might solve a woman's problems, but making private affairs public (which starting legal proceedings would certainly do), could be a daunting prospect. The decision of whether to sue for broken promises of marriage was one to be carefully weighed.

Suing for separation was also a choice that a husband or wife would not make lightly. Divorce as we now know it was not an option, but it was not impossible for spouses to effectively extricate themselves from an unhappy union. Marriages could be annulled on the grounds of a previous impediment, for instance if there was a valid pre-contract to another party or if the couple were related in a forbidden way. This was the only way spouses could escape the bonds of marriage completely, freeing them to remarry. A marriage could be partially dissolved, however, by applying for a divorce of bed and board. This arrangement did not dissolve the holy bonds of matrimony, but allowed both parties to live separate lives, each with their own individual household. The law did not allow for remarriage, but they would, at least, not be forced to spend time together. Such a separation was only granted on the grounds of cruelty or adultery. Given that annulment and separation were hard to obtain (because of costs involved and *coverture*), the initiator of proceedings to separate would have to carefully consider the possibility that the process would end in failure.[23] The possibility that the end result of such proceedings would be your continuing to live with a partner you had openly expressed a desire to desert may well be an intimidating enough prospect to deter most potential litigants from even starting a lawsuit.[24]

Towards the end of the sixteenth century, a successful suit, on the other hand, not only released a wife from an unhappy marriage but might also give her some financial freedom, as a separation of bed and board was usually accompanied by an award of alimony.[25] Such an award was usually permanent, and the amount varied depending on the husband's income, the wife's portion upon marriage and the reason for the separation. If the couple had children, maintenance costs could be added to the total sum.[26] Because a separation of bed and board did not technically end *coverture*, a woman's financial freedom was not guaranteed, however: without alimony she could struggle to keep any earnings if her husband claimed them for his own.[27] Those couples that did seek legal judgement regarding either annulment or separation accepted the fact that they must hang out their dirty laundry for all to see. Interestingly, it was a route adopted by the lower ranks and the elite alike.[28] Some, however, chose a less public and expensive way of resolving their marital problems, through the mediation of neighbours, friends and family. Such mediation could be somewhat casual by nature, such as when a neighbour steps in to enable and ensure conversation between the two antagonistic parties, but it could also be a more formal process involving the intervention of arbitrators.[29] The goal in each case was to settle matters outside of court. This kind of dispute resolution could help keep the behaviour of a violent husband or adulterous wife under control, but it could not ensure the separation of holy matrimony, nor could its agreements, such as the payment of alimony, be enforced. If mediation failed or if one of the parties reneged on their promises, there was no option but to seek redress in the courts.[30]

Whichever manner of dispute resolution was chosen, failed courtships and marriages were food for gossip and the parties involved would therefore have to expect great interest in the details of their lives. Such was the case with the quickly deteriorating marriage between Anne Lake (1599x1601–30) and William Cecil, Baron Ros (1590–1618). The nature of the conflict between the two spouses was thought to be sexual: in his letters, John Chamberlain makes references to an alleged blackmail plot between Lady Ros and her mother on the one hand, and Baron Ros on the other. The women were said to have threatened to reveal that the Baron was impotent, and to register this as grounds for the annulment of the marriage. When this scheme failed to bear fruit, the Lake women went one step further, publicly accusing Baron Ros of having illicit sexual relations with his step-grandmother, who they also claimed had attempted to poison Lady Ros. Lady Ros, in turn, was accused of incestuous relationships with her brother.[31] Following a suit in Star Chamber, which was presided over by James I himself, Lady Ros was found guilty of slander and sentenced to prison, as well as a hefty fine. The case attracted widespread public interest: Anne Clifford noted in her diary that 'there was spoken extraordinarie fowle matters of my Lady Ros' who was 'counted a most odious woman', while William Davenport's commonplace book includes a libel ridiculing Lady Ros, narrating the 'shame' the loss of 'her beard' (her pubic hair), caused by her promiscuous behaviour, had brought her.[32] The backlash Lady Ros faced after her attempts to extricate herself from her unhappy marriage is somewhat extreme, but the case shows how private matters could quickly become public upon seeking a separation. To avoid scandal of this (or less extreme) kind, women, whether as *feme sole* or *feme covert*, carefully shaped the narratives they told in court in order to minimise the damage to their reputations when involved in matters over courtship or marriage.

The narrative strategies women employed are presented in two sections: the first half of this chapter concentrates on *femes soles* and the courtship phase, and the second has the breakdown of marriage and *femes coverts* as its focus. Each section first looks at the life-writing of an early modern woman to highlight the strategies used in her text, before turning to legal records in order to demonstrate how female litigants employed similar storytelling techniques.

Part I: Courtship

In the sixty-one folios that constitute the 'True accountt' of Anne, Lady Halkett (1623–99), the author looks back on her life.[33] Despite being written some years before she died, probably *c.*1677–8, the manuscript abruptly stops mid-sentence in 1656, leaving the remaining forty-three years of her life unaccounted for.[34] Several folios in the middle of the manuscript have been ripped out, possibly by Halkett herself.[35] The remaining text focuses on the author's various courtships and her involvement in political affairs of the time. A great part of the text is dedicated to Halkett's relationship with Colonel Joseph Bampfield, who employed Halkett's help with his political endeavours, including their smuggling of the Duke of York (the future James II) out of England. The couple also became romantically involved, although the exact status of their relationship remains obscure. These various romantic and political engagements had left Halkett vulnerable to gossip, and presumably in an attempt to counter this, she set about writing down her life's story. The 'True accountt' gave Halkett the perfect opportunity to present her version of events, in which she was able to excuse her behaviour and choices.[36] Halkett used various strategies to do so.

The first part of her account is dedicated to her various failed courtships and Halkett uses conditional clauses to retain her agency as she discusses them. In the search for a suitable partner, Halkett had to strike a balance between honouring her parents' wishes, following her own desires and pleasing her suitor. She explains how she informed one of her dalliances, Thomas Howard, that she 'was 2 or 3 yeare older then hee & and were there no other obiection yett that was of such weight with mee as would neuer lett mee allow his further adrese'.[37] When Howard does not accept Halkett's refusal, she tells him that 'hee need neuer expect I would marry him withoutt his father and my Mothers Consentt; if that Could bee obtained [9][38] I should willingly giue him the Sattisfaction hee desired'.[39] This condition would be hard to meet; it is clear from Halkett's account that the couple could not count on his father's or her mother's approval. Whether Halkett genuinely wanted to marry her suitor or was simply stringing him along, the use of such conditional phrases gave Halkett the opportunity of continuing to see him, while keeping her 'legitimate' reasons for rejecting his offers of marriage as a card to be played at her leisure. Halkett was equally disingenuous following her mother's ordering her to stop seeing Howard, meeting him while blindfolded so as not to disobey this maternal directive.[40] She thus juggled the wishes of her parents and those of her suitor alongside her own agenda.

The second strategy Halkett employed is that of selection. In her 'True accountt', Halkett consciously and openly leaves out the years of her childhood, 'for I hope none will thinke they Could bee either vicious or Scandalous'.[41] She also skips over her life as James Halkett's wife. Judith Kearns has argued that 'the *Memoirs* are carefully and deliberately constructed to justify behavior that has left Halkett vulnerable' – and this behaviour seems to have taken place between the period of her coming of age and her entering marriage.[42] As such, Halkett only includes those parts of her life that might be a cause of scandal and does her best to rewrite history in such a way as to excuse her conduct and make herself appear virtuous.[43] The periods of her life that are free of sin, or those periods she feels she has a good excuse for, are left mostly unaccounted for. What Halkett chose to cover in her 'True accountt' was thus subject to selection, something Halkett foregrounds throughout her text, presumably in part to suggest that what remains was entirely true and honest.

The stories she does tell are, of course, entirely her choice. Halkett claims to remember exact words spoken years after an actual conversation took place, as such asserting her truthful authority. This allows her to present other statements to be taken at face value by the reader. There is a notable absence of discursive detail in the descriptions of her various courtships. Halkett remains, for instance, deliberately vague regarding the promises exchanged between herself and her suitor, Colonel Bampfield. All Halkett is willing to share with her readers is that she 'had beene puplickely Maried to him', leaving the exact nature of their marriage contract, and thus the exact nature of her sin, obscure.[44] She thus remains deliberately vague when describing potentially shameful behaviour on her part, while offering the kind of detail that makes her seem truthful and accurate at other times. This suggests that the author is highly selective in the information she shares with her readers, and the way she presents such information.

Thirdly, Halkett uses her memoirs to vindicate herself and assert her social credit. Her role in the civil war, and particularly her affair with the married Colonel Bampfield, had left Halkett open to criticism. Writing her 'True accountt' allowed her to explain and excuse the choices she had made. In order to do so without seeming immodest, Halkett uses the reports and judgements of others regarding her character and conduct to glorify herself. As Kearns points out, Halkett 'at significant points in the action [. . .] presents herself as having received the support of another person, generally someone in authority or well-regarded, or even more tellingly, as having won such a person over'.[45] Sir James Halkett, for instance, spots her virtue, as she describes how his 'eyes were so perceptable as to see & Loue iniured Vertue vnder so darke a Cloud[, a]s incompassed mee aboutt'.[46] Besides complimenting her future husband for his good judgement, Halkett craftily inserts a statement about her own virtue. Conversely, she refuses to discredit Bampfield, even when she has every reason to do so. Rather, she lets other people in her story refer to Bampfield as 'the most vnworthy person Liuing', and that 'though he were now [41] Likely to dye yett none pittyed him'.[47] In her reliance on second-hand, but ostensibly reliable, reports of Bampfield's unworthiness, she discredits her former suitor without appearing in any way vengeful. If anything, repeating the approbation of others while maintaining her own decorum may have made her seem all the more honest, and thus all the more badly treated.

Anne's marriage to the wealthy Sir James Halkett helped to redeem her potentially scandalous past behaviour. But before she could accept him as her husband, Anne wanted to get her financial affairs in order. She declined all of James Halkett's propositions of marriage, because she wanted to 'bring noe trouble' to her future husband. She did not meet with James Halkett 'in order to Conclude [their] Mariage' until she had 'Sattisfied all that I knew any thing was due to'.[48] The emphasis Halkett puts on the trouble she went through to settle her debts prior to marriage reveals her awareness of the importance of credit; a woman's financial situation was closely linked to the way she was perceived and spoken about and it could be damaging to her reputation if she were to marry with debts.[49] Moreover, it pre-empts any potential accusations of marrying for money. Halkett thus makes a conscious effort to present herself in the best light possible, using both her financial and social credit.

It is not that Halkett is selective when it comes to her 'True accountt' as much as it is what she selects (and actively omits) and how she does so that is of importance here. We might expect a woman such as Halkett to be able to wield the sorts of rhetorical strategies described here, and perhaps assume that they are characteristics limited to female discourse as found in diaries and autobiographies. It is striking, therefore, that these same three strategies (using conditions, applying selection bias and asserting credit) are to be found in the legal records of courtship disputes. The continual appearance of these strategies in the records suggests that a woman in the socially precarious position of having been jilted saw them as the best strategies available to her. In this sense, therefore, we can view Halkett's 'True accountt' as a manifestation of a broader cultural tendency in the self-representation of unmarried women and the strategies used as precursors to the socially delicate world of the autobiography.

'Conditional promises'

Most eligible young women were not completely free in their choice of husband. Rather, they depended on the consent of their parents or other 'friends' to find a suitable match, even if the law did not stipulate such parental consent.[50] Parental control was thus not absolute, but conditional. By accepting it, a woman claimed her parents' goodwill, while by refusing or circumventing it, she sacrificed this goodwill, potentially alongside her reputation and marriage portion. Conversely, claiming a lack of agency could be a powerful strategy, which, ironically, gave women the upper hand in a law court. Those women who had some agency in their choice of marital partner could assert it by claiming that they lacked that very same power: by telling their suitors they were willing to marry them on the condition that their parents gave consent, women could present their not-to-be husbands with a false image of obedient submission to their parents, while diverting the blame. Once they were tired of their suitors' attention, the women simply had to tell them that they would not receive consent for their match. As such, women were able to take control over the courtship phase and use the expectations of the man against them, by for instance stringing their suitors along and accepting gifts and money for the duration of the courtship, while having no intention of marrying their suitor at all. As has been demonstrated by Laura Gowing, women often used conditional clauses in their response to a marriage proposal.[51]

Women who were accused either of rescinding their promise to marry or of denying their reputed marriage vows frequently used this strategy. Joan Baker, for example, stressed that she was quite clear with her suitor John Hawarde when 'she made him a promise to marry with him if she could get her mother's goodwill or else not'.[52] In like fashion, Alice Allen told Henry Becher that if they could 'get her father and mother's good will she would marry with him and otherwise she would not'.[53] When Thomas Mannsbridge asked Margaret Purdue if she could find it in her heart to take him to her husband and 'do forsake all other for his sake', she answered that 'she would first know her friend's good will whether it were a fit match for her or no'.[54] We have already seen Anne Halkett make a similar statement to her suitor Thomas Howard.[55] In these cases, women denied their own agency to escape legal sanction in the form of the court's assertion of either the alleged marriage or promise to marry as legally binding. Moreover, by claiming they did not have the power to betroth themselves without parental consent, women were able to counter their legal opponents' claims that a valid marriage (or promise thereof) had been procured, and in doing so, they simultaneously demonstrated that they were virtuous and dutiful daughters (and thus virtuous and dutiful wives-to-be). The simple denial of agency, therefore, could be used, counterintuitively, to empower a woman during the courtship phase. By offering their suitors a conditional promise of marriage, on the condition that their 'friends' would give consent, women could buy themselves more time to consider the proposal or give them a way out when they decided the man in question did not make a suitable match after all, as they could simply claim the conditions of the promise had not been met. As such, a promise of marriage based on the condition of receiving parental consent is a crafty rhetorical strategy in itself.

Ellen Nixon was a young woman who seemed well aware of the limitations and opportunities attached to the denying and affirming of agency. Her former suitor John Cartwright started proceedings against Thomas Nixon, her father, after he learned that his fiancée had married another man.[56] One of the legal issues of the case concentrated on the question of whether Ellen Nixon's marriage to Peter Morrall – the other man – was valid. In order to determine this validity, the court required insight into the role of Ellen's parents. According to one of the deponents, a John Howell, Ellen's mother Maude Nixon was privy and consenting to the marriage between her daughter and Peter Morrall, even though she had previously given her good will to the marriage between Ellen and John Cartwright.[57] Deponent William Mullocke sketched Maude's role even more clearly, accusing her of visiting the Cartwright house in order to persuade John Cartwright to take back the tokens of affection he had given Ellen during their courtship – something John refused.[58] In doing so, Mullocke paints Maude as a typically meddling mother.[59]

Whatever Maude's role in the affair, it is plain that Ellen herself was far from being an innocent party. Despite telling Johane Mullocke that her parents had a 'liking for someone who neither she nor anybody else could like' (meaning John Cartwright), Ellen Nixon was, according to other deponents, keen to accept several tokens from John, including a pair of gloves to be worn on the wedding day, a silk girdle, knives and a hat from London. The final item was allegedly sent for by John on Ellen's explicit request.[60] In her personal answer, Nixon tries to paint a picture of herself as the dutiful daughter. She stresses that, although she did not want to marry Cartwright, 'at that time fearing to offend her said Friends she this defendant seemed to consent'.[61] She also tells Margaret Baylye that 'she would do as it should please her friends but she could never love [John Cartwright]'.[62] Only when 'the complainant coming unto this defendant and finding her very sad, said unto her these words or the like in effect Ellen if thou like any man better than me I pray thy take him', does she make any claim to considering herself free to act as she wished: 'this defendant thinketh and as her counsel informeth her she was at liberty considering she never made the complainant any but conditional promises'.[63] As such, Nixon tries to clear her name by insisting that she did not do anything wrong: at the moment she entered into marriage with Peter Morrall, Cartwright had already given her his blessing. And in any case, she never made anything except 'conditional promises', although Nixon does not elaborate what this conditional character consisted of. She thus skillfully plays with the concept of agency: she uses it to her advantage in establishing conditional promises, in presenting herself as a dutiful daughter by pretending to submit to her parents' wishes when in fact she does not and by her insistence that she did not even consider denying Cartwright until he gave her permission.

Another young woman whose family sought to assert their choice of husband over hers was Anne Fryer. In 1578, she was summoned to defend herself before London's consistory court by her former suitor Peter Richardson.[64] In her personal answer Fryer outlined the pressure placed on her to marry according to her family's wishes. Fryer told of how her father was the most active in this, 'earnestly persuading her to yield her consent', harassing her and even resorting to 'using withal some threats'. Fryer's reluctance to comply with her father's wishes stemmed from her previous commitment to marry a Richard Robinson, who was at sea at the time that Peter Richardson was pressing his suit. Although Fryer admitted to being 'moved [. . .] somewhat (although against her will)' under the influence of her family, she still refused to abandon her previous engagement in Richardson's favour. At a dinner party at her grandmother's house, Richardson put Fryer on the spot, asking her outright to give him her hand. Fryer resorted to trickery, presenting this insistent suitor with her left hand as she had already given 'her right hand with her faith and troth in the way of marriage to Richard Robinson'. And when one of her uncles asked Fryer if she would take Richardson as her husband, she 'answered yes: meaning indeed to have taken him to her husband, if that Richard Robinson had not claimed her former promise to him by her'.[65] While Fryer's 'yes' seems unambiguous, the 'if' signals the conditional element of her sentence: were she not promised to Robinson, she would have married Richardson. The conditional is thus found in the court records, but not at the dinner party, where she answered 'yes'.

Fryer, however, had no intention of marrying Richardson. She could, of course, have simply told her family and suitor this clearly and unambiguously, but responds as she does to maintain the fiction of obedience. By not telling her family and suitor that she had already promised herself to another man, she made use of another strategy that recurs frequently in courtship litigation: that of selection bias.

Selection Bias

Part of a narrator's role is to orchestrate the events in their story. This includes the careful selection of information in order to maintain the goodwill of the audience, the better to persuade them. This selection can include the simple avoidance of facts that might harm the litigant's case, the paying of lip service to other facts and the use of hyperbole and emphasis to exaggerate the importance of yet more facts.[66] A story is always one-sided, especially when a story is told with the intention of persuading an audience, as is vital in court.

The primary audience for litigants would be the sitting judge(s). To convince that judge of the truth of their story, a litigant needed to address the requirements for the formation of a valid marriage and in doing so prove whether or not those had been met. These requirements, then, form the basic ingredients for the stories litigants of marriage suits told. Women would have been well aware of these, as there was a widespread appreciation of and contact with the law in early modern England.[67] Awareness of the laws surrounding marriage was particularly widespread, given the many debates on the matter, both in the religious and political spheres, and the fact that marriage was an institution that would affect almost everybody at some point or other. Furthermore, mortality rates ensured that many would have direct experience of it more than once during their lifetimes.[68] It seems that only the most socially isolated of women could possibly be unaware of the pitfalls of marriage, and thus what sort of things they ought to address in their bills of complaint, answers and depositions, should the need arise. Knowledge of the factors that could make or break a case were key to making intelligent selection decisions when composing a narrative.

Since a lawsuit necessitated one to defend one's actions, we might expect women who found themselves amidst a legal battle regarding their conduct in courtship to take the opportunity to be as descriptive and detailed as possible in their accounts. Details of vows, actions taken and tokens received were exactly the information that might indicate whether a contract had been made or a promise had been broken. The time spent on each of these elements, or the extent to which certain features were ignored, is often revealing.

This is demonstrated in the 1601 case of *Ashe v Bedcotte*. Elizabeth Bedcotte is accused by her former suitor, John Ashe, of breaking her promise of marriage. She has no trouble admitting that John Ashe was a former suitor of hers and she also acknowledges that she did indeed receive several tokens of affection from him, although, according to her, they were not valuable and had already been returned to Ashe before he exhibited his bill of complaint.[69] The emphasis on the value of gifts is a reaction to the audience to be persuaded – the suit was taking place before the Court of Requests, the so-called poor man's court. Since John Ashe claims that his courtship of Bedcotte has put him in a state of 'very great loss and almost undoing', Bedcotte would naturally contest the value of the tokens received, even before stating that they had been returned in any case. Bedcotte avoids describing the nature of their courtship in any detail, as she 'further confesseth that she doth now refuse to marry with him and she thinketh she hath good cause so to do and lawfully may do both by Law and conscience'. She continues by desiring 'the opinion of this honorable court; whether against her this honorable court will proceed any further to examine this cause or no and humbly craveth to be dismissed of this injurious suit with her costs and charges in this suit most wrongfully sustained'.[70] Bedcotte thus keeps the detail she supplies to a bare minimum. We may infer that her legal strategy is only to respond if not doing so would harm her defence. The rhetorical effect of this approach – spending as few words and little time as possible on the matter – emphasises the key argument of the case: that the whole matter is hardly worth any attention at all. Where Ashe claims that Bedcotte has acted 'most fraudulently, dishonestly and unconscionably', Bedcotte's response is that not only are these accusations nonsense as she returned the (worthless) tokens to Ashe, but that her refusal to marry Ashe was allowable both by law and conscience.

Elizabeth Bedcotte's strategy of brevity is by no means unusual. Similarly, a defendant named Elizabeth Frith rebukes her suitor's accusations in the shortest way possible by saying that he 'hath had talk of matrimony with her and she said to him that he should be as welcome to her as any other man should be' and one Jane Salisbury simply states that William Lloyde 'was a suitor unto her in the way of marriage and she always denied him of his suit'.[71] Both women answer their suitor's accusations with the minimum of words. We see a related strategy in the personal answer of Elizabeth Church.[72] Church is sued by Mathew Levett, a former suitor for her hand in marriage. Although Levett 'by and by asked of her if she could find in her heart to love him', she claims 'she could make him no answer (so soon)' without the consent of her aunt and uncle. The suitor is persistent, but Church 'made him always the like answer'. Deponents describe how Church eventually gives in to Levett's wishes and promises him to 'take the Mathew Levett to my husband to have & to hold from this day forward in sickness & in health till death us do part' in a marriage ceremony.[73] Church, on the other hand, claimed that she did not remember any form of ceremony taking place between herself and her alleged husband. Although she remembered Levett taking her by the hand and speaking to her, 'what answer she did make unto it she doth not now remember for she was so sore amazed'. Her answer acted as a road block to further cross-questioning: she could fall back on her alleged memory loss with each question she did not want to answer. Since there were several witnesses who could testify to Church's presence and behaviour at the marriage ceremony, denial was not a workable option for her. In the presence of damning witness testimony she resorted to the shortest way to cut it off, claiming that the surprise wedding ceremony affected her mental faculties, temporarily blocking her memory and perhaps also her judgement.

While in some cases brevity was chosen as the best strategy to close down further enquiry, at other times supplying a detailed version of events might be considered the better approach, especially for a litigant who needed to amass evidence of her good character. This could be particularly useful if there was a large amount of evidence piled up against somebody and their accuser was aiming to destroy their reputation. The 1610 *Moore-Perrie c Warren* case is a good example of this: both parties give a detailed account of their version of events and various deponents are called upon to collaborate the parties' narratives. The case forms the backbone to the third recurring theme in courtship cases: asserting social credit. Such assertion requires the building up of evidence and testimonies and can lead to lengthy accounts.

Asserting Social Credit

Especially during the courtship phase, a woman was left vulnerable to gossip about her behaviour. Too much familiarity with a man, for instance, could ruin a young girl's chances on the marriage market, while too little affection could make the suitor give up. The legal process brought a particular kind of scrutiny upon the actions and demeanour of a woman. As Douglas Walton points out, a 'defendant's only argument may be her good reputation, demonstrated by her past actions and good character shown by them'.[74] This was not lost upon early modern women: in legal records we observe women styling themselves as virtuous and blameless and their legal opponents as the opposite. In order to convince a judge that their version of events was the more accurate, litigants (both defendants and complainants) naturally sought to present themselves in the best light possible. The fine line between vindication and boasting had to be carefully managed, however, as too great an insistence on one's good character could be seen as immodest, a characteristic considered unbecoming in early modern English women.[75] Tip the scales too far in one direction and one's integrity would become open to question, and with it, one's reputation.

The widow Margaret Moore-Perrie seemed well aware of this when she sued Richard Warren before the consistory court of London in 1610.[76] The lawsuit between them centres around the question of whether a legitimate marriage had been procured between the two. The couple met for the first time in the tavern the Black Spread Eagle in Wapping, London, and their relationship seems to have developed rapidly, which, as Eleanor Hubbard points out, may well have been because of their high level of drunkenness.[77] Deponents on behalf of Moore-Perrie present Warren as the initiator of proceedings. In fact, they suggest that Warren was so taken by the widow that he neglected to enquire into the situation of his newly beloved until after their marriage had been procured – on the very same evening that they had met. Moore-Perrie's testimony showed her as equally infatuated with Warren, so much so that she put complete trust in him. One of Moore-Perrie's witnesses, a Johannes Johnson, relates the following:

> this Jurat's [someone who has sworn an oath] wife would have had the said Richard Warren to break a piece of gold between him & the widow, & to give her the one half & keep the other, & the said Warren said he had not a piece of gold there, & thereupon the said Margaret said what need no any gold I dare take his word for I am persuaded he will not go from his word, or such like speeches passed between them.[78]

Moore-Perrie is depicted here as a trusting woman: she takes her suitor as a man of his word. The statement perhaps suggests she is naïve, but ultimately it reflects her in a good light: it acts as a character witness because it suggests to the judge that she has no ulterior motive for wanting to marry Warren, and also that as she trusts, so can she be trusted. Warren may not have had a piece of gold available to act as a material witness to the marriage, but according to this witness he promised Moore-Perrie that this current lack would be met in the future with a much larger token in the form of real estate:

> He, the said Richard Warren, said to the said Margaret Perrie also More that if she would be contented to marry him he would give her that house, meaning the house called black spread eagle wherein they were, & the said Margaret said she was contented to be married to him, & there upon the said Richard Warren said (. . .) I do frankly give thee this house in token that we are man & wife & it shall be thine & other houses more.[79]

According to this witness, Warren offered his new wife the tavern of his own free will – Moore-Perrie did not solicit it nor did she at any stage inquire into Warren's financial situation. The implication is clearly that Moore-Perrie married Warren out of genuine affection rather than avarice.

Since Johnson is Moore-Perrie's witness, it is of course not surprising that he both corroborates her story and paints a favourable picture of her. Indeed, both Johnson and the widow's other witnesses can be accused of partiality; as lodgers in her house, they all stand to lose something should they displease her and gain something should their landlady take possession of the tavern following their testimony. As Hillary Taylor has demonstrated based on records of the Court of Star Chamber, material dispensations and economic gain were reasons for would-be deponents to either testify, or to refrain from doing so, on behalf of their social and economic superiors.[80] Indeed, swearing on oath, as witnesses had to do, was no guarantee that their testimony was true, nor was it regarded as indicating as such, as Barbara Shapiro has shown.[81] J. A. Guy has noted, moreover, that 'perjury was rampant in the English bill courts'.[82] As well as providing Moore-Perrie with an excellent reference, Johnson also gives us reason to believe that we may reasonably suspect the reliability of his testimony: in his statement, he confirms that his landlady approached him regarding his testimony and asked the witnesses 'if they heard not Warren promise her marriage & what speeches they heard between them'.[83] Female litigants may not have had the freedom shown by autobiographers and diarists such as Anne Halkett as they simply ignored events or wrote people out of their stories as they saw fit, but they could still secure a similar control over their stories by selecting and influencing those individuals who were going to tell it – their witnesses.

While Moore-Perrie makes an effort to demonstrate that she had no ulterior motive in marrying Warren, he is more careful in the selection of his spouse: several deponents testify that Warren 'asked her if she were out of debt & she said she was & then he said he would have her to his wife if she had but the clothes on her back'.[84] Another witness corroborates this story and several witnesses emphasise Moore-Perrie's solid financial affairs prior to the alleged marriage. However, here too, we can assume that Moore-Perrie has coached her witnesses, whose dependence on her may have made them willing to lie on her behalf.

Truthful or not, these statements in the Moore-Perrie case show us the importance of 'social credit' in early modern society and especially in the early modern courtroom. Warren's alleged inquiry into his future wife's solvency demonstrates how closely connected a woman's financial situation was to the way she was perceived and spoken about. In particular, and as Halkett's 'True accountt' shows, it could be damaging to a woman's reputation and standing if she were to marry with debts; again and again in legal records we see women's financial status placed under scrutiny before entering marriage. As Craig Muldrew has suggested, early modern society placed value not only on the ability to repay a debt, but the whole economy of trust that surrounded this; it was this trust that earned you 'social credit'.[85] One's social credit determined whether a household was able to obtain financial credit and without it, a household could not thrive.[86] This goes some way to explaining the emphasis placed on a woman's financial situation upon entering marriage. Settling her debts before marriage ensured that those debts would not transfer to her husband and household, and that bad credit would not affect the future of her family and household either financially or in terms of social standing. Social credit took time to build, but allowed for financial credit. Demonstrating fiscal responsibility could act as shorthand in court and demonstrate a litigant's social (and moral) responsibility. Stressing the attempts they made to organise their financial affairs prior to marriage can thus be seen as a strategy employed by women in court to establish moral credibility. For Margaret Moore-Perrie, making sure the judges on her case knew her financial status prior to her supposed marriage was solid was not only a way of showing that she did not marry Warren for the money, but also that she was a woman of good reputation and thus obviously not lying. As such, Moore-Perrie's deponents help paint her character in a more favourable light. It is no accident that the witness statements concerning Moore-Perrie should focus so much on her financial situation and the one she thought she was about to enter.

The reliance on witnesses, however, also served another function: to maintain the appearance of modesty. Conduct books described the ideal woman as modest, silent and humble.[87] By voicing their own virtues and exhibiting their proper behaviour in a public legal proceeding, women would act contrary to those moral prescriptions. To let witnesses do the praising allowed litigants to circumvent this predicament, but still reach the desired goal. Deponents could function equally well when they put the opposition in disregard by means of *argumentum ad hominem*.[88] Building on the idea that white looks whiter when put next to black, such an attack on the character or personal attributes of the legal opponent helps to put the litigant in a better light. While this type of character assassination was not a frequent occurrence in pre-marriage litigation, when it did happen, it was primarily carried out by witnesses rather than the female parties in a suit.[89] The method needed to be employed carefully, as the use of *ad hominem* arguments could easily backfire. If the female litigant's argument was perceived as an overly aggressive attack on her former suitor, this reflected badly on her credibility.[90] The need not to appear quarrelsome or vengeful was especially great for a jilted woman. This is where witnesses could play a useful role, as they, of course, were not the ones on trial. We see this in action in the Moore-Perrie case, where one deponent claimed that she heard 'a girl said there goeth Waren they call him dirty Dick'.[91] Whether Moore-Perrie had any role in finding such a useful witness is hard to say, but the allegation against Warren's moral rectitude serves her well as it implicitly invites the court to contrast this with her own, unimpeachable behaviour.

Women involved in courtship litigation thus tended to take a relatively amicable approach towards their legal opponents. Rather than looking to attack their former suitors, they simply denied the charges made against them. Should character assassination be necessary, then this could be left to their deponents. Conversely, women involved in suits for separation took a very different approach. These types of suits were much less friendly, and character assassination formed more the rule than the exception. Wives were accused of adultery, unruliness and even poisoning; husbands were similarly accused of adultery, but cruelty and violence were the main accusations. These were accusations that could not be dealt with in an amiable manner; these issues invited an offensive approach.

Part II: Marriage and Its Breakdown

Around the year 1610 Margaret Cunningham (d. *c.*1630) wrote her autobiographical *A Pairt of the Life of Lady Margaret Cuninghame*.[92] The text opens as follows:

> I was married upon the 24th of Januwary 1598, and I remained with my Lord my Father three years, without receiving anything of my husband's living, but was furnished by my Lord my Father in my abulziement [clothing], and all things needful.[93]

In this first sentence, the Scotswoman sets the mood and scene that characterise the rest of her autobiography; from the moment the couple enter into marriage, her husband refuses to fulfil his duties as a husband. It seems to have been the continual negligence and cruelty that James, Master of Evandale, displayed towards his wife that drove her to write her autobiography. Nothing significantly changes over the duration of the work, as the final sentence is written in much the same spirit: 'The nixt tryste [meeting] not being come, I remain destitute at the present of any money to sustain me, my bairns and familie, remaining in Libertoun the 29 of Sept. 1608'.[94] As such, Cunningham's entire autobiographical work can be read as a charge against her husband.

Cunningham's open attack on her spouse is surprising in a social environment in which wives were expected to remain silent and in a state of spousal subjugation.[95] More startling still is the fact that she appears to have consciously courted public attention with her story, hoping to gather support for her decision to seek a legal separation from her husband.[96] To vindicate her choices in the eyes of the public, Cunningham employs two strategies. Firstly, she makes her husband look bad by exposing him as a cruel and philandering spendthrift. Conversely, Cunningham portrays herself as an innocent victim, left desolate and in despair, unable to function as a normal housewife and mother. The second strategy visible in Cunningham's autobiographical text ties in with this portrayal of herself as a weak and vulnerable woman. In the painting of such a self-portrait Cunningham denies herself the agency that she is patently displaying by picking up her pen. The dissonance between these two facts is apparent throughout her autobiography.

Once again, however, we see that such strategies were not peculiar to the autobiographer; female litigants deployed strikingly similar strategies in their pleadings. Despite the seeming overlap with the narrative techniques employed in courtship cases, we find here a distinction in degree. Whereas female litigants in courtship cases established autonomy by using conditional phrases, in separation cases, women actively and unequivocally described themselves as free agents. Similarly, the relatively amiable approach chosen in courtship cases is exchanged for a more offensive one here; *femes coverts* seeking alimony or an annulment aimed to utterly discredit their husbands. These two strategies are inextricably linked. This is largely due to the distinct legal status of the married woman. Since women were prohibited from suing their husbands under the common law, their rhetorical strategy before church and equitable courts was, necessarily, two-fold. Firstly, they had to persuade the court that they should be given the right to present their case regardless of the principal of *coverture*, which prevented married women from suing without their husband's approval. If this request was granted, women would then have to attempt to demonstrate that they were in the right to seek a *de facto* separation – equity courts could not grant formal separations, but did allow informal, private separations to stand.[97] To persuade the equitable courts to hear their case, women would have to tackle the issue of their status as *femes coverts*. Rather than letting this hold them back, women used the principle of *coverture* to make their case even stronger by arguing that, although they were not supposed to, they were forced to resort to suing their husbands as a result of their treatment at these men's hands. This approach meant that the legal battles between husbands and wives were, without exception, adversarial in nature.[98] In order for a litigant to win the suit, the legal system invited them to credit themselves and discredit the other party. Where a couple would, during their marriage, be perceived as one unit, these suits for separation see both husband and wife going out of their way to demonstrate that the other party has violated their part of the marriage contract. In order to sway the court in their favour, female litigants were required, or given the opportunity, to create a written account of their marital life.

Establishing Legal Autonomy

Though to persuade a court to hear their suit meant establishing their legal autonomy as separate from their husbands and outside the bonds of *coverture*, the best strategy for ensuring divorce of bed and board and subsequent alimony was to appear as weak as possible. This simultaneous assertion of both weakness and strength, this denial and affirmation of agency, formed a vital element of a woman's pleadings in cases where the litigants were married. While the principle of *coverture* prevented women from acting as their own legal entity, women could also use it to their advantage. By demonstrating that they had held up their end of the marital bargain, but their husband had not – thereby breaking the bonds of marriage – women could show that their appeal should be admitted. One might expect this emphasis on *coverture* to be the input of these women's lawyers. However, early modern women were well aware of their legal status and can thus be expected to understand the necessity of challenging their status as *feme covert*.[99] Moreover, if such challenges were present in a formulaic insertion, we would expect it to appear in every example of a woman suing her husband in the Court of Requests. This is not the case, however, and those who do make use of this strategy all choose a different wording to explain their point.[100]

In 1609 Elizabeth Egginton sued her husband Frauncis and his father John before the Court of Requests.[101] After her first husband died, Elizabeth lived quite comfortably for the space of two years. Then she met John Egginton, who offered Elizabeth the hand of his son in marriage, 'whereupon your said Subject being a weak and simple woman and altogether relying and trusting upon the fair promises of the said Iohn Egginton the father was contented and condescended to the said marriage with the said Frauncis Egginton'. Elizabeth's statement does more than simply demonstrate that she was lured into the marriage by the sweet promises of the father of her future husband. By making use of almost tautological words in describing herself ('weak and simple') and the relationship between herself and her father-in-law ('relying and trusting'), Elizabeth puts deliberate emphasis on her supposed vulnerable and trustworthy nature and thereby on the expectation that Egginton would behave wisely and honourably. This naivety is not presented as a character flaw: it is not Elizabeth's weakness that is problematic, the issue is that her husband forsakes his marital duties.

That Frauncis indeed refused to honour his wife becomes clear in Elizabeth's description of their marriage, which turned out to be an unhappy one. Written with the advantage of hindsight, Elizabeth's statement asserts that she now realises that Frauncis was motivated purely by the opportunity to acquire Elizabeth's money and property.[102] At first, Frauncis only uses 'threatening and menacing speeches' to try to convince Elizabeth to give up her wealth. When that does not work, Frauncis resorts to violence. He starts to 'beat, hurt, wound and maim your said Subject in diverse places of her body whereby your said Subject is made unable to labour and work for her maintenance'. When Elizabeth still does not give in, Frauncis tells his wife that he will

> cause or procure your said Subject to be killed and that the death of your said Subject should be obscured and not made known, that your said Subject should be burned in an Oven that thereby it might not be known what was become or happened to your said Subject.

The story Elizabeth relates is a shocking one. Not only is she in danger of her life, but the only solution open to her (apart from seeking legal redress) is to escape from her husband's cruel clutches, which leaves Elizabeth 'enforced to beg her bread and ready to perish for want of food and sustenance'. Her decision to sue in a court of law, then, is represented as an act of basic self-preservation. Besides gaining sympathy from her audience by portraying her husband as a monster, Elizabeth's story also emphasises her husband's failure to keep up his end of the marriage contract. Although legally Elizabeth is still a *feme covert*, the bonds of marriage have already been severed by Frauncis' refusal to perform his duties as a husband. The implicit logic is that Frauncis has thereby forced his wife to sue him, even though she knows she cannot do so according to the tenets of common law:

> for that your said Subject is not able to bring or maintain any Action by the strict Course of the common Laws of this Realm, for that your said Subject being a *feme Covert* cannot bring the same against her husband nor against the said John Egginton his father (without naming the said Frauncis her husband) who hath offered and done her, your said Subject, a great part of the wrong which she hath received.[103]

Elizabeth demonstrates here that she is aware of her complicated legal position: she cannot sue either Egginton before a common law court, because of the rules of *coverture*. It is exactly for this reason that Elizabeth emphasises, and perhaps even exaggerates, the hardship she has endured. Elizabeth thereby shows that her lack of agency is two-fold. She is both without legal agency ('your said Subject is not able'), and bereft of literal agency. She is a victim of a conspiracy between her husband and father-in-law, who coerced this 'weak and simple' woman into a marriage within which she was terrorised and threatened with death if she did not hand over her money and property. It is impossible to know whether Elizabeth's appeal was effective: no court order survives to reveal who won the case.

Just as women knew full well the restrictions placed on litigation between husbands and wives by common law, so did their husbands. Therefore, when Anne Perrye sued her husband John and pleaded with the court to be heard, it is hardly surprising that her legal opponent emphasised her legal rights and restrictions: 'by the Common law of this Realm no *feme Covert* is enabled to sue without her husband'.[104] The way in which Anne tries to convince the court to let her continue her suit regardless is a persuasive rhetorical strategy in itself. Her bill of complaint reads: 'for that she is a *feme covert* and may not sue alone at the common law, but humbly prayeth consideration of her Cause and that her suit may be allowed, and that she *&* her said children may be relieved in this honourable court'.[105] Anne makes clever use of *anaphora*, or the repetition of the same word or phrase in successive clauses, sentences or lines.[106] The repetition here is of the word 'may'. The court would certainly agree with the first clause in which she uses the word 'may': here it is immediately followed by the word 'not' and makes a true statement that *femes coverts* were not allowed to sue without their husband according to the common law. However, the structure is repeated twice again without the addition of 'not', first as a request that her suit 'may be allowed', and that she and her children 'may be relieved'. Given that the court might feel morally compelled to allow the latter (that she 'may be relieved'), they are therefore obliged to permit the former.

Anne Lloyd uses a similar strategy to persuade the court to order her husband to provide for her and her child's maintenance, but adds a subtle twist.[107] Anne first stresses her awkward situation: she 'was by her own means and not otherwise glad for safeguard of her life to depart away from him: without any manner of exhibition, allowance or maintenance for her or her poor young Infant'. Why Anne fears for her life becomes clear in an earlier suit, where her husband Humfrey admits that several incidents have taken place between him and his wife, such as him giving her 'two or three blows' with a 'small stick' when he found her 'Drinking in a private Chamber in the house of the arlate Thomas Sanhon with a Couple of vagrant persons'.[108] After she left,

Humfrey consequently decided to 'bar her and her infant of any manner of exhibition, maintenance or means to live upon and of all succour and help to supply her necessities and extreme wants'. Once again we see the wife stressing how her husband has failed to uphold his contractual and moral obligations as a husband and father, thereby implicitly freeing her of her legal obligation to him. Her victimhood, ironically, makes her claim to legal agency much stronger and emboldens her: 'for that your said subject is a *feme covert* and in point of law not answerable, yet being thus used and denied her competent maintenance both for herself, her child and family is forced to sue your highness for a Competent relief, maintenance and exhibition according to her and her child's degree and calling'. Like Anne Perrye, Anne Lloyd uses her children as exhibits of her husband's moral failings. In so doing, both women make their children stand in court beside them, albeit virtually. Since her husband is unwilling to provide for his family, Anne Lloyd is forced to address 'your highness'. As such, she effectively substitutes one figure of authority for another: her husband for the queen. If her husband refuses to take care of his family, Anne, as a good mother ought to, will find other means. To make her situation even clearer, Anne adds: 'therefore your poor subject being pressed to these extremities must and doth appeal unto your sovereign highness'.[109] Anne's husband is not impressed by her arguments, and gives the following reply:

> she might have complained of him to the justice of the assizes of the said County or unto any of her neighbour Justices of the peace in the same shire where they both dwelled and so have procured him with sufficient sureties to have been bounden unto the peace, if not unto his good behaviour, which had been a fitter and a shorter course then to come from thence two hundred miles and here to complain.[110]

Humfrey's complaint illustrates that Anne did not choose the usual course of action by turning to the Court of Requests. She did so, perhaps, because of Requests' reputation as a tribunal that took a favourable stance towards women or for the fear that local justice would not have ruled in her favour, perhaps because of a personal connection. Indeed, he was right to try to convince the masters of Requests to deem the case inadmissible: the court honoured its reputation by allowing Anne to present her case before them and eventually ruled in her favour, ordering Humfrey to pay maintenance to his wife.[111]

Isabell Birley, on the other hand, explicitly presented herself as a *feme sole* in her husband's suit against her.[112] Some ten years earlier Isabell had requested the consistory court of Chester for a separation on the grounds of his 'very dishonest Course & Conversation of life And living Notoriously in adultery with one Margrett Harrison'. According to Thomas, this separation was one of bed and board. Isabell, however, claims that the court 'pronounced, adjudged & declared [her] to be free & Clear of the said marriage & the bonds thereof'. According to her legal counsel, 'the said marriage is fully dissolved & she the said Isabell by the said sentence is made sole'.[113] Whether or not the marriage was completely dissolved is important for the new suit filed by Thomas before the Court of Requests. In this suit, Thomas tries to reclaim certain goods and chattels that Isabell has, according to him, taken possession of illegally. This, of course, partly explains why Isabell is so eager to stress her status as *feme sole*. If the court considers her to be tied by the bonds of *coverture*, the goods in question would still technically be owned by Thomas. The court sided with Isabell and ordered Thomas to recompense the legal costs she had sustained as a result of his 'wrongful vexation'.[114]

Taken together, the cases of Elizabeth Egginton, Anne Perrye and Anne Lloyd demonstrate that early modern women found ways around the common law's proscription of spouses from suing one another. In doing so, they fashioned themselves in whatever manner would prove most favourable to the particular circumstances of their suit; as a *feme covert* or *feme sole*, as a weak and simple woman, or quite the opposite. Once women had been granted permission to present their case at their chosen forum, the battle for maintenance or enforcement of the separation settlement began. This battle was, without exception, characterised by its adversarial nature, which culminated in the reciprocal hurling of *ad hominem* insults.

The *Ad Hominem* Attack

When a man and woman were joined in matrimony, they traditionally promised each other 'to have and to hold from this day forward, for better, for worse, for richer, for poorer, in sickness and in health, to love and to cherish, till death us part'.[115] Alongside these general vows, each spouse also had his or her own obligations towards the other partner. Women would pledge obedience to their husbands and husbands were expected to protect and provide for their families. The joining of two individuals was considered quite literally as their merging into one identity. This was especially true in the eyes of the law. When one of the couple sought to end the bonds of marriage, what was formally seen as one unit in the eyes of the law had to be forcefully made into two separate legal identities again. In order to convince the judges that such a legal rupture was necessary, litigants tried to showcase the ways in which their spouses failed to live up to their marriage vows and the accompanying expectations surrounding marriage, and perhaps the most effective, and certainly most common, method of doing so was through simple invective.[116]

That accusations often came as blunt statements of wrong-doing is demonstrated in the case of *Foye c Foye* (1579).[117] When Peter Foye asked the consistory court of London to order his wife to return to him that they might live together as husband and wife ought, she replied that 'her said husband hath broken the bonds of marriage and committed adultery with another woman. She had departed from him as is deduced in the said article and so meaneth to continue from him for ever'.[118] So far as Jane Foye is concerned, her husband's failure to honour the obligation to be faithful to her represents a *de facto* and unilateral rescindment of the contract of marriage, and as a result there was no longer a contract for her to honour. By breaking 'the bonds of marriage', Jane asserts that her husband has lost any claim on her to act the way a model wife is supposed to.

Johane Spraggyn was much more elaborate in describing how her husband had violated his part of the marriage contract when she sued him in 1595 before the Court of Requests in London.[119] According to Johane, the couple were already 'separated & appointed to live asunder' by court order from the Court of Arches; the new suit, initiated by Johane, concerns money and goods. In her bill of complaint, Johane is quick to point out her lack of agency in choosing Martin as her husband, as she 'did at the instance of her friends marry and take to husband one Martyn Spraggen'. She is also quick to point out the difference between herself and Martin: whereas she is 'descended of good parentage', Martin 'being a man of base birth and as bad Condition [. . .] reported him self to be of great maintenance and good descent'.[120] Johane thus claims that Martin has tricked her 'friends' into requiring that she marry him, by presenting himself to be of better parentage than in fact he is. Martin, on the other hand,

> thinketh it was no disparagement for her, being a tapster's daughter, to be married to the son of an honest yeoman, especially the complainant having not one penny to her portion nor yet clothes worth the naming to her back at the time of her marriage.[121]

While we cannot know which spouse is telling the truth, this, in many ways, is beside the point. What is interesting is the way they go about making their cases. Johane is eager to present herself in a good light, which necessarily means discrediting her husband. Martin himself observes this strategy when he states that 'the said complainant in her said bill of complaint maketh protestation for her credit, alleging against the credit of this deponent that he was of base birth and that she, the said complainant, was descended of good parentage'. As such, Martin cleverly turns Johane's use of *argumentum ad hominem* around. Rather than giving her credit, she now needs to be careful that the court will not perceive her as a quarrelsome scold.

Not content to merely cast aspersions on Martin's backgound, Johane also denounces his behaviour as a husband. After having lived amicably enough for the space of nine years, Johane claims that Martin started to abuse his wife 'by daily beating and misusing her besides diverse other Injuries and wrongs done unto her, whereby she could enjoy no quiet nor peace'. Not only does Martin mistreat his wife, but he also 'lewdly spent and Consumed the money by them received therefore to the extreme impoverishment & utter undoinge of your poor Subject forever'. Moreover, his prime goal in life seems to be 'seeking the Ruin and overthrow of' his wife, using a 'Crafty & subtle devise' to ensure her complete undoing.[122] Johane's story regarding her husband's behaviour does more than simply appeal to sympathy: it shows that Martin has long ago stopped fulfilling his marital obligations and that the two should no longer be seen as a married couple – nor be treated as such.

The examples in this chapter show that the *ad hominem* attack was often tied to the implicit argument that the husband had cut the marriage bonds. So it is in the case of Anne Lloyd, whom we have already met. Anne ('being a gentlewoman of good birth and parentage') disparages her husband by revealing his poor treatment of her. Indeed, she claims she is 'daily and hourly in peril to be diversly spoiled and cast away if she should cohabit with him'. By openly portraying Humfrey as a bad and dangerous husband, Anne clearly seeks to discredit him:

> in all the course of the time of her marriage with the said Lloide your said Subject lived free in the Eye of the world from any suspicion of hard usage or cause of dislike between her and her said husband and yet in all that time endured at her said husband's hands vile and inhuman manner of dealing.

She goes on to claim to have been 'day by day by her said husband assaulted, beaten and wounded most pitifully'.[123] Anne is careful to point out the discrepancy between public appearance and what actually happens behind closed doors. This is an important intervention, as it counters any potential testimony from her husband's witnesses, who would undoubtedly claim that they had never seen Humfrey attack or abuse his wife. Anne thus employs a technique that Walton refers to as 'lip service selection': she addresses an opposing argument ('nobody ever saw Humfrey assault Anne') and immediately pre-emptively counters this possible line of argument ('he only hurt her in private, never in public').[124] By doing so, she makes her opponent's argument less strong, while simultaneously strengthening her own story.

Elizabeth Garthe resorted to the *ad hominem* attack when she was entangled in a lawsuit with her husband over land and goods.[125] The Garthes had received a separation of bed and board, but that did not end their (legal) disputes. In 1602 Robert Garthe started proceedings against his wife in order to get back diverse important papers and household goods which she had allegedly stolen. Elizabeth states in her pleading that she is willing to return all to her husband,

> in Case the Complainant would acknowledge & Confess the several wrongs offered unto this defendant, & publicly right this defendant in her good name & reputation, which the Complainant by dishonest & undue means hath sought & endeavoured to take from her, being more dear & of far greater worth unto this defendant then the value of the said goods & premises or all the lands the Complainant hath Can recompence or Countervail.[126]

Elizabeth's statement demonstrates the importance of reputation for an early modern English woman. By refusing to return the goods, Elizabeth makes it inevitable that the couple will end up in court yet again. The maintenance of her reputation is apparently so important to Elizabeth that she is also willing to spend money on legal representation and court fees to ensure it; money, as she stresses in her personal answer, that she does not have as her husband has deprived her of it.

The other 'several wrongs' that Elizabeth talks about in her personal answer comprise defamation, physical abuse and other forms of violence. According to Elizabeth, her husband

> lived very unquietly with this defendant, taking occasion oftentimes to abuse her, the said defendant, otherwise than was fitting or decent for the husband to behave him self towards his wife, this defendant always demeaning herself very obediently & dutifully to the said Complainant as became her, & did from time to time, in hope of better usage of the Complainant, suffer & bear to her great grief & discontentment the wrongs & injuries offered unto her by the said Complainant. Nevertheless, the said Complainant, still persisting in his froward & perverse humor & disposition towards this defendant, did in no sort Cease his former Courses but further endeavoured the disgrace & destruction of this defendant by slanderous defamation of her, this defendant, & many other ungodly practices, offering violence unto this defendant, whereby she stood in fear of her life, the particulars of which said practices & endeavours this defendant for modesty doth forbear to mention in this honourable Court.

In this fragment, Elizabeth discredits her husband while simultaneously crediting herself. Through her use of *synonymia* (the use of several synonyms together to amplify, explain or add emotional force) by stacking up words connoting suffering ('suffer & bear', 'great grief & discontentment', 'wrongs & injuries'), Elizabeth creates an image of insufferable burden.[127] Despite this cruel behaviour, Elizabeth nevertheless stood 'obediently & dutifully' by her man as a good wife is supposed to. Where Elizabeth thus behaved as a model wife, her husband acted contrary to what is 'fitting or decent'. Robert not only fails to cherish and love his wife, but actively seeks her 'disgrace & destruction'. Once more we see a woman manipulating the expectations of what it meant to be a good husband or wife. With her pairing of near-synonyms, Elizabeth draws a picture of a woman carrying more and more weight, until the point arrives when she can bear it no longer and she is forced to seek relief in the legal system. Elizabeth thus creates a sense of crisis: she can no longer be a good, obedient and dutiful wife when her husband continues to display 'froward & perverse humor & disposition' towards her. Elizabeth's subsequent counter-demand of the court to correct her husband's perverted, unnatural behaviour is thus described as pure necessity and a result of her desire to protect her reputation. In doing so, she stresses her husband has inverted the norms of normal husbandly behaviour.

As these cases demonstrate, suits between husbands and wives can best be described as adversarial. Wives fought to tip the scales of justice in their favour, by demonstrating that their husbands had failed to keep up their end of the marriage contract. By describing the various ways in which their husbands failed to live up to their marital obligations and hereby perverted the natural order between husbands and wives, these women tried to convince the courts that the bonds of marriage had already been broken. The *ad hominem* attack is one of the ways in which they sought to establish this, and while we often see this in other types of trial, the process of establishing legal autonomy by demonstrating a man's failure to fulfil the role of husband relies on this form of 'argument'. These attempts constitute acts of life-writing, in which litigants described their own virtuous lifestyle as well as the alleged immoral life of their spouse. The adversarial nature of these acts was largely a function of the arena for which they were designed: the courtroom. However, outside of the courtroom, disillusioned spouses did not have to turn to such binary oppositions.

An Unhappy Marriage

Despite Elizabeth Delaval's attempts at finding romance and a suitable marriage partner, which were discussed in the opening section of this chapter, her eventual marriage to Robert Delaval (1647–82) was arranged by her father. When it proved unsuccessful, Elizabeth did not seek separation:

> I was so foleish at that time of my life as to beleive it t'was in my power to change any custume he had that I did not like, and to be very much disoblidged when I found my selfe mistaken, so that this begining of a maryed life was very disagreable to me, but I knew there was no remedy and therefore resolved to suffer it with the most patience.[128]

Rather than seek redress, Delaval chose endurance. It would be twelve years until Elizbeth was granted the relief of widowhood, when Robert died in 1682.

Although Delaval chose patience over a separation suit, her memoirs employ the same kind of arguments women use in their separation suits. Delaval, too, emphasises how her partner violated the bonds of marriage: 'my husband broke the vow's he had made to me then because intemperate life and other sins of his were offences against our God'.[129] The primary difference between Delaval's memoirs and the suits of separation is an introspection that the adversarial nature of the courts could not allow:

> Iff I had taken the right course when I found my selfe unhappy at first in my mary'd life, by grieving truly at what ever Mr. DeLaval did amiss which was offensive, and had taken away with a kind concern to represent my thoughts mildly to him, tis very probable his love to me might have made my just endeavours prove successfull; but (alasse) on the contrary I have by another sort of behaveour, with proud ill natured words, to often tempted him to fall into the fury of a mad and sinfull passion, and thus have been accessary to his iniquities and miserably increased my own.[130]

Outside the context of the law courts, there was less need for Delaval to justify her desire for separation. Therefore, there was also no reason for her to stress her own virtue in this situation. Instead, the purpose of her *Meditations*, to represent and acknowledge her sins, leads Delaval to scrutinise her own behaviour.[131] Had she chosen to actively seek judicial separation from her husband, however, we can assume she would have styled herself more along the lines of those women involved in suits of annulment, separation and alimony: an innocent, humble and frail wife in the thrall of an unprincipled, dishonourable and faithless husband. The meditative diary, then, allows Delaval both more and less freedom in shaping her account than a legal pleading could. For where a meditative diary leaves little space for its author to call out a neglectful or abusive husband, the court gave a voice to those women suffering abuse and the space to counter their abusers. Legal records, then, may be impaired, mediated and ultimately one-sided, but they are still valuable resources that allow us insight into the lives of early modern women, particularly of their ability and willingness to work within the systems open to them to ameliorate their conditions within marriage or, indeed, to assert no little influence over the selection of their eventual marriage partner. These insights are of a different kind than more traditional forms of life-writing can offer. The constraints placed upon them by the necessarily adversarial court system may perhaps make the stories women tell less directly honest than other forms of life-writing, but in acknowledging these constraints we can read lives in a way impossible within, say, an autobiography. By paying attention to the strategies that court records share with other forms of life-writing as much as where they diverge we can gain a fuller and more nuanced picture of the lives these women led.

Notes

1. The *Meditations* are kept at the Bodleian Library, MS Rawl D78. All citations here are taken from Elizabeth Delaval, *The Meditations of Lady Elizabeth Delaval, Written Between 1662 and 1671*, ed. by Douglas G. Green (Northumberland Press Limited, 1978).
2. Delaval, *Meditations*, p. 27.
3. Ibid.
4. Marie-Louise Coolahan, 'Redeeming Parcels of Time: Aesthetics and Practice of Occasional Meditation', *The Seventeenth Century*, 22(1) (2007): 124–43, at 125.
5. Raymond A. Anselment, 'Feminine Self-Reflection and the Seventeenth-Century Occasional Mediation', *Seventeenth Century*, 26(1) (2011): 69–93, at 74; Femke Molekamp, *Women and the Bible in Early Modern England: Religious Reading and Writing* (Oxford University Press, 2013), p. 215); Susan Wiseman, 'Elizabeth Delaval's *Memoirs and Meditations*: Textual Transmission and Jacobite Context', *Early Modern Women: An Interdisciplinary Journal*, 10(1) (2015): 68–92, at 74.
6. See, for a discussion of how Delaval's *Meditations* is influenced by the romance genre, Margaret J. M. Ezell, 'Elizabeth Delaval's Spiritual Heroine: Thoughts on Redefining Manuscript Texts by Early Women Writers', in Peter Beal and Jeremy Griffiths (eds), *English Manuscript Studies 1100–1700*, Volume 3 (University of Toronto Press, 1992), pp. 216–37. Raymond A. Anselment, by contrast, emphasises the spiritual and secular dimensions of Delaval's life-writing ('Feminine Self-Reflection', 71–4).
7. Delaval, *Meditations*, p. 112.
8. T. E., *The Lawes Resolutions of Womens Rights* (London: 1632), STC 7437, p. 6.

9. Only the last pages (201–12) are concerned with Delaval's marriage. At the time of composing her work (which was not at the time of the events Delaval is describing), then, Delaval paid more attention to her courtships than to her marriage.
10. Of the 117 cases considered in this chapter, 90 concern courtship suits. The actual disparity in occurrence of the two suits might be greater, as one needs to actively search for cases concerning marital problems, which are relatively scarce. In order to minimise selection bias, I have chosen cases from various law courts, regions and dates. However, because of the nature of the suits that this chapter is concerned with and jurisdictional governing, records from church courts as well as the Court of Requests feature heavily. Moreover, as Cordelia Beattie reminds us, because of the 'grey area between singleness and marriage', quantification is difficult (Beattie, '"Living as a Single Person": Marital Status, Performance and the Law in Late Medieval England', *Women's History Review*, 17(3) (2008): 327–40, at 337).
11. T. E., *The Lawes Resolutions*, p. 7. In practice, people got married at a more mature age: the average woman married when she reached her mid- to late twenties, and it was 'not law but social custom' that determined what was seen as a fitting moment to enter into marriage (Martin Ingram, *Church Courts, Sex and Marriage in England, 1570–1640* (Cambridge University Press, 1987), p. 129). See also, B. J. Sokol and Mary Sokol, *Shakespeare, Law, and Marriage* (Cambridge University Press, 2003).
12. 'Canons (1604), Section C', www.anglican.net/doctrines/1604-canon-law. Importantly, though, the canons did not declare marriages without consent void, meaning that this particular canon could not be enforced (see Sokol and Sokol, *Shakespeare, Law, and Marriage*, p. 33).
13. T. E., *The Lawes Resolutions*, p. 52. T. E. adds that 'matrimony is not accounted consumate, until there go with the consent of mind and will conjunction of body'.
14. Subha Mukherji, *Law and Representation in Early Modern Drama* (Cambridge University Press, 2006), p. 17.
15. See for a discussion and overview of this: Nancy Mohrlock Bunker, *Marriage and Land Law in Shakespeare and Middleton* (Fairleigh Dickinson University Press, 2014), pp. 93–4.
16. Rebecca Probert, *Marriage Law and Practice in the Long Eighteenth Century: A Reassessment* (Cambridge University Press, 2009), p. 44.
17. On the difference between the two contracts, see A. D. Nuttall, '"Measure for Measure": The Bed-Trick', *Shakespeare Survey*, 28 (1975): 51–6.
18. John Webster, *The Duchess of Malfi*, ed. by Leah S. Marcus (The Arden Shakespeare, 2009), 1.2.385–6.
19. Ibid., 4.1.35–6. For a discussion of contemporary attitudes towards, and the status of the Duchess' marriage, see Leah S. Marcus, 'The Duchess's Marriage in Contemporary Contexts', in Christina Luckyj (ed.), *The Duchess of Malfi: A Critical Guide* (Continuum, 2011), pp. 106–18. On the status of the clandestine marriage contract of the Duchess in Webster's

play and various of its adaptations, see Rachel E. Holmes, 'A Widow's Will: Adapting the Duchess of Amalfi in Early Modern England and Spain', *Studies in Philology*, 116(4) (2019): 728–57.

20. For more about clandestine marriages, see R. B. Outhwaite, *Clandestine Marriage in England, 1500–1850* (The Hambledon Press, 1995).
21. According to Barnabe Rich, the 'infallible marks of a virtuous woman' were 'modesty, bashfulness, silence, abstinence, sobriety: she must be tractable to her husband', see Rich, *The Excellency of Good Women* (London: 1613), STC 20982, p. 32.
22. See chapter 3 for more on bastardy.
23. Tim Stretton, 'Introduction', in Tim Stretton (ed.), *Marital Litigation in the Court of Requests, 1542–1642* (Cambridge University Press, 2008), pp. 1–24, at 4. On cost of separation, see Elizabeth Foyster, *Marital Violence: An English Family History, 1660–1875* (2005; Cambridge University Press, 2009), p. 21.
24. For more about marriage and separation, see Joanne Bailey, *Unquiet Lives: Marriage and Marriage Breakdown in England, 1660*–1800 (Cambridge University Press, 2003); Katie Barclay, *Love, Intimacy and Power: Marriage and Patriarchy in Scotland, 1650–1850* (Manchester University Press, 2011); K. J. Kesselring and Tim Stretton, *Marriage, Separation, and Divorce in England, 1500–1700* (Oxford University Press, 2022).
25. Ralph Houlbrooke has shown that in the period 1520–1570, long-term alimony was rarely mentioned in church court records (*Church Courts and the People during the English Reformation, 1520–1570* (Oxford University Press, 1979), pp. 68–9). On the development of the law of separation, see Kesselring and Stretton, *Marriage, Separation, and Divorce*.
26. Lawrence Stone, *Road to Divorce: England 1530–1987* (Oxford University Press, 1990), p. 210.
27. Stretton, 'Introduction', p. 4.
28. See, for instance, Jane Whorwood's suit against her husband: *Whorwood c Whorwood*, Lambeth Palace Library, Court of Arches, E5/29; E4/122; A10 f 87v; Eee 5 f 218v-220r; Ee 4 f 101r-107v; and the case of *Dame Margery Acton v Sir Robert Acton* (TNA, REQ 2/14/53 (1552) (edited case papers available in Stretton's *Marital Litigation*, pp. 29–32).
29. Eleanor Hubbard, *City Women: Money, Sex, and the Social Order in Early Modern London* (Oxford University Press, 2012), pp. 186–8. For mediation in cases of marital disharmony in the long eighteenth century, see Joanne Bailey, *Unquiet Lives*, pp. 32–5.
30. Mediation and arbitration did not usually leave a paper trail. If these extrajudicial methods failed and the case was brought before a law court, the litigants and deponents sometimes shared details regarding their failed attempts at reconciliation. Formal legal records therefore sometimes contain information about such informal proceedings, but it is otherwise hard to gather more information about them. For an example, see *Elizabeth Moore c Philip Clark*, LMA, DL/C/233, fo. 194r (1631), discussed, alongside other examples of arbitration, in Hubbard's *City Women*, p. 187.

31. Susan D. Amussen and David E. Underdown, *Gender, Culture and Politics in England, 1560–1640: Turning the World Upside Down* (Bloomsbury, 2017), p. 39.
32. Alastair Bellany, 'Cecil, Anne, Lady Ros (1599x1601–1630)', *Oxford Dictionary of National Biography* (25 May 2006). Accessed 18 March 2024; John Chamberlain, *The Letters of John Chamberlain*, ed. by Norman Egbert McClure, Vol. 2 (The American Philosophical Society, 1939), pp. 80, 92–3, 132, 134, 144–5, 148, 207, 220, 222, 235, 247, 302, 408; TNA, STAC 8/111/26 *Thomas and Frances Cecil v Thomas and Mary Lake & Anne Cecil* (1619); Anne Clifford, *The Diary of Anne Clifford, 1616–1619*, ed. by Katherine Acheson (Garland Publishing, 1995), pp. 100, 109; William Davenport, commonplace book, Ches. & Chester ALSS, CR 63/2/19, fol. 20r.
33. Following Nadine Akkerman's lead, I opt for 'True accountt' when referring to Halkett's autobiography/memoirs. See Akkerman, *Invisible Agents: Women and Espionage in Seventeenth-Century Britain* (Oxford University Press, 2018), p. 185.
34. BL Add. MS 32376.
35. Both John Loftis (*The Memoirs of Anne, Lady Halkett and Ann, Lady Fanshaw* (Clarendon Press, 1979), p. 3) and Effie Botonaki (*Seventeenth-Century English Women's Autobiographical Writings, Disclosing Enclosures* (Edwin Mellen Press, 2004) p. 77) suggest it was Halkett herself who molested her text.
36. For more about Anne's civil war involvement, see Susan Wiseman, *Conspiracy and Virtue: Women, Writing, and Politics in Seventeenth-Century England* (Oxford University Press, 2006), pp. 320–33; Diane Purkiss, *The English Civil War: A People's History* (Harper Perennial, 2007), pp. 443–50; and Akkerman, *Invisible Agents*, pp. 182–203. On the constructed nature of Halkett's 'True accountt', see Judith Kearns, 'Fashioning Innocence: Rhetorical Construction of Character in the Memoirs of Anne, Lady Halkett', *Texas Studies in Literature and Language*, 26(3) (2004): 340–62; Sheila Ottway, 'They Only Lived Twice: Public and Private Selfhood in the Autobiographies of Anne, Lady Halkett and Colonel Joseph Bampfield', in Henk Dragstra, Sheila Ottway, and Helen Wilcox (eds), *Betraying Our Selves: Forms of Self-Representation in Early Modern English Texts* (Palgrave, 2000), pp. 136–47.
37. Anne, Lady Halkett, 'The Autobiography of Anne, Lady Halkett, 1677–78', p. 57, in Suzanne Trill (ed.), *Lady Anne Halkett: Selected Self-Writings* (Ashgate, 2007).
38. The number indicates the start of a new page.
39. Halkett, 'Autobiography', p. 58.
40. Ibid., p. 63.
41. Ibid., p. 55.
42. Kearns, 'Fashioning Innocence', p. 341.
43. Interesting in that light is the intentional removal of certain potentially incriminating pages from the manuscript; not only are the pages that describe the first meeting between Halkett and her suitor Joseph Bampfield

missing, also the folios describing the moment after she discovers Bampfield's wife is still alive are torn out. Unfortunately, it is unclear who violated the manuscript – it may have been the author herself, or perhaps one of her family members – but in any case we might reasonably suppose that the vandal considered what was written on those pages too scandalous for anybody else to see.

44. Halkett, 'Autobiography', p. 131.
45. Kearns, 'Fashioning Innocence', p. 352.
46. Halkett, 'Autobiography', p. 131.
47. Ibid., p. 80.
48. Ibid., pp. 132; 138.
49. We see a similar desire to settle debts prior to marriage in the diary of Elizabeth Delaval: 'I disputed the mater very earnestly with my aunt when I found it was both my father's will and her's to make me change my state of life and ty me up in bond's I never wou'd have chose, and which I desier'd might not be made so much the heavyer by a load of debt's' (*Meditations*, p. 69).
50. See also Diana O'Hara, '"Ruled by my Friends": Aspects of Marriage in the Diocese of Canterbury, *c.* 1540–1570', *Continuity and Change*, 6(1) (1991): 9–41, for more on the influence of family and friends on the courtship and marriage phases, including the offering and withholding of consent.
51. Laura Gowing, *Gender Relations in Early Modern England* (Routledge, 2014), p. 35.
52. *Hawarde c Baker*, WSRO, Ep/I/11/1, f. 7v (1568).
53. *Becher c Allen*, WSRO, Ep/I/11/1, f. 29v (1573).
54. *Mannsbridge c Purdue*, WSRO, Ep/I/11/1, f. 33 (1574).
55. See Halkett, 'Autobiography', p. 58. Rather than using her own family's lack of consent as a reason not to get married, Elizabeth Delaval pointed to her suitor's family's reservations: she refused to 'privately' marry the object of her affection, because she 'was not capable of doing it, haveing a nicenesse in my conscience which hinder'd me from marrying any body contrary to the consent of there parents' (*Meditations*, p. 167).
56. TNA, REQ 2/31/37, *John Cartwright v Thomas and Maude Nixon and others* (1592).
57. TNA, REQ 2/31/37, *Cartwright v Nixon* (1592), deposition of John Howell.
58. Ibid., deposition of William Mullocke.
59. Meddling mother figures form a recurring theme in legal proceedings in the courtship phase, see for instance Katherine Jernegan's role in the marriage between Charles Forth and Elizabeth Jernegan (TNA REQ 2/46/25, *Robert Forth v Henry Jerningham and Elizabeth Forth* (1595)); and Elizabeth Church's sister-in-law in the match making between Elizabeth and Mathew Levett, *Levett c Church* (1572), LMA, DL/C/211/1, ff. 102v–104r.
60. TNA, REQ 2/31/37, *Cartwright v Nixon* (1592), deposition of Johane Mullocke; deposition of Margaret Baylye, deposition of Rendull Bathowe.
61. Ibid., answer of Peter and Ellen Morrall.
62. Ibid., deposition of Margaret Baylye.

63. Ibid., answer of Peter and Ellen Morrall.
64. LMA, DL/C/629, *Peter Richardson c Anne Fryer* (1579), ff. 99v–100v. For an elaborate discussion of this case, see Hubbard, *City Women*, pp. 119–20. See also: Gowing, *Domestic Dangers*, p. 144.
65. Ibid., answer of Anne Fryer, f. 100r.
66. Douglas Walton, *One-Sided Arguments: A Dialectical Analysis of Bias* (State University of New York Press, 1999), pp. 91–114.
67. B. J. Sokol and Mary Sokol, *Shakespeare, Law, and Marriage* (Cambridge University Press, 2003), pp. 2–3; Tim Stretton, 'Women, Property and Law', in Anita Pacheco (ed.), *Early Modern Women's Writing* (Oxford: Blackwell, 2002), pp. 40–57, at 53; Paul Griffiths, 'Punishing Words: Insults and Injuries, 1525–1700', in Angela McShane and Garthine Walker (eds), *The Extraordinary and the Everyday in Early Modern England: Essays in Celebration of the Work of Bernard Capp* (Palgrave Macmillan, 2010), pp. 66–85, particularly at 70.
68. Sokol and Sokol, *Shakespeare, Law, and Marriage*, pp. 2–3.
69. TNA REQ 2/65/55, *John Ashe v Elizabeth Bedcotte*, bill of complaint of John Ashe (1601).
70. Ibid., answer of Elizabeth Bedcotte (1601).
71. LMA, DL/C/211/1, *William Hill c Elizabeth Frith* (1573), answer of Elizabeth Frith, f. 123v; LMA, DL/C/211/1, *William Lloyde c Jane Salisbury* (1573), answer of Jane Salisbury, f. 119r. For more on this case, see Gowing, *Domestic Dangers*, p. 145.
72. LMA, DL/C/211/1, *Mathew Levett c Elizabeth Church* (1572), answer of Elizabeth Church, ff. 102v–104r. For an elaborate discussion of this case, see: Gowing, *Domestic Dangers*, pp. 151–3.
73. Ibid., deposition of Wilhelmus Teloston, f. 98r; see similar relations in the deposition of Thomas Bucknell, ff. 99r–100v; and the deposition of Wilhelmus Howell, ff. 100v–102r.
74. Douglas Walton, *Witness Testimony Evidence: Argumentation, Artificial Intelligence, and Law* (Cambridge University Press, 2008), p. 23.
75. Rich, *The Excellency*, p. 32.
76. LMA, DL/C/219, *Margaret Moore-Perrie c Richard Warren* (1610), ff. 80v–87v; 161v–169r.
77. Hubbard, *City Women*, pp. 245–6.
78. LMA, DL/C/219, *Moore-Perrie c Warren* (1610), deposition of Johannes Johnson, ff. 80v–83r, at 81v.
79. Ibid., f. 81r.
80. Hillary Taylor, 'The Price of the Poor's Words: Social Relations and the Economics of Deposing for One's "Betters" in Early Modern England', *Economic History Review*, 72(3) (2019): 828–47.
81. Barbara J. Shapiro, 'Oaths, Credibility and the Legal Process in Early Modern England: Part One', *Law and Humanities*, 6 (2012): 145–68.
82. J. A. Guy, *The Court of Star Chamber and Its Records to the Reign of Elizabeth I*, Public Record Office Handbooks, No. 21 (H.M. Stationery Office, 1985), p. 27.

83. LMA, DL/C/219, *Margaret Moore-Perrie c Richard Warren* (1610), deposition of Johannes Johnson, ff. 80v–83r, at 83r. Although perjury was deemed a crime (see 5 Eliz I c. 9 s. 6), no statute deemed the coaching of witnesses by a litigant a felony. As such, the deponents ran the risk for falsifying testimony, not the litigant who encouraged them to lie under oath.
84. Ibid., deposition of Elizabeth Lane, ff. 86r–87v, at 86r.
85. Craig Muldrew, *The Economy of Obligation: The Culture of Credit and Social Relations in Early Modern England* (Macmillan, 1998), p. 3.
86. Ibid., p. 149.
87. See, for instance, Rich, *The Excellency*, p. 32; Peter de la Primaudaye, *The French Academie* (London: 1586), STC 15233, p. 512; Giovanni Michele Bruto, *The Necessarie, Fit, and Convenient Education of a Young Gentlewoman* (London: 1598), STC 3947.
88. When employing *argumentum ad hominem*, the 'proponent argues that the respondent has a bad character (. . .) and then uses this allegation to try to get the audience to conclude that the respondent lacks credibility', Walton, *One-Sided Arguments*, p. 244.
89. There are, of course, exceptions. See, for instance, Margaret Bennett's statement that she 'doth not intent to marry with [Richard Leache] as well for his lewd talk of her and also for his unchristian life', personal answer of Margaret Bennett, *Leache c Bennett*, WSRO, Ep/I/11/2, f. 17 (1573).
90. Walton, *One-Sided Arguments*, p. 87.
91. LMA, DL/C/219, *Moore-Perrie c Warren*, deposition of Elizabeth Lane, ff. 86r–87v, at 87r.
92. Repository of work: National Library of Scotland (MS 874, ff. 363–84; and MS 906). All quotations in this chapter are taken from Margaret Cunningham, *A Pairt of the Life of Lady Margaret Cuninghame that She Had with her First Husband, the Master of Evandale, as it Was at First Written with Her Own Hand*, ed. by C. K. Sharpe (James Ballantque and Co., 1824).
93. Cunningham, *A Pairt of the Life*, p. 1.
94. Ibid., p. 11.
95. Cunningham was bound, too, by the Scottish equivalent of English *coverture*, although the Scots *jus mariti* afforded women 'the potential for more freedom under the law' than *coverture* (Deborah Simonton, 'Community of Goods, Coverture and Capability in Britain: Scotland versus England', in Anna Bellavitis and Beatrice Zucca Micheletto (eds), *Gender, Law and Economic Well-Being in Europe from the Fifteenth to the Nineteenth Century: North versus South?* (Routledge, 2019), pp. 31–46, at 43). See also Cathryn Spence's '"For his interest"? Women, Debt and Coverture in Early Modern Scotland', in Cordelia Beattie and Matthew Frank Stevens (eds), *Married Women and the Law in Premodern Northwest Europe* (The Boydell Press, 2013), pp. 173–90, at 177–8 and Rebecca Mason, 'Women, Marital Status, and Law: The Marital Spectrum in Seventeenth-Century Glasgow', *Journal of British Studies*, 58 (2019): 787–804, at 789.

96. Faith Lanum, 'Biography of Margaret Cunningham', *Perdita* online database. Accessed 18 March 2024.
97. On informal separation, see Beattie, 'Living as a Single Person', 333; Kesselring and Stretton, *Marriage, Separation, and Divorce*, pp. 5; 14; 51–68.
98. See Walton, *Witness Testimony Evidence*, p. 163, and Stretton, *Marital Litigation*, p. 15.
99. See also Sokol and Sokol, *Shakespeare, Law, and Marriage*, pp. 2–3.
100. For comparison, see *Acton v Acton* (TNA, REQ 2/14/53 (1552)), in which Margery Acton does not refer to her inability to sue her husband at common law at all; Issabell Osmoderly, on the other hand, does not explicitly mention *coverture* when she writes that she was 'not able nor can by the law attempt or commence any suit against her said husband but only in your highness' right honorable courte of Requests', *Issabell Osmoderly v William Osmoderley* (TNA, REQ 2/24/82 (1553)) (for a full set of case papers of this suit, see Stretton's *Marital Litigation*, pp. 33–4). This contrasts with, for instance, the statement of Elizabeth Egginton, who explicitly refers to her status as a *feme covert* (TNA, REQ 2/414/40, *Elizabeth Egginton v John Egginton and Frauncis Egginton* (1609), Elizabeth's bill) (for the complete case papers, see Stretton's *Marital Litigation*, pp. 221–32).
101. TNA, REQ 2/414/40, *Egginton v Egginton and Egginton* (1609).
102. Elizabeth explains that she is 'lawfully seized in her demesne as of fee *sibi et suis* according to the Custom of the said Manor of Pattingham' and that the tenement and land in question are meant for 'the only use and behoof and for the maintenance and Livelihood of your said Subject Elizabeth and her heirs for ever'. Frauncis wants his wife to transfer these rights unto his name.
103. TNA, REQ 2/414/40, *Egginton v Egginton and Egginton* (1609), Elizabeth's bill.
104. TNA, REQ 2/416/93, *Anne Perrye v John Garbet and John Perrye* (1614), John Garbet's answer (full case available in Stretton's *Marital Litigation*, pp. 235–40).
105. Ibid., Anne's bill.
106. Martin Gray, 'anaphora', *A Dictionary of Literary Terms* (Beirut: Longman York Press, 1992), p. 23.
107. TNA, REQ 2/234/61, *Anne Lloyd v Humfrey Lloyd and John Bradshaw* (1596) (see also Stretton's *Marital Litigation*, pp. 171–90).
108. LMA, DL/C 222, *Anne Perry c John Perry* (1614), John Perry's account, ff. 239r–v. For more on this case, see Gowing, *Domestic Dangers*, p. 210.
109. TNA, REQ 2/234/61, *Lloyd v Lloyd*, bill of complaint of Anne Lloyd.
110. Ibid., demurrer of Humfrey Lloyd.
111. TNA, REQ 1/19, pp. 116–17, *Lloyd v Lloyd*, court order.
112. TNA, REQ 2/422/19, *Thomas Birley v Isabell Birley and Henry Cornoe* (1616) (edited case papers available in Stretton's *Marital Litigation*, pp. 241–8).
113. TNA, REQ 2/422/19, *Birley v Birley and Cornoe*, answer of Isabell Birley.

114. TNA, REQ 1/28, f. 467r (p. 979), *Birley v Birley and Cornoe*, court order.
115. The book of common prayer, 'The Fourme of Solempnizacion of Matrimonye' (1559), justus.anglican.org/resources/bcp/1559/Marriage_1559.htm. Accessed 18 March 2024.
116. For more about the reciprocal nature of marriage vows in a Scottish context, see Barclay, *Love, Intimacy and Power*, p. 180.
117. LMA, DL/C/629, *Peter Foye c Jane Foye* (1579), f. 99r.
118. Ibid., answer of Jane Foye, f. 99r.
119. TNA, REQ 2/273/67, *Johane Spraggyn v Martin Spraggyn* (1595). This case can be found, from beginning to end of the suit, in Stretton's *Marital Litigation*, pp. 121–70.
120. Ibid., bill of complaint of Johane Spraggyn.
121. Ibid., answer of Martin Spraggyn.
122. Ibid., bill of complaint of Johane Spraggyn.
123. TNA, REQ 2/234/61, *Lloyd v Lloyd*, bill of complaint of Anne Lloyd.
124. Walton, *One-Sided Arguments*, pp. 98–100.
125. TNA, REQ 2/210/17, *Robert Garthe v Beniamyn Tichborne and Elizabeth Garthe* (1602) (see Stretton's *Marital Litigation*, pp. 193–216).
126. Ibid., answer of Elizabeth Garthe.
127. Gideon O. Burton, 'synonymia', *Silva Rhetoricae*, http://rhetoric.byu.edu. Accessed 29 January 2023.
128. Delaval, *Meditations*, p. 206.
129. Ibid., p. 209.
130. Ibid., p. 210.
131. Ibid., p. 26.

Chapter 3

Sex and Slander

Regardless of whether they were maids, wives or widows, women's sexuality was everybody's business. An immoral single woman was a whore, jade, queen or bawd; an immoral wife rendered her husband a cuckold.[1] Because of the conjunction of social credit and actual credit, the potential damage that could result from malicious gossip or outright slander was immense – the risks involved in defending oneself against such rumours very real. While gossip was traded throughout the social echelons, from the royal household to the poor, some people had better means of dealing with gossipmongering than others. Princess Elizabeth, the future queen of England, had to deal with rumours and gossip that followed her alleged sexual affair with Thomas Seymour. As a response to these rumours, Elizabeth's governess had been replaced, because she was deemed to have had a bad influence on the young princess. Elizabeth was worried that the appointment of a new governess would only affirm the rumours and cause the people to say that she 'deserved throwgth my lewde demenure to have such a one' (i.e. a new governess). She therefore desired the Lord Protector to let her retain her old governess, as well as 'to sende forthe a proclamation in to the countries that the refraine ther tonges declaringe how the tales be but lies it shulde make bothe the people think that you and the counsel haue greate regarde that no suche rumors shulde be spreade of anye of the Kinges Maiesties Sisters'.[2] Clearly, the scandal surrounding Elizabeth did not leave her unaffected. As the king's sister, she was in a position to request a top-down approach to quashing the rumours. But how did other, less well-positioned women deal with rumours about their sexual behaviour?

Literate women could produce a written counter-narrative. One such example is the autobiography of Alice Thornton (1626–1707), which she seems to have penned in direct response to the various slanders against her.[3] Thornton shared this text with certain friends and family members.[4] Clearly, whatever allegations and remarks were made about Thornton, she strongly felt the need to vindicate her reputation.[5] An educated gentlewoman like Thornton had the means to construct such a counter-narrative of her life. Illiterate women and those not minded toward writing autobiographical texts also had the possibility of clearing their names by going to the law courts.

This chapter considers the relationship between sex and slander in the representation of women in early modern legal records, both in terms of how women were characterised by others and how in turn they presented themselves. Writing about early modern sexual slander *an sich*, however, is no easy task. A woman subject to sexual slander might take her slanderer to court in order to clear her name. However, if the court dismissed the charges, it might imply that the accusation were true, and the law may then turn its attention to the sex crime itself.[6] The act of sex and the way it was spoken about, therefore, were intertwined in complex ways. Despite the difficulty of separating act and speech in the legal context, this chapter is structured in two distinct parts. It demonstrates first the ways in which certain sexual acts rendered women vulnerable to being discredited, before examining the subtle and indirect ways such acts were invoked in legal courts. While the courtroom offered women a place in which they might exert some level of agency and present a face of their choosing, women accused of sexual deviance often effaced themselves in their pleadings, relying on strategies of elision, evasion and the shifting of agency rather than crafting elaborate self-portrayals. Perhaps unsurprisingly, in cases of sexual slander, women typically portray themselves as innocent victims lacking power and influence.

Sexual Transgressions and the Law

When they were accused of fornication (any sexual encounter outside of the marital bed), women mostly faced charges of pre-marital sex, adultery or prostitution. Invariably, in such cases, the burden of guilt and punishment fell disproportionately upon the shoulders of the woman.[7] Accusations of these types of sexual immorality, be it in the courtroom or outside it, left women vulnerable to losing their good name and fame. Only by considering the risks attached to losing one's good name can we comprehend the ways in which female sexuality is talked about in the early modern law courts.

Pre-Marital Sex

The policing of pre-marital sex in early modern England was governed by a complex set of concerns, concerns which arose from a heady combination of moral absolutism and rather more pragmatic issues of financial management.[8] Sexual indiscretions were largely tolerated by the authorities unless they resulted in one of two threats to the local order: bastardy or overt promiscuity such as prostitution.[9] Illegitimate children were a financial burden on the parish and community in which they were born. If the parents were absent or could not contribute to the child's upbringing, the child was dependent on community charity. After the introduction of the Poor Laws, the parish was to dedicate a part of its poor rates to the child.[10] The laws that were designed to deal with bastardy were based on the idea that illegitimate children were the victims of their parents' sexual immorality and that they required financial support. This arrangement weighed heavily on the parishes and, perhaps naturally, the ecclesiastical authorities and the local communities would often join together in attempts to trace absent parents and force them to accept their parental duties, either by taking the child in or by offering regular monetary contributions to its upbringing. The communities were helped in their efforts by laws that helped in tracking down and punishing the parents of illegitimate children.

A 1576 statute made a first attempt to curb both fornication and the births of illegitimate children:

> Concerning bastards begotten and born out of lawful marriage (an offence against God's law and man's law) the said bastards being now left to be kept at the charge of the parish where they be born, to the great burden of the same parish, and in defrauding of the relief of the impotent and aged true poor of the same parish, and to the evil example and encouragement of lewd life.[11]

Although the wording of this statute focuses first on its moral aims, the larger part of this quotation is concerned with the social ramifications of fornication: placing a financial burden on the parish and the diverting of funds away from the deserving poor. In order to avoid this kind of unwanted consequence, the statute aimed to make both the 'mother and reputed father of such bastard' take financial care of the child. In practice, however, it could be difficult to prove who was the father and get him to acknowledge his responsibilities.[12] As a result, the primary obligation for support was, in effect, placed on the mother.[13] In 1610 a further step was taken aimed at alleviating parishes from the expenses of helping provide for illegitimate children.[14] Statute 7 Jac. I, c. 4 allowed for mothers of illegitimate children to be sent to a house of correction. Although this would not immediately diminish the financial burden on parishes, it could have a deterrent effect on women and their willingness to engage in fornication. The statute did not provide any form of punishment for the alleged father, further reinforcing the existing prejudices against unmarried mothers.

More often than not, however, the matter of decreasing the financial burden illegitimate children placed on the parishes was most easily solved by tracing the absent father, who could then be bound over by the court and forced to make regular payments of child support. In order to escape the public embarrassment of being publicly declared as the absent father, men had the option of paying off their 'debt' privately. Women could not escape public punishment so easily, because for them it came in forms other than mere monetary contributions. Punishments for bastard-bearers included public confessions, whipping and imprisonment. In the words of G. R. Quaife, '[p]unishment for bastardy fell heavily on the woman'.[15]

Why, then, would women risk all of this by agreeing to having pre-marital sex? Of course, some women may not have had a choice. Such was the fate of one Johan Hinson. When her parents were out of the house, an unknown servingman came in and called her up to a room. When she entered the room 'he stopped her mouth with a handkerchief and there on a bed had the Carnal knowledge of her body and then ran forth'. Hinson seems to have escaped unwanted pregnancy, but was forced to gain treatment at a hospital to rid herself of the disease the man gave her.[16] Others claimed to have only agreed to intercourse after receiving a promise of marriage from their lovers. Indeed, the promise of marriage was an often-heard explanation when accused of pre-marital sex in court.[17] There was also a possibility that the man in question might have died before the marriage could take place. This was the reason provided by Johan Burges, who had to appear before the court of Bridewell prison in 1605 to account for her fatherless child. Johan 'saith the father of it was one to whom she was sure but he died before they could be married'.[18] And, of course, some women simply did not think through the risks or took them for granted to satisfy their desires. Whatever the reason, the law was much harsher towards women engaging in pre-marital sex than towards their male partners.

Adultery

Pre-marital sex was only one of the various forms of sex considered problematic. Adultery, too, was a concern, particularly for the church courts. Quite apart from its inclusion in the Ten Commandments, couples were further warned against its dangers in sermons and conduct literature: the clergyman Henry Smith called adultery the 'disease of marriage' and claimed 'adulterers are likened to the devil'; in his advice book *Of Domesticall Duties*, William Gouge deemed adultery 'one of the most capital vices' and a 'heinous sin'.[19] Extra-marital sexual activity was thought to be so problematic that it could be a ground for separation *a thoro et mensa*.[20] Indeed, according to *The Lawes Resolutions of Womens Rights*, 'by Divine and Common Law, the only sufficient cause [of divorce] is adultery and fornication'.[21] Several bills were introduced throughout the sixteenth and early seventeenth centuries to devise a statute punishing adultery, but none of them made it through parliament until 1650. Although the exact nature and form of legislation could not be decided upon until this date, for several decades prior to the bill's introduction parliamentarians seemed to agree that adultery needed to be punished severely.[22]

The 1650 Adultery Act satisfied the desire for more severe punishment by decreeing extra-marital intercourse to be a capital offence.[23] The death penalty could only be incurred by adulterous wives; under the statute philandering husbands were punished by three months of incarceration. As such, the act introduced into law a bias that until then had largely been present in prosecution and social custom. Although the letter of the statute suggests that draconian measures were being introduced, the practice was somewhat different: this largely symbolic piece of legislation was abandoned at the Restoration.[24] Starting legal proceedings for separation on grounds of adultery was not a common occurrence. Given the public and exceptional nature of such a trial, this is not surprising, as few men would choose to make their wives' indiscretions (and, with that, their own failure as husbands) more public than was necessary. Most men would therefore settle matters themselves. Some would do so by beating their wives, which allowed husbands to reassert their authority, as long as the violence was not excessive.[25] Cheating wives could also be punished by their husbands by being denied access to their children.[26] Involving the courts invited not only ridicule but also rather more direct forms of punishment.

As the Adultery Act illustrates, while both men and women committed adultery, it was deemed all the more offensive an act in women, possibly because of the threat it posed to family and lineage.[27] However, when their wives cheated on them, men would receive a form of punishment, too. Adulterous women not only subverted the household order, but also the social order: men who could not control their wives were mocked as cuckolds. Edmund Garrett was one such man.[28] He was on the receiving end of a 'written and published' libel: 'Garrett no man, what then? an ox: his wife she hath what? the French pox: a lovely couple and a brave, a pocked queen, and an horned knave'. The libel repeatedly refers back to Garrett's horns as a symbol of his cuckoldry, mentioning for instance that 'if he before had ran away his horns in every bush would stay, where now most freely it may pass, not like an ox but like an ass'.[29] The horns may not be the only visible sign on both parties: the libel suggests both husband and wife are marked by the pox. While Garrett is ridiculed for being unable to prevent his wife from committing adultery, he, too, seems to have been unfaithful, as he used to 'stay in every bush'. Now that he has been infected by his unfaithful wife, however, no one will have him and his horns. The main source of ridicule, however, remains Garrett's failure to subordinate his wife, the ultimate humiliation for a man.[30]

Prostitution

Prostitution was the sexual offence that was taken most seriously by the authorities, not least as 'the charge undermined an adversary's social as well as moral standing'.[31] Prostitution was 'greatly developed' in early modern England, and in London in particular, although it had been outlawed by Henry VIII's 1546 proclamation.[32] Before this, prostitutes worked outside of London to avoid the authorities – once it had been made illegal, they were forced to move and they relocated to ale houses, inns and covert houses of ill repute inside the city walls.[33] By the early seventeenth century, London was scattered with prostitutes, making the offenders hard to track down and deal with for the authorities. The spread of prostitution was further enabled by the rapid growth of London's population. Poverty, too, played its part. Impoverished women were often forced to resort to selling their bodies for money in order to sustain themselves and their families. As a result, there were various kinds of prostitutes active in early modern London, ranging from the more professional type, who worked under the supervision of a bawd, to the amateur (who offered her services whenever and to whomever it suited her), to the poor, vagrant streetwalkers. England's countryside and villages were not free from prostitution either, although the lower density of potential clients meant that it was probably less widespread.[34]

As with pre- and extramarital intercourse, it was not so much the sexual act itself that made authorities anxious, but the accompanying threat of disturbing the peace and disrupting the social order. As an illicit financial transaction, prostitution was invariably accompanied by other criminal activities. The association of prostitution with poverty meant that 'Cony-catchers' were a constant danger, picking the pockets of naïve men lured into the stews, as were more violent and direct means of robbery.[35] These concerns were no doubt exacerbated by the regularity with which inns and ale houses doubled as brothels, which ensured that customers were often drunk.

Prostitution was a predominantly female profession. Although the narrator of Moll Cutpurse's 'autobiography' envisioned herself as the bawd to a group of male sex workers, this vision only emphasises how it was predominantly women who sold their bodies for money: this inversion of the *status quo* seems to be a calculated attempt to shock her readers.[36] Jennifer Panek has argued that it is likely that professional male prostitutes did operate in early modern London, but even when a man accepted money to have intercourse with a woman, it was she who was deemed a whore.[37]

Quite apart from the risks run by prostitutes in simply carrying out their profession, arrest added the possibility of public humiliation to the list. Punishments included having their heads shaved and being carted through the streets. Visitors of brothels stood more chance of being sued for disturbing the peace. Sometimes the community in which a prostitute was active decided to punish her of its own accord, rather than leaving it up to the authorities.[38] Although prostitution is a social act (for it requires two people), the male client in this equation did not face the public penalty that condemned prostitutes did. The sexual double standards seen in the punishments meted out to the prostitutes but not to their clients is merely an indication that, when it came to ascribing agency to early modern women, society was only happy to do so in cases of sexual malfeasance.

Women accused of sexual impropriety thus faced two punishments: that of the legal system and that of societal custom. This latter punishment was partly meted out by women; the very group which bore the brunt of the blame. Indeed, society had its own double standards, visible in, for example, plays. While on Shakespeare's stage female bonds can materialise and come to the fore in the face of accusations of infidelity, in real life, women accused of infidelity seemed to have had other women as their hardest critics.[39] This placed women in an even more difficult position, as they were forced to evade all talk of their sexual behaviour. At the same time, talking about other women's fornication was encouraged if it could root out such behaviour and prevent parishes and communities from facing financial and social repercussions. It was because a woman's sexual status or activity was so often employed to categorise and condemn her that it was crucially important to have effective strategies against such accusations. The following section explores how women countered both formal accusations against them brought by the authorities and cases of informal gossip circulating in their communities regarding alleged sexual impropriety. Legal proceedings allowed women the space to shape an account of themselves in opposition to these damaging accusations and labels, but because society already viewed women as culpable, they were forced to make use of strategies of elision and evasion, and the shifting of agency. As such, the self-portraits that emerge in these cases regarding sexual crimes are ones of a self-effacing kind: women describe themselves as innocent, powerless victims.

Sins of the Tongue

By analysing legal proceedings initiated by women who felt they had been the victim of slander, libel or defamation, alongside those of women who were formally accused of sexual promiscuity, what follows demonstrates that the need to defend their honour allowed women to leave records of their lives in legal archives. Because 'legal relief for defamatory words depended not only on the nature of the words themselves, but also on the quality of the person of whom the words were spoken', slander cases allowed the victims of defamation the space to assert their own version of themselves.[40] This makes it possible to see how ordinary women fallen victim to sexual slander presented themselves and their experiences. In the process of giving their account, and in the face of legal and societal constraints, women wrote themselves into the court records.

Sins of the tongue could be committed in various forms. Any spoken words that could offend the defamed person would constitute as 'slander', but only when the slanderer had said something particularly offensive or upsetting, or perhaps when there was a pre-existing grudge that needed to be settled, would slander become subject to judicial process.[41] If the words were not spoken, but written down, they would be perceived as 'libel'. Libel could also take place *sine scriptis*, when it came in the form of gestures, symbols or images, rather than in script. In practice, however, both 'slander' and 'libel' were used interchangeably, as the distinction between the two had not yet fully crystallised in the early modern period, as can be seen, for example, when people spoke about 'libellous slander' or 'slanderous libel'.[42] 'Defamation' was the legal term used to describe both libel and slander in the church courts, although people used the term for non-ecclesiastical forms of slander and libel, too.[43]

England witnessed an explosion in litigation concerning slander and libel: the number of defamation suits in the church courts quadrupled during the second half of the sixteenth century.[44] This explosion of business in the ecclesiastical courts occurred at the same time as the more recent common law action for slander gained ground. While the common law courts awarded damages if the plaintiff could substantiate that the alleged slander had resulted in economic loss, the church courts offered a forum for the tarnished reputation that was not necessarily matched by loss of income. As this was often the case for sexual slander, the type of slander most endured by women, female victims of slander tended to be drawn to the church courts to counter loss of reputation.[45]

Still, this explosion in slander suits is perhaps surprising when we consider the issue of cost. To put a defamation suit before the church courts cost around £8 and could drag on for up to four years.[46] The Court of Star Chamber would also deliver a verdict in a slander case, but at even greater cost.[47] Nevertheless, one's personal reputation was of such import that people were willing to sacrifice large portions of their time and money to preserve it from the vagaries of the gossip-mongers. This is directly related to the status of early modern England as a society where everything centred on personal credit. Business and trade ran on a system of credit, promissory notes and understandings that were entirely dependent on trust. An individual's reputation, therefore, would determine their ability to function in society.[48] Just as any failure to deliver on a financial level would tarnish a reputation, so would allegations of more personal backtracking – a promise, whether financial or social, was still a promise. If an individual lost the trust of their community, it could have grave implications for their professional dealings. An allegation of fornication, for example, could thus have serious financial implications, so the motivation to challenge and dispel defamatory claims or rumours was strong.

Similarly, false charges of, for example, adultery were sometimes uttered in the hope of getting a quick financial reward.[49] This is illustrated by the Star Chamber case of *Clerke v Essex*, brought to the court by the attorney general.[50] Susan Clerke, wife of John Clerke, accused Humphrey Essex of threatening her with 'death, reproach and slander': he 'would in plain terms accuse her to be a common whore'. According to Clerke, Essex told her that 'he knew well how dear and precious her reputation was to her' and that 'there was no way for her to redeem her Credit and good name from perpetual Infamy and reproach but to give unto him the said Fifty pounds'. Refusing to give into blackmail, Susan called on her brother for help. Her brother's subsequent intervention (which Essex states involved the use of weaponry) persuaded Susan's antagonist to make good on his threats and he purposed to make her 'Incontinency and adultery with the said Gilbert Armestronge and Thomas Webb' known to anyone who will listen. With Essex now spreading his poisonous rumours abroad, Susan resorted to the courts, where she hoped to prevent these rumours from destroying her reputation. Essex was right when it came to how 'dear and precious' her reputation was to her, he merely miscalculated the manner in which she would strive to protect it. In this lawsuit, Susan is described by the attorney general as 'being fifty years of age or thereabouts even hath even from her childhood hither unto been of so virtuous and sober conversation that she was never in all the Course of her life ever touched with the least blemish of Incontinency or lightness but hath Contrariwise gained to herself the general report of a most grave and virtuous woman'. Clerke, through the attorney general, is able to turn the bill of complaint into a concise mini-biography. Essex, however, claims Susan invented the blackmail attempt. If this was the case, then Susan's bill is an attempt to recast herself as a virtuous woman in order to counter the rumours about her sex life that were in circulation. The fact that there is no verdict extant for this case is especially tantalizing, but this is far from uncommon in cases brought before Star Chamber.

Let's Talk About Sex

The act of having sex and the speaking about this act are so intertwined in early modern England that the two feed into one another. Institutions with criminal jurisdiction, like Bridewell prison, but also the church courts, acted upon mere gossip and innuendo: the suggestion that somebody had behaved lewdly could give rise to a legal investigation. Slander was often countered in the law courts. The results in both cases are essentially the same: a person discussed in terms of their sexual promiscuity would have a likelihood of ending up in court, either as complainant in a slander suit or as subject of a criminal prosecution. In both cases, gossip forms a foundation for the lawsuit.[51] For these reasons, this section draws on cases dealing with sexual impropriety as well as sexual slander.

To understand how and why women shaped the testimonies about their own sexuality in the way they did, we must first consider how accusations of illicit sexual activity aimed at women were phrased and framed. The purpose of sexual slander, to shame and ridicule, partly accounts for the way women defended themselves against such aspersions. The same holds true for women formally accused and incarcerated on suspicion of fornication: the humiliation of their situation shaped their accounts. Embarrassed about being the subject of sexual innuendo and forced to recount details from their private lives, women produced terse accounts of the sexual acts they admit to or deny the charges altogether, portraying themselves instead as virtuous and chaste. In the records that have been analysed, from courts with both criminal and civil jurisdiction, most notably Star Chamber and Bridewell prison, two key tactics are foregrounded in trial accounts when it comes to talking about sex: elision and evasion, and the shifting of agency.

In line with the double standard present in the laws on sexual immorality, women are the ones to whom agency is usually ascribed when their sexual behaviour is discussed. This ascription can be achieved by calling somebody a whore. Both in its technical meaning (as a woman prostituting herself for hire) and its more general definition (of an unchaste or lewd woman), the word 'whore' placed blame and disgrace on the head of the woman.[52] Indeed, many of the insults aimed at women suggested, implicitly or explicitly, her whoredom. Notably, this extension of the *ad hominem* was often employed by women, against women. Elizabeth Copsheafe, for example, allegedly called Brigite Frost a 'whore, a burnt arsed whore & a pocky whore & hast had the french pox'.[53] The repetition of the words 'whore' and 'pocky'/'pox' is notable, as if in the piling up of words the guilt of the woman is somehow proved. It is a rhetorical gesture that occurs frequently. In the 1610 dispute between Alicia Rochester and Jane Lilham, some claim Rochester referred to Lilham as 'a whore & an arrant whore & a common carted whore & thou art my husband's whore', while others insist that Rochester also said that Lilham 'was carted through Newcastle', suggesting she had been prosecuted for whoring in that city.[54] The multiplication of accusations in one voice is further multiplied by several other, notably female, voices. The repetition of slurs by a number of people served to emphasise the message in the absence of actual proof that Lilham had indeed slept with Rochester's husband.[55] When Joane Knipe wanted to discredit her ex-mistress she opted to describe both her and her daughters as whores in similar fashion, saying that:

> your said subject Marye was dishonest, unchaste of her body; And that she was overfamiliar with divers persons, & that she & her said daughters used to daub or paint their faces; And the said Joane then also said that your said subject's daughters were all of them whores; And that the house (meaning your subject's said house) was never without a whore.[56]

Knipe uses five different ways of describing Mary Bulver as a whore and as such, mounts up accusations to prove the latter's guilt: not only is Bulver sexually immoral (1), she is immoral with various people (2), she flaunts her immorality by wearing make-up (3), she has made her daughters into whores (4) and her house has been turned into a brothel (5). Although Knipe's description of her ex-mistress's whoredom is more carefully constructed than the repetitious insults made by Copsheafe and Rochester, the strategy in both is the same. In these insults, the slandered party is referred to as a whore not once, but several times and in slightly different wordings that still come down to the same thing: that the person spoken about is a whore. The freely bestowed repetitious slurs literally replaced any proof that the defamed had engaged in fornication.

More than simply being called whores, women accused of fornication and extramarital sex were portrayed as predatory, promiscuous and scheming in the court records. Johan Bradley, for example, was brought into Bridewell 'great with child', having testified that 'one William Hering servant with her said Master is the Father thereof'.[57] The Bridewell governors are mild in their treatment of the young William Herring, a tailor's apprentice, after he confesses to having had sex with Bradley. Considering that the boy is 'but 15 years old and as he saith [was] drawn to this lewdness by the alurement of the said Johan', his punishment is that he ought to pay some money for the benefit of the poor of Bridewell, as well as to 'put in sureties to discharge the city of the child'.[58] Although it is clear that both the servant boy and the Court of Governors deem Johan Bradley the seducer of a young man, it is less clear how Bradley views the matter: the court clerk has not penned down her defence to her alleged 'alurement'.

A similar kind of predatory agency is attributed to women in cuckoldry libels. One example of this can be found in the lawsuit initiated by Henry Cunde, vicar of Montford, in 1605.[59] He had been married for nine years to his wife Johan, when the following libel was circulated about her in Montford and its surrounding areas:

> Commendations I will send now at a word / Unto the priest of Monford / [. . .] Sir priest although thou art wise enough / I will give thee some counsel but yet I must laugh / Thou hast a fair wife as I hear tell / But before I would be a cuckold I would drive her to hell / Be ruled by me man and hear what I say / for thy wife she will have a trick of false play / With many a one which comes to and fro / She will cast a rolling eye on them before they go / Master vicar when you are from home / The parson is ready to supply your room / The keeper also will not be behind / If she say him nay she is unkind / Vicar I tell thee it is not long agone / Since the keeper had thy wife to show her a son / [. . .] Thy wife were meet a minstrel's wife to be / unmeet for a minister I do tell thee / Thou knowst vicar, six children thy wife hath had / And never a one to light / for fear they should be like their fathers was not this a cruel spight / [. . .][60]

Although the writer of the libel claims to be offering some friendly advice, it is clear that their intentions are far from innocuous.[61] While the text suggests it is the vicar who is the victim, his wife (whether she was an adulteress or not) is the one who is being slandered for her alleged promiscuous behaviour and therefore both the vicar's failure to subordinate his wife and her unruly behaviour are mocked. Notably, the libel asserts Cunde's wife's agency: by 'cast[ing] a rolling eye' she has invited 'many a one' into her bed, including the parson and keeper, and it is she who has 'a trick of false play'. By association, the vicar has failed to assert his position as head of the household. In order to fix this, the libeller suggests he '[b]e ruled by me', instead of his wife.

In his pleading, the vicar takes care to counter this idea that he is ruled by his wife. His wife, he shares with the court,

> with whom your said Subject lived for diverse years together in great love and kindness, without any blemish, reproach or infamy, which said Johan during her marriage and the *coverture* between her and your said Subject did so loyally and dutifully behave herself toward your said Subject and so modestly and housewifelike govern your subject's house and family, that neither your said Subject nor any of her neighbours did or ever could charge, accuse or suspect her of any spark of light, lascivious or Immodest behaviour, muchless of any dishonest vice or offence.[62]

By mentioning not just their marriage, but also the principle of *coverture*, the vicar points out that his marriage was undertaken in line with the patriarchal system: he controlled his wife, not the other way around. He continues in describing her as the perfect spouse. Not only was she loyal, dutiful, modest and capable of governing the house perfectly, none of those who knew her well would be able to say anything bad about her. The vicar takes special care to emphasise all of his wife's passive and feminine qualities, which are in contrast with the allegations made against her: the Johan Cunde presented in the libel is far from the perfect wife and spends her time actively pursuing men and disregarding the bonds of marriage. The intention of the vicar's evidence is to absolve her from blame and suspicion, and thus redeem his reputation.

The men Cunde is said to have relations with are left unjudged and unaccountable in the text: all blame is laid on Johan Cunde for her promiscuous behaviour and, by association, on her husband for his failures as head of the household. She is in no position to answer the libel, as she has since passed away. Publicly disgraced and painfully reminded of her miscarriages, the libel took a heavy toll on her. Cunde explained the disharmony the libel had caused between him and his wife: 'great variance, discord, debate and dissention was like to grow, and did grow, betwixt your said Subject and his said late wife', who depended 'greatly upon her credit and honesty and never willing to violate the same or the bonds of a true and faithful wife toward her husband, and finding herself unjustly accused and depraved took such an inward grief and sorrow that she presently fell sick and pined, wasted and consumed away, and shortly afterward died'.[63] Cunde's bill, by suggesting a correlation between the libel and his wife's death, shows just what the impact of harming a woman's reputation could be. As Anne Thompson reminds us, it is impossible for contemporary readers to assess Johan's character, but 'just for a woman to be talked about in this way was itself degrading'.[64]

In sum, we notice two main attributes in the accusations of sexual sin against women: it often involved a piling up of slurs, particularly accusations of whoredom, and the concomitant attribution of agency, often of an unfeminine and predatory kind. Although it is easy to disgrace others with sexual slander, discussing one's own sexual transgressions seems to have been accompanied with more reluctance and embarrassment, as will be discussed in the following section. The modes of discourse discussed in this section invoked particular 'answers' from the accused women. Two strategies in particular can be found in the legal records of women accused of illicit sexual behaviour, both by slanderers and the authorities, namely the use of elision and evasion, and the displacing of agency.

Defence Strategies

Elision and evasion are key when it comes to discussions of sexual behaviour in the courtroom. Indeed, descriptions of sex and sexuality in the legal records are usually terse and cursory; it is rare to find records of women speaking openly and explicitly about their sexual encounters.[65] Alice Partridge, for example, recounts that she went to a 'chamber where one Allen was, and she further saieth that afterwards the said Wilkinson's wife fell out with the said Allen'.[66] The sexual act that took place in the chamber is completely omitted from the story. Ellinor Grobye, accused in a libel of turning her inn The Sign of the Hind into a brothel in which both she and her daughters worked as prostitutes (who, reputedly, 'between your legs will sing a bawdy song / and be your companion all the night long'), does not counter the specific sexual allegations made against her, but instead portrays herself more generally as someone who 'hath lived in good fame and credit amongst her neighbors and endeavoured to maintain her self and her children in good and orderly fashion to the uttermost of her power'.[67]

When women did provide details, this was likely to be the result of the nature of their legal proceedings. Specifically it mattered if the case was concerned primarily with the acts of illicit sex or with sexual slander. In cases of sexual transgression, proceedings could force prisoners and deponents to be explicit in their descriptions. The nature of the alleged crime, an illicit sexual activity, could require the suspect to talk about this in great detail. The where, when, how and with whom needed to be established in order to determine the extent of guilt. Conversely, slander suits centred on the words spoken, and turned away from the underlying sexual activity on which the slander was based. The uttered words are disputed, not the activity. In these cases, litigants are explicit when they describe the slander, but are free to completely ignore the sex act. This is particularly the case in criminal slander suits before the Court of Star Chamber, where truth was no defence to accusations of slander or libel.[68] Here, litigants are less likely to go into detail about their sexual behaviour and instead focus on how the slander or libel has affected their reputation.

Laura Gowing has argued that women's ability to talk about sex in the courtroom 'depended crucially on marital status and age'. She found that, in their depositions concerning sexual assault, children use a more varied, precise vocabulary to refer to sexual acts than wives, who use less explicit words and descriptions in their testimony.[69] In general, adult women (regardless of whether they were married, widowed or single) were more restrained in their descriptions of sexual activities, or more skilled in euphemistic language, than young, inexperienced girls. Indeed, as Renato Barahona has noted in his study on sex crimes in early modern Spain, descriptions of the actual act and the specific bodily organs involved are paradoxically absent.[70] Young girls' sexual inexperience may have caused court clerks and commissioners to ask for more detail than they would with more experienced women, who were presumed to know what they were talking about.

The type of lawsuit as well as the age and experience of the litigant are thus factors that help explain the level of detail in an account, but it is reductive to think that the courtroom context is the sole cause of women's use of elision and evasion in their records. There are important parallels to be found between early autobiographical writings and legal records in the lack of detail and the strategies of elision and evasion employed in the description of sexual acts. This suggests that such strategies go beyond the spoken word and that there were normative ways in which women treated sex that pertained to writing as much as public speech. Women do discuss their marital routines, pregnancies, childbirths and lyings-in in their diaries and autobiographies, but mentions of sexual activity are conspicuously absent. While it is clear, for example, that Alice Thornton penned her various autobiographical texts in response to slanderous rumours spread about her and her family, she obscures the exact nature of the slander. '[T]o sattisfy all my freinds of my life and conversation,—that it was not such as my deadly enymyes sugested', Thornton sends one of her autobiographical texts to her mother's 'cairefull servant' Dafeny, who showed the manuscript to various others.[71] One of them, at least, 'pittied my case, saing that I had ever bin a most virtuous woman all my life, and now to be soe abused, did wound her very hart'.[72] That the slander concerned Thornton's virtue also becomes clear at other points in her autobiography: she emphasises that her 'unspotted virtuous life' speaks for her and that her husband was convinced of her 'faithfull and entire conjugall fidelity' to him.[73] This seems too strong a response merely to counter the malicious gossip that 'if [her] husband were dead [Thornton] would be married within a month to Mr. Comber';[74] it is certainly possible, if not likely, that there were stronger attacks on her virtue, but that she chose to gloss over the finer details.

In fact, the closest we get to finding uncensored erotic passages in women's life-writing in English are in the accounts of their intimate relationship with God.[75] This self-censorship of sexual affairs manifests itself in the letters between Maria and Thomas Thynne. In a response to her husband's 'wanton letters', Maria Thynne writes: 'know that I have not, nor will not forget how you made my modest blood flush up into my bashful cheek at your first letter, thou threatened sound payment, and I sound repayment, so as when we meet, there will be pay, and repay, which will pass and repass, allgiges vltes fregnan tolles'.[76] The sexual message is relayed in the language of commerce, attempting to obscure the sexual undertones, or, conversely, accentuating them. Alison D. Wall, editor of the letters, suggests the non-English phrase means 'you will rise up' and may be written in (bungled) Latin 'to make a vividly sexual comment, hidden from prying eyes'.[77] Whether this use of a foreign language is meant to be coy, flirtatious or both is hard to say, but Samuel Pepys uses a similar technique in his diary. He describes his adulterous affairs in a polyglottal mix of French, Italian and Spanish: 'I by water to Westminster-hall and there did see Mrs. Lane, and de là, elle and I to a cabaret at the Cloche in the street du roy; and there, after some caresses, je l'ay foutée sous de la chaise deux times, and the last to my great pleasure.'[78] It is unlikely that Pepys used different languages in order to hide his affairs from his wife, as she was skilled in French, and because at least some of these erotic passages were also written in longhand, she would have no trouble deciphering them. It has been suggested that the mystique of writing in languages other than English might have enhanced the secretive nature of his affairs.[79] But it is also possible that, despite the diarist's obvious pleasure at seducing so many women, Pepys was confronted with a form of embarrassment or sense of textual decorum. Not capable of putting his sexual affairs to paper in the vernacular, he turned polyglot to write down those things that he could not freely discuss in English.

As women were well aware that engaging in illicit sexual activities could harm their reputations, they therefore took measures to conceal anything untoward, not just in their language, but also in their actions. Alice Partridge, for instance, changed her name when she entered into the employment of the bawd Agnes Wilkinson as a prostitute.[80] Wilkinson, who had turned her house into a brothel, was the one who suggested to Partridge that she would 'change her name from Partridge to Alice Woodstocke, saying else it would be a discredit unto her'.[81] While we might expect the nature of legal proceedings to almost guarantee that litigants remain unforthcoming with regard to such details as would prove incriminating, the use of elision and evasion outside the legal arena suggests that fear of shame and humiliation, too, shaped legal accounts and the way that women talked about (or refrained from doing so) their own sexuality in private.

Alongside this use of elision and evasion, a second strategy is foregrounded in the legal records left behind by women accused of illicit sex, namely shifting agency. This shifting of agency was discussed in the previous chapter, where we saw the technique used by single women to avoid marriage to unwanted suitors and by married women when they attempted to separate from their husbands. In cases of sexual impropriety, however, the strategy was used as an answer to the double standard in the law and in society that attributed almost sole agency to women for a crime that required two people. To counter this (implicit) accusation of agency, women maintained an air of passivity when discussing their sexual activities and, moreover, they attempted to locate the agency for sexual acts with another. One example is Amey Bennett, a former servant girl who was promised marriage by John de Lane, also a servant. He gave her two rings, a gold one and one with a diamond, 'which said rings (as this examinant saith) the said John de Lane took from her again after he had had his desire of this Examinant's body and would not restore them again'. John de Lane confirmed the trick he played on Amey Bennett and 'confesseth he gave the said Amey those Rings to have the use of her body'. As a punishment, the Court of Governors of Bridewell ordered John de Lane to provide for the child or children Bennett might bear as a result, as well as to cover the costs of her period of lying-in.[82] In this narrative, Bennett portrays herself as passive. She is given the rings as a token of marriage, which are subsequently taken from her again, and her body is 'use[d]': the girl claims to have had no agency over the events that befell her. Instead of a case revolving around sexual impropriety, Bennett successfully turns it into one concerning courtship and marriage.

Blame is not only shifted onto the men women had sex with; other women, too, could be attributed blame. One example of shifting blame to another woman is given by Anne Whetherall, mother of what is thought to be an illegitimate child. In Bridewell prison, she 'confesseth that she hath wrongfully charged Master Phillipes with it [e.g. her child], for that she was thereunto allured by a woman which counselled her to it. And said master Phillipes had ability to keep it And to give her money', thus blaming an unnamed woman.[83] The real father of her child, Whetherall now tells the Board of Governors, is in fact the man she married a couple of months previously, when she was already pregnant with his child, as they had engaged in pre-marital intercourse. A witness corroborates this version of events and claims Anne Whetherall 'did it by evil counsel and was sorry for it'. Her husband, too, affirms the story, as much as he can, by stating that 'the child is of his own getting, to his knowledge'.[84] Whetherall's strategy in front of the judges seems to have been carefully calculated, whether by her alone or in collaboration with her husband. Seeing an opportunity for financial advancement, she is willing to let a random person believe that he is the father of her child (although the two must have had illicit relations together to make the man believe the story). Rather than taking full responsibility for her actions, Whetherall attributes all agency and thus blame to the unknown woman who provided 'evil counsel'.

We see this shifting of blame, too, in the case of Judith Vincent, who claimed she was tricked into prostitution by her mistress Dorothy Clevely, who had 'most wickedly betrayed' her.[85] According to the servant girl, her mistress had instructed her 'to go with one master Bisshoppe, being a priest (. . .), saying that he should bring her to a place where she should be retained into service'. Clevely orders her servant to wash her feet and put on clean clothes, for 'if she tarried all night at the place where he would bring her, she should peradventure lie with some gentlewoman of the house, and that such another one would be loath to lie with her if her Feet were foul & her smock not clean'. This story sounds perfectly innocuous and Vincent follows her mistress's instructions without scruples. Instead of sharing a bed with a gentlewoman, however, Judith Vincent has to spend the night with one Edmund Verney (who checks her feet before bedding her). The following morning Verney gives the servant girl four shillings and promises her that Mr Bisshoppe will buy her a petticoat. Vincent has to give the money to her mistress, but does receive the petticoat. After that, Dorothy Clevely urges her servant girl not to discuss what had happened with anybody else: 'if she did disclose this matter, she would cause her to be so punished as all other should take example by her'. This is clearly blackmail, but Clevely's threat invokes the type of public penance that would await Judith Vincent if she were to be prosecuted for her crime, namely public humiliation. Despite this prospect, however, the girl cannot hold her tongue and shares the information with another maid, after which Clevely 'called her whore, wherewith she had her self much offended, by cause she was brought to her folly by her mistess' conspiracy, and being betrayed by her policy'. Clevely's response implies that only in speaking of her action does Vincent become a whore; silence is protection. Here we see how difficult it is to separate the prosecution of sexual offences from the prosecution of sexual slander: only in speaking of it does the sin come to light. Moreover, it is only after Vincent has been called a whore by her mistress that she seems to realise and articulate how her whoredom was imposed on her and she in turn accuses her mistress of acting as her bawd.[86] One act of speech begets another and another: speaking of the illicit act begets the slander of whoredom from Clevely, which in return receives the accusation from Vincent of pimping. It is therefore fit that the conclusion of the trial results in two more speech acts: double confession. Although Clevely denies the accusations at first, the Bridewell's court clerk records her revising her story: 'the said Dorathie confesseth the whole matter in such order as is by the same Judethe confessed, for which the said Dorathie had correction'. The case also shows the dangers of going to court: by doing so, rumour can be made reality. The adversarial nature of the courtroom is rehearsed in the original arguments, revealing women's rhetorical flair outside of that same courtroom.

Shifting of blame is also the approach taken by servant girl Eme Fynch. While working for Alice and Richard Robinson, Fynch was engaged in sexual activities with various customers of her employers' victual shop. This was not, as the servant girl stresses, voluntary: Fynch tells the Bridewell governors that 'her Mistress would often times force her to go up into a room to be naught with divers men which resorted to the house'.[87] Fynch gives an example of one such incident:

> a young man, a bricklayer, who resorted to the house came in and asked if he should drink a pot of beer & this Examinant answered 'yes, if he would', and bid him sit down in the one of the rooms below; but he refused so to do and would have gone up, then this Examinant perceiving his lewd intent said her Master & Mistress were both asleep on the bed; then the said Bricklayer was presently going forth of the house and turning him about he espied this Examinant's Master & Mistress coming indoors; and he said 'are those they that were on the bed asleep?'; then the bricklayer sent for an ale pie which they ate and then he would have a pint of wine; which this Examinant's master himself went for; and in that time when her master was gone for the wine; her mistress caused her to go up with the Bricklayer, and there the said

> Bricklayer had the use and carnal knowledge of this Examinant's body & he gave her eighteen pence which her mistress took from her as soon as the bricklayer was gone away.

The servant girl thus claims to have been forced into prostitution by her employers. By claiming that her mistress took the money from her, the girl further portrays herself as a mere commodity, whereas Alice Robinson is turned into a bawd. Robinson, however, denies running a brothel and instead claims Fynch is a promiscuous woman. According to Robinson, 'one Thomas Casey, a Plasterer in Gutter Lane, came into her house (herself & her husband being forth); and one Eme Finch, her maid, being in the house a washing, & there & then the said Thomas Casey had the use & carnal knowledge' of her body.[88] The mistress's narrative does not involve the mention of money, by which she suggests that her servant girl is simply unvirtuous. She thus shifts blame entirely on her employee and refuses to acknowledge any responsibility. The two women are therefore locked in a battle over agency, in which each of them accuses the other of a lewd act, while dismissing their own culpability and claiming to be a passive party.

Although none of the men Fynch has slept with (whether voluntarily or not) is attributed any kind of agency in the accounts of either woman, the language used to describe the sexual relations that have taken place suggests something different: it is Fynch's male customers who have 'the use and carnal knowledge' of her body. Sex between men and women is often described in this way, with the man actively 'using' the body of the woman. Apart from surrendering their bodies, women are described as playing no active part; men are almost invariably the subject and women the object when it comes to describing sexual relations. This formulaic phrase seems an almost mechanical insertion in court records documenting illicit sexual behaviour. Indeed, when we find the phrase used in early modern drama it is in a thoroughly legal context.[89] The legal inconsistency is perhaps worth noting: if it is in fact the courts that impose this kind of language, it implicitly contradicts the laws they are meant to uphold, for while punishment befalls the woman, the language used assigns agency to the man. Even if this phrase was wholly formulaic, it would serve the women accused of sexual lewdness well, as it placed agency with the man.

That it was possible to diverge from this standardised formulaic phrase, however, is demonstrated by the variations of this phrase that gave women more agency, which we occasionally also find jotted down by clerks in legal records. Mary Warren and William Mason, for example, did 'lie together and had carnal knowledge one of the other's bodies', and Judith Tailor, who is described in the courtbooks as 'a lame creature', is brought into the Bridewell on account of 'abusing her body with one Thomas Smithe'.[90] In this case, it is Judith Tailor who is the subject and the man who is the object.

In the rest of her story, however, Tailor portrays herself as passive in the face of a man, Smithe, who is portrayed as holding all the power. When questioned, Tailor told the Bridewell governors that

> she lay in Shoreditch under a stall, And there the said Thomas Smithe came between three & four of the clock in the morning and found her laying under a stall of whom she saieth she was afraid, And then the said Thomas asked her what she did there, & she told him that she could get no lodging, whereupon she [*sic*] willed her to go home with him.[91]

Tailor makes it clear that the initiative lay with Smithe and is initially quick to dismiss all suggestions of illicit behaviour: although she was at Smithe's house for 'two days, but she saieth he never had the use of her body'. She is thus insistent that she had no intention of prostituting herself. Instead, poverty and fear of her life forced her to go home with an unknown man, and upon his invitation. However, towards the end of her testimony Tailor suddenly changes her story: 'she confesseth she went up into the chamber to make his bed, & now she confesseth he had the use of her body', for which she receives 'correction'. Tailor's late (and possibly forced) confession does not render her previous story completely untrue, as it can also reinforce her earlier claims of poverty and fear. Having accepted Smithe's offer of a roof over her head, she may have been too afraid to decline his advances towards her, in case he would turn her out on the street again. Tailor's dependency on Smithe becomes painfully clear. While she is accused of abusing her own body, her narrative suggests that the second phrase ('the use of her body') is more accurate: it is Smithe who is the actor, even though Tailor receives the punishment.

One case where the law seems to have been unequivocally on the side of the female litigant was that of Elizabeth Guy. This upsetting case gives numerous reasons why the court would have been sympathetic, including the accused's age and active resistance:

> being of the age of eleven years, daughter of widow Guye dwelling in Pincocks Lane, brought in & examined saieth, that one Roberte Archer, servant with Thomas Maddoxe, on Monday last was [illegible] brought her by enticement to Hoggesdon from London into the field, & their they two continued two days, two nights, & in that time he had the use of her body thrice, once in a ditch & twice in a field, & she pushed him away & cried when he was doing of it but he would not away or leave her.[92]

This eleven-year-old child could not stop Robert Archer from raping her three times despite having 'pushed him away', as well as crying 'when he was doing of it'. Her assailant 'saieth & confesseth that the same is true, did so use the said Elizabeth'. Robert is punished for his ravishment of the young girl by being 'set to labour' in Bridewell, while 'the said Elizabeth [is] delivered to her mother'.[93] The girl's age explains why she receives no punishment: twelve was the age of consent for girls; the abduction of unmarried girls under the age of sixteen was prohibited in the 1558 Act; and in 1487 legislation had been passed making the abduction and rape of an heiress a capital felony.[94] The question of agency therefore did not even arise, as the law automatically placed all blame on her assailant.

Apart from these special circumstances, when women were protected by the law because of their age or inheritance, women portrayed themselves as lacking agency and falling victim to the immoral designs of others in an inversion of the double standard present in the law on illicit sex. These others could be the men who had 'the use of their bodies' or the women whom they trusted or worked for. Women thus portrayed themselves as innocent victims rather than the active, lustful creatures the law, and wider society, presumed them to be according to the legal double standard. The agency women displayed when suing others for slander was thus dismissed when they talked about their own sexuality. If these techniques were so common, however, this raises the question of whether there was any space for women in sexual slander cases to provide autobiographical details.

The Life of Eleanor Gresham

Following Natalie Zemon Davis, various scholars of legal records have pointed out that the legal process threatened the individual stories of women with homogenisation.[95] Indeed, it might be logical to assume that if women made use of these strategies of elision and evasion, and shifting blame, all legal records of the kind that have been analysed in this chapter are more or less streamlined and that instead of having a space within which they sought to construct a narrative of their own life, women merely conformed to a standardised idea. It is true that, in constructing a narrative best able to convince their audience, these women often used similar strategies. The individual ingredients of their stories, nevertheless, remain unique. Even within these narrative frameworks, it was possible for women to use the legal system to shape the way they wanted to be remembered. We can see this clearly from the case of Eleanor (also known as Ellen) Gresham, who initiated a suit in Star Chamber against her neighbour Evan Lloyd and his wife, whom she suspected and accused of slander and libel.[96] In her various case papers, Gresham leaves a trail of autobiographical details, giving their reader insight into her colourful life.

In 1613 Gresham found a libel written 'at large on a piece of paper' fastened

> upon the top of the door of your said subject's dwelling house and leave the same to the open and public view of all the neighbours and passengers traveling to and fro by your subject's said house, who read the same as they passed by, and being known to be a libel caused company to flock and repair thither to the hearing and reading of the same.

The piece of paper contained the following text:

> within this door dwelleth a very notorious whore, let no body else bear the blame for Ellen Gresham is her name, she doth her self so much abuse that she keepeth a house worse than the stews, Moll Cutpurse is a good one, Ellenor Gresham is a worse, take heed how you come thither for she will cut your purse, her husband is at sea, she plays the whore on land, she went to mistress Lynsey and cozened her of her bond, Megg Marshall is a good one, Ellenor Gresham is a better, And between those two whores we have entitled this letter, Ellen Gresham pawned her gown and for one night's lodging she cozened a cloth maker of ten pounds, Moll Cutpurse, Moll Clevely, Megg Marshall and mistress Nell, And of all these whores Ellen Gresham bears the bell. Finis.

The libel suggests Gresham is guilty of a diverse range of offences: it lists her as a prostitute, a cutpurse, an adulteress, a cozener and a thief. It also deems Gresham guilty by association in mentioning Moll Cutpurse, alias Mary Frith (1584/9–1659), who was considered to be a serial offender and general disturber of the public peace. The main allegation in the libel, however, is that of Gresham's being a whore, which is repeatedly referred to. This accusation follows the strategy we have seen in the second part of this chapter: the stacking up of repeating accusations fills the void of actual proof. In her response to the libel, Gresham makes use of the strategies of elision and evasion, as well as the shifting of agency: in her bill of complaint she does not discuss her own sexuality but merely claims she is an honest person and good neighbour, suggesting in the process that it was not she but her neighbours who caused the loss of her good name and fame.

The suit she initiated in Star Chamber is the sequel to earlier legal disputes fought out before the Court of Chancery between Gresham and her legal opponents, the Lloyds. As such, this particular suit forms only one part of a larger legal battle. Sadly, the relevant Chancery records seem to be no longer extant; the legal records in the Star Chamber suit, however, refer back to the older Chancery cases. Gresham had appeared in Chancery three times previously and each time a writ was issued binding her to good behaviour. Three times she failed to comply and three times she was detained in prison. These facts were confirmed by both herself and her opponents. By filing a suit before a different forum, Gresham may have hoped to set the record straight and to demonstrate that what was said about her by her legal opponents, a story accepted and confirmed by Chancery, was a mere fiction. In a lengthy bill that lists both herself and her husband as the complainants, Gresham sets forth in elaborate fashion all the insults to her reputation made by Evan and Agnes Lloyd. These comprise the various charges made against her before Chancery, including the suggestion that Gresham has 'taken a house of a very honest man, when he came to demand his rent she ran at him with a halberd and had there slain him had he not fled (. . .) and to this day hath not paid the rent due'; that she lives a 'very bad life and never cometh to church to receive the communion this seven years and upwards, she hath troubled many of her neighbours, some by charging them of common Sorcery, hags and witches, and did call their names in question and could make not any due proof thereof'; and that 'she hath cozened one Richard Ameys, a citizen and a young man, by drawing him into her company and accused him with incontinency on her self, making him believe that she was with child by him'. She is also referred to as a 'matchmaker' who 'sold one widow unto three several men', and who is 'acquainted with common Sorcerers, cunning men, and women and fortune tellers'. In short, Gresham is depicted as the very worst of all possible neighbours.

What all the accusations have in common is that the acts they describe have the potential to disturb the peace. Social order is dependent on people's acceptance of their place in society, but that order can be challenged and brought into disarray by various kinds of deviance.[97] This is exactly what Gresham is accused of by her neighbours. She is portrayed as a 'moll', or a displaced figure, a poor woman 'with no clear social place or identity' – a female rogue.[98] There is a proper sense of displacement: while Gresham claims that she had attempted to fit in, she did not succeed in the eyes of the libel's author(s). If these authors are not the Lloyds, who vehemently deny the accusations of slander aimed at their address, then that would mean that there were even more people who felt she did not belong or wanted her to leave the neighbourhood. Indeed, the accusations that are enumerated in the bill at Gresham's address suggest that she had a number of enemies within her neighbourhood.

The Lloyds, in turn, deny the allegations made against them. In their answer to Gresham's elaborate bill, they stress the vexatious nature of the suit. Although claims of vexatious litigation are made often in Star Chamber proceedings, the Lloyds offer several arguments to back up their claim. According to the Lloyds, the matter before the court had been referred to the lawyer Sir Henry Montague in June of the previous year, and was thus already settled.[99] In this case, Montague had dismissed Gresham's complaint, deeming the bill 'very insufficient'. Montague ordered the defendants their expenses against Gresham who, according to the Lloyds, 'hath not payed the same costs and yet notwithstanding hath since exhibited a new Bill'. According to the Lloyds, then, the newly filed bill is vexatious because the matter has already been decided, but also for other reasons:

> this honourable court, as these defendants hope, will not think it reasonable that the said Ellenor shall vex a multitude of her neighbours with a tedious and long Suit without her said husband's privity, who hath almost for the space of two years been at sea in the East Indian Fleet and so could not give allowance to the exhibiting of any of the said Bills.

Rather than having a legitimate cause for initiating proceedings, the Lloyds thus consider the suit a form of harassment, aimed only at 'vex[ing] a multitude of her neighbours'. They also point out that, although William Gresham's name is on the bill, it is impossible for him to have approved the suit, given that he is currently at sea, and has been for the last two years. They thus question the legitimacy of the suit in its entirety: without her husband's approval, a woman, after all, was not allowed to initiate legal proceedings before the Court of Star Chamber.[100] The Lloyds' answer thus questions the legitimacy of Gresham's bill for several reasons. Their version of events finds possible support in the Surrey County Council records, where we find a writ of exigent issued against an Eleanor Gresham 'for certain transgressions and contempts' in 1615.[101]

Gresham herself, on the other hand, denies 'vexing' her neighbours and being a 'moll'. Instead, in her bill of complaint Gresham appears keen to rectify the picture that has been painted of her by the Lloyds and that has been affirmed by the Court of Chancery. Because these records are no longer extant, it is Gresham's self-portrayal before her chosen forum that has outlasted all other narratives – presumably the outcome she had intended, though perhaps not in this manner. In repeating all her alleged wrongdoings and immoral behaviour in her lengthy bill of complaint, Gresham presumably aimed to demonstrate how severely her good name had been tarnished. Moreover, it provides evidence of her self-representation: the listed accusations must be repeated because they do *not* reflect her life or personality. In this listing of falsehoods, Gresham seeks to establish both the truth of who *she* is and also of who her neighbours are. From the material included in Gresham's account we can compile an 'official' biography, thus completing the process she began in court: Eleanor Gresham was married to William Gresham, of the parish of St Saviours in Southwark, Surrey, who was a dyer by profession. Their marriage was amiable ('to their great and mutual comforts lived married together in the state of Matrimony as man and wife') and solid (efforts made 'to work a divorce betwixt your said subjects' had all failed). Although she always endeavoured to be 'an honest woman without the least blemish, spot or reputation of any man', she did not get on with all of her neighbours: the Lloyds vexed her with multiple suits in Chancery, leading to three spells in prison. Firstly, she was 'arrested and imprisoned in the prison of the White Lion in Southwark' based on a 'writ of special supplicant' against her. She was released because of 'her good behaviour', but soon after committed to the White Lion again, this time 'for a long time'. A third spell in prison followed after a grand jury had 'taxed [her] to be a common barratrix and disturber of your Majesty's peace'. Shortly afterwards, in March and April 1613 to be exact, the libel started circulating. All of this demonstrates not Gresham's wickedness but instead presents the Lloyds as 'lewd, troublesome and evil disposed persons', who 'beggered' Gresham and her husband with a 'multiplicity of suits in law and driven them out of their said dwelling and place of their present abode'.

Despite Gresham's vehement attempts at influencing the record, a contemporary account of the case suggests that the court agreed with the Lloyds on at least one aspect of their defence, dismissing the case on the grounds that Gresham had failed to secure her husband's approval to begin the suit.[102] Nevertheless, Gresham's case demonstrates that, even though they were fighting a legal system that effectively held them in contempt, women were able to actively shape their stories – with the help of their legal advisers and penmen – and leave traces of themselves in the archives that express their own views of their own lives. It also allows us to chart how she constructed her own narrative, employing the commonly used tactics of elision and evasion, and the shifting of agency, to portray herself as she wished to be perceived. These strategies, moreover, could be wielded in such an individual manner by the women involved that they do not settle into a series of formulaic or homogeneous entries into the legal record, but are instead a set of generic conventions around which women could shape their narratives and self-representations. In the case of Eleanor Gresham, it led to the creation of a vivid written portrait of the self, in a forum chosen by herself, with the clear desire to fashion an image of herself that countered the public opinion about her. Perhaps the fact that her case is discussed here suggests that she might have succeeded, if only by making us question the truthfulness of the Lloyds.

Notes

1. On the gendered nature of (sexual) slander, see Laura Gowing, 'Gender and the Language of Insult in Early Modern London', *History Workshop Journal,* 35 (1993): 1–21; J. A. Sharpe, *Defamation and Sexual Slander in Early Modern England: The Church Courts at York*, Borthwick Papers no. 58 (Borthwick Publications, 1980).
2. Felix Pryor, *Elizabeth I: Her Life in Letters* (University of California Press, 2003), pp. 20–1.
3. Charles Jackson, 'The Preface', Alice Wandesford Thornton, *The Autobiography of Alice Thornton: of East Newton, County, York* (Andrews and Co., 1875), pp. v–xv, at xii. See also the *Alice Thornton's Books* project, which is in the process of creating a digital edition of the four different versions of Thornton's autobiography: Cordelia Beattie, Suzanne Trill, Joanne Edge and Sharon Howard. 'Alice Thornton's Books: Remembrances of a Woman's Life in the Seventeenth Century', *Alice Thornton's Books*. Accessed 5 December 2023. It is high time such a new edition is prepared: Jackson's version is 'a responsibly edited, albeit limited version of Thornton's original autobiography', which rearranges material from three of the manuscript sources into one text (Raymond Anselment, 'Seventeenth-Century Manuscript Sources of Alice Thornton's Life', *Studies in English Literature,* 45(1) (2005): 135–55, at 137). https://thornton.kdl.kcl.ac.uk/.
4. Alice Wandesford Thornton, *The Autobiography of Alice Thornton: of East Newton, County, York* (Andrews and Co., 1875), pp. 258–60.
5. Thornton does not elaborate on the exact nature of the slander (for this see Anselment, 'Seventeenth-Century Manuscript Sources', 136; and Anselment, '"My first Booke of my Life:" The Apology of a Seventeenth-Century Gentry Woman', *Prose Studies*, 24(2) (2001): 1–14, at 2–3).
6. George Eystone, for example, brought charges of libel against his legal opponents as he feared the rumours spread about his 'incontinency' and 'foul and lewd' behaviour would get him into trouble with the church courts. His worries were not unfounded: his legal opponents petitioned several courts on account of the various accusations against him (TNA, STAC 8/132/9, *Eystone v Rey et al.* (1616), Eystone's bill).

7. Keith Thomas, 'The Double Standard', *Journal of the History of Ideas,* 20 (1959): 195–216; Gowing, 'Gender and the Language of Insult'; Bernard Capp, 'The Double Standard Revisited: Plebeian Women and Male Sexual Reputation in Early Modern England', *Past & Present,* 162 (1999): 70–100; A. Lynn Martin, *Alcohol, Sex, and Gender in Late Medieval and Early Modern Europe* (Palgrave Macmillan, 2001); Jennifer Jordan, 'Her-story Untold: The Absence of Women's Agency in Constructing Concepts of Early Modern Manhood', *Cultural and Social History,* 4 (2007): 575–83; Johanna Rickman, *Love, Lust, and License in Early Modern England: Illicit Sex and the Nobility* (Ashgate, 2008).
8. Faramerz Dabhoiwala, *The Origins of Sex: A History of the First Sexual Revolution* (Oxford University Press, 2012), pp. 28–31.
9. G. R. Quaife, *Wanton Wenches and Wayward Wives: Peasants and Illicit Sex in Early Seventeenth Century England* (Croom Helm, 1979), p. 181.
10. Eleanor Hubbard, *City Women: Money, Sex, and the Social Order in Early Modern London* (Oxford University Press, 2012), p. 88.
11. 18 Eliz. I, c. 3.
12. Ibid.
13. Helen I. Clarke, *Social Legislation* (Appleton-Century-Crofts, 1957), p. 349.
14. Mark Jackson, *New-Born Child Murder: Women, Illegitimacy and the Courts in Eighteenth-Century England* (Manchester University Press, 1996), p. 31.
15. Quaife, *Wanton Wenches*, p. 225.
16. Bethlam Royal Hospital Archives (BRHA), BCB 5, f. 3r.
17. Quaife, *Wanton Wenches*, p. 59.
18. BRHA, BCB 5, f. 26r.
19. Henry Smith, *A Preparative to Marriage* (London, 1591), STC 22686, pp. 83–4, 14; William Gouge, *Of Domesticall Duties* (London, 1622), facsimile reproduction in *The English Experience*, Number 803 (Walter J. Johnson, Inc., 1976), pp. 218, 221.
20. Anthony Fletcher, *Gender, Sex and Subordination in England 1500–1800* (Yale University Press, 1995), p. 110. See also the previous chapter on courtship and marriage for more on separation of bed and board.
21. T. E., *The Lawes Resolution of Womens Rights* (London: 1632), STC 7437, p. 65.
22. Rickman, *Love, Lust, and License*, p. 23.
23. 'May 1650: An Act for suppressing the detestable sins of Incest, Adultery and Fornication', in C. H. Firth and R. S. Rait (eds), Acts and Ordinances of the Interregnum, 1642–1660 (London, 1911), pp. 387–9. British History Online, www.british-history.ac.uk/no-series/acts-ordinances-interregnum /pp387-389. Accessed 18 March 2024. This act is the result of longer-standing concerns about sexual transgressions and it finally passed after six years of debate. See Veronika Christine Pohlig, 'Adultery in Early Stuart England', unpublished PhD dissertation (Freien Universität Berlin, 2009), p. 2, for more on this.

24. Keith Thomas has found only four records of death sentences under the 1650 Act, see Keith Thomas, 'The Puritans and Adultery: The Act of 1650 Reconsidered', in Donald Pennington and Keith Thomas (eds), *Puritans and Revolutionaries: Essays in Seventeenth-Century History Presented to Christopher Hill* (Clarendon Press, 1978), pp. 257–82, at 258. For more on the act in general, see Abby Chandler, *Law and Sexual Misconduct in New England, 1650–1750: Steering Toward England* (Routledge, 2015), pp. 49–51; David M. Turner, *Fashioning Adultery: Gender, Sex and Civility in England, 1660–1740* (Cambridge University Press, 2002), p. 4.
25. Joanne Bailey, *Unquiet Lives: Marriage and Marriage Breakdown in England, 1660–1800* (Cambridge University Press, 2003), p. 5; Susan Amussen, '"Being stirred to much unquietness": Violence and Domestic Violence in Early Modern England', *Journal of Women's History*, 6(2) (1994): 70–89; Elizabeth Foyster, 'Male Honour, Social Control and Wife Beating in Late Stuart England', *Transactions of the Royal Historical Society*, 6 (1996): 215–24. On the defence strategy of using violence as a response to adultery, see Laura Gowing, *Domestic Dangers: Women, Words and Sex in Early Modern London* (Clarendon Press, 1996), pp. 219–22.
26. Bailey, *Unquiet Lives*, p. 151.
27. Merry E. Wiesner, *Women and Gender in Early Modern Europe* (Cambridge University Press, 2000) p. 297.
28. TNA, STAC 8/152/11, *Edmund Garrett v Perkins* (1610).
29. Ibid., bill of Edmund Garrett.
30. Turner, *Fashioning Adultery*, pp. 86–7. Although it was technically possible for a woman to be mocked as 'cuckqueane', the female counterpart of the 'cuckold', this was extremely rare.
31. Capp, *When Gossips Meet*, p. 192.
32. 'Ordering London Brothels Closed (Westminster, 13 April 1546, 37 Henry VIII)', in Paul L. Hughes and James F. Larkin (eds), *Tudor Royal Proclamations*, Vol. 1 (Yale University Press, 1964), pp. 365–6. The proclamation targets those people who 'provoked' and 'enticed' the youth and laboured 'to spoil and rob the true labouring and well-disposed men': women are to blame.
33. Wallace Shugg, 'Prostitution in Shakespeare's London', *Shakespeare Studies*, 10 (1997): 291–313, at 294.
34. Quaife, *Wanton Wenches*, p. 146.
35. Capp, *When Gossips Meet*, p. 67.
36. Moll Cutpurse, 'The Life and Death of Mal Cutpurse', in Janet Todd and Elizabeth Spearing (eds), *Counterfeit Ladies* (William Pickering, 1994), pp. 1–73, at 51–4.
37. Jennifer Panek, '"This Base Stallion Trade": He-Whores and Male Sexuality on the Early Modern Stage', *English Literary Renaissance*, 40(3) (2010): 357–92; Valerie Traub, *Thinking Sex with the Early Moderns* (University of Pennsylvania Press, 2016), pp. 178–9; Gowing, *Domestic Dangers*, p. 66.
38. Frédérique Fouassier-Tate, 'Fact Versus Fiction: The Construction of the Figure of the Prostitute in Early Modern England, Official and Popular

Discourses', in Richard Hillman and Pauline Ruberry-Blanc (eds), *Female Transgression in Early Modern Britain: Literary and Historical Explorations* (Routledge, 2016), pp. 51–70, 82–3.

39. Cristina León Alfar, *Women and Shakespeare's Cuckoldry Plays: Shifting Narratives of Marital Betrayal* (Routledge, 2017).
40. J. C. Lassiter, 'Defamation of Peers: The Rise and Decline of the Action for Scandalum Magnatum', 1497–1773', *American Journal of Legal History*, 22 (1978): 216–36, at 216.
41. David Cressy, *Dangerous Talk: Scandalous, Seditious, and Treasonable Speech in Pre-Modern England* (Oxford University Press, 2010), p. 19.
42. It was not until 1660 that the common law started to consistently distinguish between 'slander' and 'libel', see J. H. Baker, *An Introduction to English Legal History*, 4th edition (Oxford University Press, 2007), pp. 445–6. Both libel and slander have received considerable scholarly attention. See, for example, Fox, *Oral and Literate Culture*; Andrew McRae, 'Reading Libels: An Introduction', *Huntington Library Quarterly*, 69(1) (2006): 1–14; Alastair Bellany and Andrew McRae (eds), 'Early Stuart Libels: An Edition of Poetry from Manuscript Sources', *Early Modern Literary Sources Text Series I* (2005), http://purl.oclc.org/emls/texts/libels/; Martin Ingram, 'Ridings, Rough Music and the "Reform of Popular Culture" in Early Modern England', *Past & Present*, 105 (1984): 79–113; M. Lindsay Kaplan, *The Culture of Slander in Early Modern England* (Cambridge University Press, 1997); J. A. Sharpe, *Defamation and Sexual Slander*; Clare Egan, 'Women and the Performance of Libel in Early-Modern Devon', *Medieval English Theatre*, 38(2) (2016): 145–62.
43. Alongside these personal forms of defamation exist those defamatory remarks and statements that could have wider implications. Any words that formed a danger to the peace would be considered seditious. Sedition, however, was never defined by statute and therefore retained a controversial status. Nonetheless, the term was used both by the common people, as well as by jurists. 'Sedition' was distinguished from 'treason', with the latter being the more serious offence. For more on sedition and treason, see Cressy, *Dangerous Talk*; and the unpublished dissertation of Steven Veerapen, 'Slander and Sedition in Elizabethan Law, Speech and Writing' (University of Strathclyde, 2014).
44. Sharpe, *Defamation and Sexual Slander*, p. 4.
45. Ina Habermann, *Staging Slander and Gender in Early Modern England* (Ashgate, 2003), pp. 60–1.
46. See Sharpe, *Defamation and Sexual Slander*, p. 24.
47. J. A. Guy, *The Court of Star Chamber and Its Records to the Reign of Elizabeth I*, Public Record Office Handbooks, No. 21 (H.M. Stationery Office, 1985), pp. 62–5.
48. Craig Muldrew, *The Economy of Obligation: The Culture of Credit and Social Relations in Early Modern England* (Macmillan, 1998), p. 156.
49. Quaife, *Wanton Wenches*, p. 163.

50. TNA, STAC 8/10/5, *Attorney General at the relation of Susan Clerke v Humphrey Essex* (1610).
51. Unless, of course, people were caught in the act by the watch, in which case gossip did not play any part.
52. 'whore, n.' *OED Online*. Oxford University Press, June 2016. For more about the meaning of the word 'whore' as insult in early modern England, see Gowing, 'Gender and the Language of Insult', 3–4; and Gowing, *Domestic Dangers*, pp. 79–105.
53. LMA, DL/C/219, *Brigite Frost c Elizabeth Copsheafe* (1610), deposition of Henricus Iessom, f. 171r.
54. LMA, DL/C/219, *Jane Lilham c Alicia Rochester* (1610), depositions of Agnes Mace, Joanna Elmes, Agnes Bilton and Elizabetha Caper, ff. 196v–198v, at 196v (Agnes Mace) and 197r (Joanna Elmes). See also: Hubbard, *City Women*, pp. 178–9.
55. This repetitive use of the word does not mean it had lost its power: forced by his wife to write his mistress a letter in which he called her 'whore', Pepys initially attempted to wriggle out of this task by producing a letter 'sparing that word', eventually settling for writing it but instructing the carrier to not let his former mistress read that particular passage. Samuel Pepys, *The Diary of Samuel Pepys: A New and Complete Transcription*, Vol. IX, ed. by Robert Latham and William Matthews (Bell and Hyman, 1986), pp. 370–1.
56. TNA, STAC 8/56/17, *Bulver v Knipe alias Snipe* (1625).
57. BRHA, BCB 5, f. 17r.
58. Ibid., f. 18r.
59. TNA, STAC 8/100/18, *Cunde v Browne* (1605). For a discussion of this case, see Fox, *Oral and Literature Culture*, pp. 327–8; and for a copy of the libel, Fox, 'Popular Verses and Their Readership in the Early Seventeenth Century', in James Raven, Helen Small and Naomi Tadmor (eds), *The Practice and Representation of Reading in England* (Cambridge University Press, 1996), pp. 125–37, at p. 130.
60. I have reproduced roughly half of the full libel here, as quoted in Cunde's bill of complaint. Another version (roughly similar in its wording, but slightly differently spelled) of the libel is annexed to the proceedings.
61. The libel is signed by 'Thy very good friend Jacke Strawe'. This name reveals something of the text's possible intent. Jack Straw was allegedly one of three leaders of a peasants' revolt in the fourteenth century. The story was a popular one in English culture, retold and reshaped through the centuries. Straw was mentioned, for instance, in Chaucer's *The Canterbury Tales* and he was the protagonist of a play that dramatised the events of the peasants' rising, *The Life and Death of Jack Straw* (1593). Possibly, the author of the libel hoped to stir up a similar kind of revolt as the original Straw did by attacking a member of the clergy.
62. TNA, STAC 8/100/18, Cunde's bill of complaint (1605).
63. Ibid.

64. Anne Thompson, *Parish Clergy Wives in Elizabethan England* (Brill, 2019), pp. 233–5, at 234.
65. This conforms to the narrative models women use when accused of infanticide: these, too, lack detail, as Laura Gowing has shown (Gowing, 'Secret Births and Infanticide in Seventeenth-Century England', *Past & Present*, 156 (1997): 87–115, particularly at 105).
66. BRHA, BCB 4, f. 8r. This case is also discussed in Hubbard's *City Women*, pp. 109–19.
67. TNA, STAC 8/153/5, *Ellinor Grobye v James Ball* (1612). The case is briefly discussed in Fox's *Oral and Literate Culture*, p. 328.
68. For the different rules regarding slander that applied in Star Chamber as opposed to other courts (both secular and ecclesiastical), see Habermann, *Staging Slander*, pp. 46–7.
69. Laura Gowing, *Common Bodies: Women, Touch and Power in Seventeenth-Century England* (Yale University Press, 2003), p. 94.
70. Renato Barahona, *Sex Crimes, Honour, and the Law in Early Modern Spain: Vizcaya, 1528–1735* (University of Toronto Press, 2003), p. 58.
71. Thornton, *The Autobiography*, 259; 52.
72. Ibid., 259.
73. Ibid., 235.
74. Ibid., 236.
75. Anne Bathurst described her desire to 'ly in [God's] arms as I had done the night before' and willed him to 'kiss me with the kisses of his mouth'. Her explicitness seems to be exceptional: as far as I am aware, no other early modern diary penned by an English woman contains similar unreserved sexual desires, even if Bathurst is citing from the Song of Solomon. Mary Rich, Countess of Warwick, is less open about her feelings: at numerous occasions she describes the 'warmth' of God's love, but perhaps embarrassed about her expressions of passion, crossed some of these entries out at a later stage. Sara Heller Mendelson has argued that contemporary devotional literature was encouraging women to take on God or Christ as spouse, but the Countess of Warwick may, in hindsight, have reflected that she took this inducement slightly too far. Examples quoted from Sara Heller Mendelson, 'Stuart Women's Diaries and Occasional Memoirs', in Mary Prior (ed.), *Women in English Society, 1500–1800* (Methuen, 1985), pp. 181–210, at 194–5.
76. Alison D. Wall (ed.), *Two Elizabethan Women: Correspondence of Joan and Maria Thynne, 1575–1611* (Wiltshire Record Society, 1983), pp. 37–8.
77. Wall, *Two Elizabethan Women*, p. 38, note 3.
78. Samuel Pepys, *The Diary of Samuel Pepys: A New and Complete Transcription*, Vol. V, ed. by Robert Latham and William Matthews (G. Bell and Sons Ltd, 1971), p. 17, 16 January 1664.
79. Turner, *Fashioning Adultery*, pp. 30–1.
80. BRHA, BCB 4, ff. 8r–10r.
81. Ibid., f. 8r.
82. BRHA, BCB 5, ff. 10r, 15r.

83. BRHA, BCB 3, f. 81v. The identity of this mystery woman is not revealed in the legal records. Either the court clerk has omitted the details or Whetherall was unable to provide them with a name.
84. Ibid. f. 81v.
85. BRHA, BCB 2, ff. 155v–156v (new foliation: 179v–180v). See also: Hubbard, *City Women*, p. 108.
86. Cf, Lisa Jardine, '"Why Should He Call Her Whore?": Defamation and Desdemona's Case', in Margaret Tudeau-Clayton and Martin Warner (eds), *Addressing Frank Kermode: Essays in Criticism and Interpretation* (Macmillan, 1991), pp. 124–53, at 136–42 in particular. Jardine argues that the way private exchanges can spill over into a public space can alter the nature of an incident, changing words into events.
87. BRHA, BCB 5, 26v. For more on this case see Hubbard, *City Women*, pp. 107–8.
88. BRHA, BCB 5, f. 25v.
89. E.g. when Mirth in Ben Jonson's *The Staple of News* says: 'I would have him flat disinherited by a decree of court, bound to make restitution of the Lady Pecunia and the use of her body to his son', Ben Jonson, *The Staple of News*, ed. by Anthony Parr (Manchester University Press, 1999), 4.4.62–4.
90. Cited in David Cressy, *Birth, Marriage, and Death: Ritual, Religion, and the Life-Cycle in Tudor and Stuart England* (1997; Oxford University Press, 2002), p. 279; BRHA, BCB 2, f. 117r (new foliation: 142r). See also: Hubbard, *City Women*, p. 107.
91. BRHA, BCB 2, f. 117r (new foliation: 142r).
92. BRHA, BCB 3, f. 49r.
93. Ibid., f. 49v.
94. 4 & 5 Philip and Mary, c. 8 (1558); 3 Henry VII, c. 2 (1487). The 1487 act would only apply to this case if the girl was indeed an heiress. For more on abduction and rape of women, see Caroline Dunn, *Stolen Women in Medieval England: Rape, Abduction, and Adultery, 1100–1500* (Cambridge University Press, 2013); and Garthine Walker, '"Strange Kind of Stealing": Abduction in Early Modern Wales', in Michael Roberts and Simone Clarke (eds), *Women and Gender in Early Modern Wales* (University of Wales Press, 2000), pp. 50–74. For more about the reliability of child testimony, see Barbara J. Shapiro, *A Culture of Fact: England, 1550–1720* (Cornell University Press, 2000), p. 16; Garthine Walker, 'The Strangeness of the Familiar: Witchcraft and the Law in Early Modern England', in Angela McShane and Garthine Walker (eds), *The Extraordinary and the Everyday in Early Modern England: Essays in Celebration of the Work of Bernard Capp* (Palgrave Macmillan, 2010), pp. 105–24, at 117–19.
95. Natalie Zemon Davis, *Fiction in the Archives*; Gowing, *Domestic Dangers*; Capp, *When Gossips Meet*; Marion Gibson, *Reading Witchcraft: Stories of Early English Witches* (Routledge, 1999); Tim Stretton, *Women Waging Law in Elizabethan England* (Cambridge University Press, 1998); Garthine Walker, *Crime, Gender and Social Order in Early modern England* (Cambridge University Press, 2003).

96. TNA, STAC 8/151/7, *Gresham v Lloyd* (1613). The case is mentioned in Fox, *Oral and Literature Culture*, p. 317; and in Capp, *When Gossips Meet*, pp. 280–1. See also Malcolm Gaskill, *Crime and Mentalities in Early Modern England* (Cambridge University Press, 2000), p. 72 n205.
97. Martine van Elk, 'The Counterfeit Vagrant: The Dynamics of Deviance in the Bridewell Court Records and the Literature of Roguery', in Craig Donne and Steve Mentz (eds), *Rogues and Early Modern English Culture* (University of Michigan Press, 2004), pp. 120–39, at 122.
98. Donne and Mentz, 'Introduction', in Donne and Mentz (eds), *Rogues*, pp. 1–29, at 1.
99. According to Brian Quintrell, Montague was 'continuously in demand as a referee for all manner of domestic problems and disputes' ('Montagu, Henry, first earl of Manchester (c. 1564–1642), judge and government official', *Oxford Dictionary of National Biography* (3 January 2008). Accessed 18 March 2024.
100. Deborah Youngs has noted that, in cases where a female plaintiff's husband's name was missing from the bill, defendants often alleged in their answer that they did not need to provide an answer to the bill, but 'continued to list other reasons why the plaintiff's bills were wrong, a recognition that they realized a missing husband's name did not in itself amount to a sufficient rebuttal' (Youngs, '"A besy woman . . . and full of lawe": female litigants in early Stuart Star Chamber', *Journal of British Studies*, 58(4) (2019): 735–50, at 746).
101. Such a writ forced the person against whom the writ was issued to appear before the magistrate or suffer outlawry. Surrey County Council catalogue entry to reference 212/119/2 (e).
102. Hudson, *A Treatise of the Court of Star Chamber*, pp. 132–3. No official verdict is extent for this case, as far as I am aware.

Chapter 4

Widows

When contemplating her widowed state, Katherine Austen (1629–*c*.1683) wrote in her diary: 'Men never think their wifes may be / Necessitate by misery / Or their children be a prey / When them selues are gone away'.[1] Her lamentations were not unfounded, as entering the third stage of a woman's life, widowhood, could bring about uncertain times: quite apart from the emotional distress caused by the loss of a spouse, widowhood also had legal and financial implications. These included the need to administer a late husband's estate, the financial burden of maintaining solvency after the loss of income and the mediation of changed familial relations. A woman's new social and legal identity as *feme sole* was immediately tested by administrative changes in her life that could lead to legal suits over land, money and sometimes even her own children. Moreover, widowhood forced a woman to refashion herself in order to deal with patriarchal anxieties about her new status and the multifarious negative stereotypes that surrounded the state of widowhood, including a pernicious one concerning the 'litigious widow'. The regularity with which contemporary popular literature featured widows contributed to creating a literary trope that widows found themselves fighting against – when they were not turning it to their own advantage, of course. The result is that widows had options concerning how they wished to portray themselves in a legal context. Various models were available, including the tropes of the biblical widow and eternal wife, while they were also free to portray themselves as *feme sole* or emphasise their role as mother. Widows could therefore fashion different images of themselves according to their circumstances and needs.

This chapter first considers what widowhood entailed in early modern England, looking at its legal consequences and reflecting on the social perceptions that were attached to this new phase in a woman's life. The need to balance legal and financial imperatives with the expectations of a severely judgemental society required widows to tread carefully when initiating legal proceedings, and this is reflected in their writing style:

they often attempted to pre-empt accusations of acting as the stereotypical litigious widow by emphasising their reluctance to seek legal redress. With this first hurdle overcome, they could then make other tropes concerning widowhood work to their advantage. This chapter then analyses the different ways in which widows portrayed themselves in diaries, autobiographies and legal records. Perhaps as a result of the plethora of stereotypical widows to be found within the literature of the day, the narrative strategies employed by widowed autobiographers and litigants are markedly similar. By reading the autobiographical texts of widows such as Anne Halkett (1623–99) and Katherine Austen alongside the legal pleadings of widowed complainants and defendants, we can trace these similarities.

Widowhood in Early Modern England

After the death of her husband in 1666, Ann, Lady Fanshawe (1625–80) wrote a moving passage in her *Memoirs* on what this loss meant to her: 'O all powerfull Lord God, look down from heaven upon me, the most distressed wretch upon earth. See me with my soule divided, my glory and my guide taken from me, and in him all my comfort in this life'.[2] Not every widow was as devastated as Lady Fanshawe at the death of her husband, however. Sarah, Lady Cowper (1644–1720), for instance, described her first year as a widow as 'a State of Liberty', expressing clearly the relief felt after her husband's death, even if his passing had also caused this new state of hers to be rather precarious in financial terms.[3] While arguing against remarriage, Cowper advised her readers: 'Wear not a Straight Ring. Lead your Life in Freedom and Liberty, and throw not your Self in to Slavery'.[4] Although Cowper may have been exceptionally happy at reaching the state of widowhood, the freedom she felt after the passing of her husband may well have been an experience common amongst the newly widowed.[5] This joy may have often faded in the light of reality, however, as losing a spouse had very different implications for a woman than it did for a man. Any emotional distress notwithstanding, the death of a wife left the new widower's legal status unaffected: for a woman, however, losing a husband was a life-changing experience that affected her social, legal and financial status, and not always for the better.[6]

The unity of person created by *coverture* was normally broken only by death, and if lucky enough to survive her husband, a woman reverted back to her pre-marital state of *feme sole*, albeit now with perhaps some money or property. Having recovered a legal identity, a woman could therefore sue (and be sued), enter into contracts or make a will under her own name. Perhaps for this reason, widowhood in early modern England is often referred to as a time that brought about the greatest independence for women.[7] The writer of *The Lawes Resolutions of Womens Rights* (1632) certainly seems to agree with this point of view, as he asks his female readers: 'Why mourn you so, you that be widows? Consider how long you have been in subjection under the predominance of parents, of your husbands, now you may be free in liberties, and free *proprii iuris* at your own law'.[8] Widows, theoretically at least, had more freedom and experience, as well as greater resources, than any other category of woman in society, including those women who had remained *femes soles* throughout their lives.[9] Viewed in that light, it is not surprising that Sarah Cowper considered remarriage as akin to re-entering a state of slavery, and thus refused to countenance it.

The widow's renewed legal freedom, however, was often put to the test from the very moment it had been gained. Widows were frequently appointed as executrix of their husband's last will and testament, or administratrix of their late husband's affairs and estate if no such will had been drawn up prior to death. As such, widows were thrust into the legal arena, perhaps for the first time in their lives. When there were no creditors or when the balance of the estate remaining after the deduction of debts was positive, widowhood could bring about a certain amount of financial freedom. Had her late husband the gall to perish while heavily in debt, however, a newly minted widow might face serious challenges in overseeing his estate – or if its administration had been entrusted to another, she may struggle to maintain her living standards. There could be multiple creditors while his family or heirs added to her worries by competing with her for a share in what estate there was; she might not even be guaranteed the right to remain in the marital home. Such trials and tribulations were anything but exceptional, and if a widow was left with mouths to feed and no personal income, the legal and financial consequences of widowhood could be devastating.

While it has been suggested that as many as 45 per cent of women would become widowed at some point, a fair proportion of these would experience widowhood several times, as remarriage was common, especially in early modern London.[10] The legal problems that invariably followed the death of a husband meant that a widow was bound to have far greater appreciation of the impact any pre-marital agreements might have on her future welfare than her single or married counterpart. It is because of their experience and knowledge of the legal system that widows are well represented in the legal archives, and, like all women involved in litigation, they played the system by pressing their suits in the most advantageous forum when possible. It is perhaps unsurprising that widows appear in the records of courts all over London, making up almost half of the female litigants in the Courts of Requests, Common Pleas and Queen's Bench.[11] It is difficult to establish how well widows were represented in local suits: given the local law's preference for custom over written accounts, records are scarce. However, the records of the Court of Requests demonstrate that widows flocked to the capital to deal with local issues whenever they deemed it necessary. The Court of Requests had a reputation of being favourable to those parties that needed extra protection, such as the poor and women. As such, it was the perfect arena for widows to try their suits. Arguing before this 'poor man's' court allowed widows to tap into the tradition of the poor, biblical widow, an image with which they could hope to gain particular sympathy from the Masters of Requests.

Widows were not only well represented in the law courts; popular literature and theatre were also rife with representations of widows.[12] It is possible that this was a direct result of the threat widows were perceived as posing to the early modern patriarchal order. Naturally, a patriarchal society would view any situation in which a household was not headed by a man as a challenge to the 'order of things'.[13] Add to this the fact that widowhood would be the first time in a woman's life when she was not ruled by a man, it is no surprise that the figure of the widow was seen as a locus of conflict. Without a father or husband present, widows took over their roles as head of the household, challenging and complicating established patriarchal norms.[14] While a widow who remained single posed an obvious challenge to societal norms, so too did a widow who chose to remarry. Quite apart from the fact that a widow who re-entered the marriage market automatically confronted a potential suitor with his mortality, she was presumably less keen on accepting unfavourable conditions or financial settlements. Instead, she may have been aware of the possibilities of using trusts to protect her interests from transferring to her new husband. The widow, perhaps, knew too much to be considered entirely safe, and the position of widows, especially when it came to remarriage, was a hotly debated issue in early modern England and thus fertile ground for dramatists and other writers.[15]

The early modern stage widow was lusty, litigious and wealthy; she was both keen to remarry and a desirable object to those men seeking quick and easy enrichment. The trope of the rapidly remarrying widow would appear particularly frequently on the early modern stage. The Duchess in *The Duchess of Malfi* (*c.*1612), Widow Plus in *The Puritaine Widow* (1606), Lady Goldenfleece in *No Wit, No Help Like a Woman's* (*c.*1611) and Valeria in *The Widow* (*c.*1616) are just some examples of remarrying stage widows. The fact is, a widow simply could not win: ridiculed if she remarried too quickly, or indeed, at all, she ran the risk of being termed a whore, bawd or witch if she had the temerity to remain single. An early modern proverb stated that 'the rich widow weeps with one eye and casts glances with the other'.[16] George Chapman's widow Eudora from the play *The Widow's Tears* (*c*.1605) is an example: she vows never to marry again, and, as such, remains 'a fort of chastity', something she is praised for.[17] When Eudora does marry again, against her own vows, this is seen as proof of 'how short-lived widows' tears are'.[18] It is the characterisation of the lusty widow that Katherine Austen seeks to avoid when she writes: 'It shal never be sed I lived a widow (now almost 8 years) vnder the vaile of Hipocrisy, pretending to Honour the memory of my deceased Friend. And make it the foundation of my perticular Fortune, and raise a second bed'.[19] Contemporary medical books did nothing to discourage this commonplace; Nicholas Culpeper's *Dictionary for Midwives* (1651), for instance, claimed that a common illness of the wombs of widows ensured that they were 'mad for Lust'.[20] At the same time, the stereotypical English witch and bawd were elderly women, usually widowed.[21] Widows thus had to walk a fine line: remarriage was frowned upon, but so was staying single.

Such was the culture in which early modern widows lived: their renewed freedom was immediately put to the test by legal challenges, forcing them to stake their claims in public, while stereotypes ensured continued scrutiny of their lifestyle and choices. Women such as Austen, Halkett and Alice Thornton (1626–1707) sought to counter these stereotypes in their autobiographies, employing the only weapon at their disposal, rhetoric.[22] These same perceptions were at work in court pleadings and necessitated the same rhetorical techniques to counter them. Widows seeking to control their image, whether in autobiography or in court, had four distinct 'selves' available to them: the biblical widow, the eternal wife, the *feme sole* and the mother. They pressed these 'selves' into action to counteract the stereotyping that was wielded against them. When pressing their suit in court, of course, the first stereotype a widow was forced to confront was perhaps the hardest to dispel – the image of the litigious widow.

'Unquiet and miscontented':[23] The Loud and Litigious Widow

The 'loud and litigious' widow was a mainstay of early modern literature and drama: early modern dramatists frequently wrote litigating widows into their plays. Thomas Middleton's *The Widow* (*c.*1615) has the widow Valeria engage with the law when she tells Francisco and Attilio that she will 'take course against' them and hopes 'that law will right' her.[24] By act four of the play, Valeria is 'up to th'ears in law'.[25] Other litigious widows on the early seventeenth-century stage include John Webster's Leonora in *The Devils Law-Case* (*c.*1617) and Jacintha in *The Spanish Curate* (1622). Half a century later William Wycherley's *The Plain Dealer* (1676) featured the quarrelsome and litigious widow Blackacre, described in the *dramatis personae* as a 'petulant, litigious widow, always in law', while other characters describe Blackacre as 'a litigious she-pettifogger', 'as vexatious as her father was, the great attorney [. . .] and as implacable an adversary as a wife suing for alimony' and that 'she has no pleasure, but in vexing others'.[26] The first lines the widow speaks are full of legal terminology, with mentions of judges, suits, hearings and law-French.[27] The result of this familiar and persistent characterisation was that accusations of litigiousness in court would instantly resonate with those present, but it also meant that the widow herself would be expecting such an attack and thus could construct a defence against it. Nevertheless, a widow initiating a lawsuit always began at a disadvantage, and this held true whether she was appearing in court or merely recounting a previous suit in her diaries. It is for this reason that we find the same rhetorical strategies designed to counter expected accusations of quarrelsome litigiousness in both legal records and autobiographical writing.

The case of *Maddilowe v Barnes* illustrates what widows were up against when engaging in a lawsuit. Agnes Maddilowe sued Robert Barnes over the lease of a tenement in 1597, of which they both considered themselves to be rightful possessor, an assumption that led Barnes to evict Maddilowe from the premises. According to Barnes, Maddilowe had buried him with legal suits ever since, starting with her 'procuring him the said defendant to be called before the Justices of Assize', 'and also divers & sundry times before Justices of the peace'. After that 'the said Complainant Agnes Maddilowe not thus satisfied hath since upon some new petition exhibited (as it seems) to the Justices of Assize procured the said defendant to appear again before Justices of peace'. After these various, apparently unfruitful attempts, she 'now lastly sued with her majesty's writ of privy seal to appear & answer the matter in this honourable court, So that it doth manifestly appear the said defendant is driven to all these troubles & great expenses rather of malice'.[28] By describing her as 'not thus content' and 'not thus satisfied', Barnes portrays the widow as impossible to please and by emphasising that she had repeatedly brought him to court out 'of malice' he makes her seem quarrelsome. The overall picture painted thus fits in with the stereotypical image of the widow: quarrelsome and clamorous. At the close of the first round of the filing of case papers, after the bill of complaint and the answer, a widow like Agnes Maddilowe would be at a disadvantage. While women like Maddilowe did theoretically have the chance to counter such assertions, either orally or in a second round of responses and counter-responses, by filing a replication, the latter route imposed additional cost on the complainant. The replication would have to be drawn up and submitted, which required the additional services of lawyers. Moreover, by prolonging the proceedings a widow would run the risk of affirming her litigious image – the very image she was trying to dispel.

Accusations of litigiousness were almost always accompanied with other implied slurs against the widow's character. The most common accusations were of ruthlessness, the desire to receive her legal right regardless of the consequences and double-dealing. We see a number of such examples in the records of the Court of Requests. One can be found in the case of *Bowdon v Beaple* (1566). Alice Bowdon complained that Alexander Beaple refused to hand over the papers by which she could prove that she was the legal tenant of a certain tenement. Beaple, on the other hand, 'verily thinketh and believeth that the said complainant hath the said two copies in her own custody' – copies which would prove that he was in fact the rightful tenant of the premises.[29] Both of them thus accuse the other of withholding legal evidence. Beaple, however, has an advantage: whether or not Bowdon did indeed have this proof in her possession, by accusing her of such duplicity, Beaple implicitly places her alongside what Stretton refers to as stereotypical 'bad' widows.[30] Another case, from 1587, features a widow accused of double-charging. Marye Daughan accuses Edward Bassett of borrowing money from her first husband and failing to pay it back. After her first husband died, her second husband tried to get the debtor to pay up, but he failed too. When her second husband died as well, Daughan took matters into her own hands in order to get the debt satisfied. Bassett, however, was of the opinion that she put in a

> suit against your said Subject contrary to all equity and conscience, albeit she knoweth the said promise to be made by the said Roberte Hincke, her first Husband, as aforesaid, and also the said agreement to be made by the said John Daughan, her latter husband, as is also aforesaid, and beside that he, your said Subject, hath duly & truly made the said several payments. [. . .] by all likelihood the said Marye is privy to the said dealings of her said Husbands.[31]

According to the alleged debtor, Daughan knew very well that he was no longer indebted to her, but she decided to sue him anyway, in order to get paid twice. Indeed, the complainant accuses Daughan's husbands of duplicity, and her of inheriting it. As such, the widow's actions are described as underhand and her lawsuit as unnecessary and snide. Because in this case it is merely the word of one person against another, the negative image of the widow, so persistent in early modern culture, could help Bassett to win his case.

The stereotype of the widow who sought legal process simply because she could (rather than because she was compelled out of necessity) was not completely without foundation. Anne Clifford is a well-known example of a woman continually tied up in litigation. In total, Clifford was at law for a period spanning some fifty years, not only during her widowhood, but also before and during her marriages, leading Richard T. Spence to comment on 'her love of controversy and lawsuits'.[32] While she is often praised for her tenacious determination to claim her inheritance, her legal endeavours went far beyond the mere recovery of 'her' family estates.[33] It was during her widowed years that Clifford moved beyond trying to merely recover what she deemed rightfully hers, but instead desired to expand her wealth, influence and lands at the expense of some of her (under-)tenants as well as her relatives and parents of her goddaughter, the Corks. Spence has documented these episodes in great detail, laying out how in a bid to acquire more money and influence, Clifford built a corn mill to rival the local one.[34] By instructing her tenants to use only her mill, she placed them in a difficult position: caught in the middle of the fight between Clifford and the owner of the local mill, they were constantly at risk of lawsuits by both mill owners. This situation only came to an end when 133 tenants joined forces and petitioned the court to offer legal resolution. Spence's detailed overview of Clifford's dispute with the Corks over some Craven estates shows how this was fought out over the heads of her own tenants, too: she tried to force them into signing a new lease with her, and when they refused, she ejected them from their homes and lands.[35] In both cases, Clifford seemed willing to sacrifice her tenants' piece of mind by engaging in 'litigious warfare' with her neighbours.[36] While Clifford may have always been litigious, it seems she only turned into a vexatious litigant while widowed.

Katherine Austen, too, was caught up in extensive legal battle, though Austen's litigiousness was directly related to her being widowed, as she sued and was countersued over her late husband's manor of Highbury. Austen, in her diary, makes a point of expressing her unhappiness at being entangled in legal proceedings: 'And stil I am attended with Law shuites. Sister Austen agen and another Troublesome man. sues in forme of paupery. These make up to me a Triple Tax'.[37] While Clifford similarly pleaded reluctance when it came to pressing lawsuits,[38] she is remarkably quiet in her diaries on the matter of the prolonged litigation with her neighbours at the expense of her tenants.[39] The strategies employed by these widows (Austen pleads reluctance when it came to pressing lawsuits, while Clifford glosses over her more ruthless legal battles), suggests their mediation of the contemporary ideas about litigating widows. Their awareness of the prevalent contemporary ideas regarding widowhood may have led them to express their discomfort, or gloss over their legal pursuits entirely, in an attempt to adhere to socially desirable behaviour. It did not, however, stop them from pursuing justice in the law courts.

In the archives we can find many records of the lawsuits of widows who, like Katherine Austen, seem to have been drawn to the courts of law. One of them is Dame Mary Cheeke. Cheeke fought several battles in the courts of Star Chamber, Requests and Chancery between 1594 and 1600.[40] Although most of these suits were started by her late husband, Cheeke continued targeting his legal opponents after his death. In one case (*Cheeke v Symcocks*, 1594) the defendant, perhaps drawing on the received trope of the litigious widow, accuses Cheeke of abusing the court for her own gain: 'he marveleth at the malice & lying falsehood of such as gave instruction for the drawing of this odious & slanderous bill', referring to Cheeke, and adds that 'if the very devil should be the complainant he could no more untruly or slanderously accuse or belie this defendant'.[41] Hyperbole not withstanding, the defendant is clearly stating that Cheeke's charges are false and vexatious. We encounter something similar in *Bristowe v Bristowe* (1582). Here, Elizabeth Bristowe, the widow of the late Christopher Bristowe, was accused by her opponent, her stepson Henry Bristowe, of litigating out of sheer greed. Henry was the issue of Christopher's previous marriage, and had been appointed as executor of his father's will. Elizabeth, who had several children by Christopher, fell out with Henry following her husband's death. She accused him of throwing her and 'her said children, being his brothers and sisters, out of the doors and unto the street'. This is not only cruel, since most of her children were 'very young, not able to help or provide for them selves' and she was 'without any manner of provision for their bringing up and funding', it is also unlawful, since she considered the house as rightfully hers (as a component of her widow's part).[42] In his defence, Henry Bristowe claimed that he had made his stepmother a generous offer, which she 'did only mislike and obstinately refuse'.[43] By calling her behaviour obstinate and implying she is greedy, the stepson suggests that the legal proceedings started against him were without foundation; it was not his behaviour that should be objected against, but rather his stepmother's. Although Henry does not explicitly refer to his stepmother's widowed state, he is tapping into the familiar stereotype of the litigious widow. It is this kind of stigma that widows had to fight against when choosing to enter the legal arena. But it was also a known evil and widows knew how to deal with this kind of rhetoric.

In an attempt to pre-emptively counter allegations of litigiousness, many widows inserted a sentence in their bills of complaint accentuating their overall humble and graceful demeanour, the very opposite of the loud and vexatious widows of the stage. Alice Bowdon 'hath oftentimes of late gently desired the said Alexander Beaple To deliver her the said Copies whereby the said several estates of her husband may Appear by which she may from then forth enjoy the premises quietly as she hath done'.[44] By phrasing her efforts in this way, Bowdon emphasises that she is anything but loud and litigious. When her gentle line of action failed, even after several attempts, her only option was to start legal proceedings. Likewise, Fridefreed Norwood 'by herself and other her friends by her assignment hath divers & sundry times in very friendly sort' asked the defendants to pay her the rent they owe her.[45] Anne Knyght 'oftentimes in good & gentle manner required' her legal opponent to come through.[46] Margarett Eaton's husband 'whilest he lived & your highness' said oratrix since his death have often times gently required the said Thomas Hackett to pay unto them the said sum of sixteen pounds or to deliver them the said bill of debt'.[47] The claims are all the same: that since their gentle and humble requests had been repeatedly ignored, they had no choice but to seek redress through the courts.

That several women appear to have attempted unsuccessfully to use 'gentle persuasion' or variations thereof, before finally submitting their suit to court may indicate that this was a formulaic phrase. Indeed, variations of this phrase occur frequently in Court of Requests' suits, in bills by men and women alike. The fact that not all widows used this tactic, however, suggests that it was not a set phrase in every Requests' bill, especially as the message delivered – namely that legal proceedings were a last resort – was generally the same, even though it was subject to different modes of delivery. Dame Elizabeth Wallwyn, for example, expressed her desire to solve the issues she had with her grandson over her husband's inheritance outside of the legal arena quite explicitly. She accepted a relatively small sum as her widow's part 'for the avoiding of suit and expenses in the law', even though 'it was but a very small recompense unto your said Subject considering how greatly and richly the said Sir Richard Wallwyn [her husband] was advanced by your said Subject being at that time surmised in all things according to her calling and dignity'.[48] Since this did not settle the dispute with her grandson, she was forced to seek legal redress, despite her attempts to avoid this. While some widows implied that they were forced to appeal to the law, others made a point of stating this fact. Alice Cowper, for example, explained how 'the said defendant (bona fide), without any friend or covin to recover her own, was enforced to commence suit upon the said bill obligatory in the said court'.[49] Cowper did not emphasise her own persistent attempts at recovering what was rightfully hers, but explained that she had nobody in her life who could do it for her. Moreover, she aimed to demonstrate that her reason for going to court, collecting an outstanding debt, was entirely just. Cowper describes the debt as 'being a true and just debt which the said John Tewesly did owe unto the said Thomas Cowper', her late husband, and 'it was a true & just suit commenced upon a true debt forborn for a long time'.[50] Although these women make it clear in their bills that they would have rather avoided a lawsuit, they all choose to do so in different ways, possibly dependent on the nature of their suit.

Alongside this defensive strategy a woman could also make positive use of the widow trope in order to validate both her character and her cause. Looking at the models upon which widowed autobiographers and diarists based themselves can help us understand the strategies chosen by litigating widows. Upon meditating on her status as a widow, Anne Halkett considered that 'There is two examples of Widows w[ch] I desire to follow'.[51] Both of Halkett's examples belong to the category of the biblical widow, modelled on the widow described by St Paul in 1 Timothy 5:5–12, who lived her life in dedication to God, and is '[w]ell reported of for good works; if she have brought up children, if she have lodged strangers, if she have washed the saints' feet, if she have relieved the afflicted, if she have diligently followed every good work'. But Halkett also described her identity as plural and adaptable: she had duties as 'a Widow a Mother, & a Cristian'.[52] We should therefore pay attention to Halkett's 'plurality of lives', which is captured in a 'web of texts, available to different readers at different moments'.[53] The remainder of this chapter outlines the three 'types' of widow we see presented in legal records: the *feme sole* (and the related trope of the eternal wife), the widowed mother and the biblical widow. These three forms of self-presentation gave women the argumentative power to seek their legal rights.

Biblical Widow

The model of the biblical widow was rooted in a combination of different verses from the Bible. In 1 Timothy 5, Paul instructs the honouring of widows above the age of sixty, who are 'desolate, trusteth in God, and continueth in supplications and prayers night and day', and who are '[w]ell reported of for good works'. An example of doing good work can be found in Mark 12.38–44, where a widow receives the highest praise from Jesus for putting all her money in an offering box. The biblical widow is thus not only described as helping others: by giving away her money and material property to those less fortunate, she lives in relative poverty and is therefore in need of charity. Indeed, the biblical widow requires God's provision and she can count on him to protect her.[54] The true biblical widow is thus poor, aged and worthy of God's protection.

This biblical widow was a familiar trope in early modern England. Anne Halkett, for example, explicitly invokes the idea of the biblical widow in her 'Meditations' as an ideal that she would like to model her own behaviour on. Halkett self-consciously strove to be the kind of widow that

> St Paul Calls a Widow Indeed (Oh to bee such a one)[,] desolate (wch I vnderstand to bee alone & retired)[,] trusting in God[,] & Continuing in Suplications & Prayers Night & day. [B]lamelese, well reported of for Good workes[,] brought vp chilldren[,] Lodged strangers[,] washed the Saints feet[,] releeued the afflicted[,] dilligently followed euery good worke[. T]his Lord I desire to doe[.][55]

Halkett paraphrases 1 Timothy 5:5–10 here, but is guilty of partial textual editing. While she claims to strive to do good works and to honour God, which would make her eligible for being honoured, she conveniently leaves out 5:9, where Paul preaches against the giving of charity to a widow under the age of sixty. Halkett wrote the passage in 1670, when she had just become widowed, aged forty-eight. At other moments in her account it becomes clear that Halkett could use the financial relief of charity mentioned by Paul, however. Upon considering remarriage, she asks God for the 'strengh to resist this Temptation', even though remarriage would offer her the opportunity to be 'inabled to pay my depts & bee more vsefull to the poore'.[56] Halkett thus styles herself after St Paul's widow, by desiring to do good deeds for others despite her own precarious financial state. When, at the end of her meditation, Halkett decides against remarriage, it comes as no surprise that she refuses to accept her suitor's 'Riches' and rather chooses to 'place more true Contentt in my quiett retirementt'.[57] While seemingly adhering to Paul's instructions (urging widows to remain 'desolate'), Halkett tweaks them yet again to her own liking, for in 1 Timothy 5:14, Paul advises widows below the age of sixty to remarry. Halkett thus highlights those elements that make her resemble the biblical widow, while ignoring those features that she inconveniently lacks.

Halkett illustrates exactly how the model of the biblical widow could be strategically adopted and adapted: reconstruction in accordance with the biblical widow was attractive as a corrective to Halkett's rather scandalous past.[58] Her romantic involvement with the Royalist spy Joseph Bampfield had left her vulnerable to gossip and accusations of being unvirtuous, as Bampfield was already married to another woman during their romance, during which she 'had beene puplickely Maried to him & avouedly Liued with him as his wife', as she admits in her 'True accountt'.[59] If she had indeed married Bampfield, it would mean that in marrying sir James Halkett, Anne committed bigamy and adultery. Regardless of whether or not Halkett was, in fact, following the example of St Paul's widow, she thus had excellent reasons to describe herself as one: her disreputable image needed to be replaced with a more pious one. Halkett's alignment with the biblical widow is a strategic choice aimed at presenting her as pious and devoted, as well as worthy of protection.

The biblical widow was thus the perfect model for those widows seeking to present themselves in the most favourable way. In order to invoke the model, widows needed to portray themselves as poor, weak, in need of protection – and, preferably but not necessarily, aged. Autobiographers and litigants alike thus invoked God's promise to orphans and widows. Ann Fanshawe referred to it when she addressed God in her autobiography: 'Doe with me and for me what thou pleases, for I doe wholly rely upon thy mercy, beseeching thee to remember thy promises to the fatherlesse and widow, and enable me to fullfill thy will cheerfully in the world'.[60] Katherine Austen did something similar, by asking God to do for her what he has done for other widows: 'O God that hast heard the sighing of oppresed widdowes. of helpless orphanes heretofore here me at this time'.[61] Both Austen and Fanshawe thus petitioned God in order to alleviate their dire circumstances. The link with widows seeking relief from law courts is clear.

In order to receive this redress, both diarists and litigating widows cast themselves as helpless, dependent creatures. So did Katherine Austen claim that '[i]f the Lord is not on our side, now men rise up agen us. I if the Lord takes not our part. now that we have great opposeres. They will swallow our estate up quick, while their many devices are intended to overthrow us'.[62] And Ann Fanshawe wrote that she would 'humbly submit to thy justice', when she asked God to 'save' her, 'have pitty on' her and 'speak peace to [her] disquieted soul'.[63] Litigating women drew on a similar notion of dependency: whether maids, wives or widows, they generally made it clear that they desperately needed help by inserting a particular formula into their legal record, such as: 'your said orator is without all remedy if your great Favour be not to her extended in this behalf'.[64] Widows, however, often modified this sentence to suit their personal situation, in a further attempt to convince a court that intervention was necessary. Johane Coppe, for example, wrote in her bill of complaint that 'she having nothing else to relieve or comfort her withal being a woman of the age of threescore years and above, to her utter undoing & overthrow, if some speedy remedy be not by your majesty herein provided'.[65] By claiming that only a favourable court ruling could prevent her from becoming utterly undone (since she was both old and without the help of friends or family), the widow laid herself fully at the court's mercy. Moreover, by explicitly mentioning that she was sixty, Coppe makes it clear that she is entitled to charity, according to 1 Timothy 5. Likewise, Margaret Carter in her pleading requested 'your highness' clemency' to be 'unto her extended', to avoid her becoming 'undone'.[66]

Asserting their weakness and dependency were key rhetorical elements for these widows as they petitioned the court for assistance. Katherine Austen mastered this technique to perfection and employed it repeatedly in *Book M*. At one place she wrote: 'O God tho my enemies seek to take aduantage upon my week and destitute and helples condition A woman without Alliance of the Family to help one. Yet o God help me & make me overcome those bands that doe environe me'.[67] At another: 'Help me o lord, now I am helpless. now I am weeke by distempers of body. be strength to my body, be supportation to my minde'.[68] Litigating widows made use of these strategies, too. Elizabeth Bedell, for example, referred to herself as 'being both aged and very Impotent'.[69] Maryan Smythe, too, repeatedly refers to her age as a form of weakness, 'she being 80 years of age and not able to help her self', 'she being also an Ancient parishioner', 'a silly woman of 80 years of age' and finally 'a very Aged woman of 80 years of age & cannot travel'.[70] Alice Cowper described her lonely and solitary status, by stating she was 'without any friend'.[71] In court, a widow would seize on any way to show her general weakness, whether this was poor health, age, impotence or a lack of a functioning support network. In this way, she sought to align herself with the trope of the biblical widow and, thus, deserving of succour. More to the point, perhaps, the widow demonstrated how appropriately humble and obedient she was and that she needed the help of an authority figure, whether this be God or the Master of Requests.

In fact, the courts so rarely heard a widow describe herself as anything other than poor that the formulation of 'poor widow' became almost meaningless. The near-emptiness of the phrase was perhaps accentuated by the suggestion that not all of those petitioning the Court of Requests were as poor as they made out.[72] Widows therefore tended to qualify their assertions of poverty with a note of their 'many children'. So was Margerie Themilthorpe 'very poor and overcharged with many children',[73] and Anne Davie claimed that 'your highnes' said poor subject hath many poor fatherless children, whereof sundry of them been of few yeares and very chargeable to your highnes' poor subject to bring up'.[74] Ann Fanshawe, in her diary, expressed similar problems with taking care of her children after her husband's death, which emphasises once more the parallel between pleading with God and the judge: 'Have pitty on me, O Lord, and speak peace to my disquieted soul now sinking under the great weight, which without thy support cannot sustaine itself. See me, O Lord, with five children, a distressed family'.[75]

The greater the strain caused by the dependents, the greater the widow's poverty, of course, so litigants would latch onto any way of demonstrating how their own, particular circumstances were especially bad. Agnes Bridges describes herself as 'a very old woman and not able to get her living, having two sons, the one blind and the other lame',[76] while Margaret Carter had to 'maintain her self and her poor mother and two children',[77] and Elizabeth Thomas had an entire family – whoever that may include – to think about, as she described how her legal opponent's behaviour could potentially lead 'to the utter undoing of her, her poor Children and family'.[78] Age, the number of children or other dependants and specific expensive circumstances such as ageing mothers or disabled children were thus used to justify calling oneself a 'poor widow'.

In order to stress the direness of their financial situation, widows often characterised their poverty in explicit contrast to the wealth, cunning or rapaciousness of their legal opponent.[79] In doing so, they were aided by the setup of the Court of Requests, which held jurisdiction over cases 'where the Plaintiff's poverty, or mean estate, was not matchable with the wealth, or greatness of the Defendant'.[80] Johan Fowles, for example, referred to herself as 'a very poor and needy widow' and to her opponent John Sencler as 'A worshipful esquier'.[81] Margaret Pralyng ploughs a similar furrow, though rather than accentuate her opponent's social status, and therefore his relative wealth, she employs a strategy often used in marriage separation cases, and denigrates his moral rectitude, contrasting her status as a 'Widow very simple and ignorant lest altogether friendless and Fatherless' with 'the defendant's very cunning crafty and subtle people'.[82] The self-same strategy can be found in the diary of Katherine Austen, who styled herself as 'week as a child to Contest, with my potent Aduarsaries'.[83] Moreover, she claimed to be 'in the hands of potent men. Men skilful. to distroy of subtil men, who lay traines to ruine the widow and Fatherles'.[84] This juxtaposition serves two functions: on the one hand it makes the widow appear even more helpless, on the other, it questions her opponent's morality, making them into somebody using their power and skills to destroy a poor, needy widow.

Women would not plead poverty as a matter of course, however. Dame Mary Cheeke, for one, refrained from commenting on the nature of her financial state in her numerous pleadings. She did, however, describe the wealth of her real estate, as such almost showcasing her lack of poverty. She appears to be suing not because her financial well-being depended on it, but because she was being defrauded and simply found that unfair and unacceptable.[85] Other widows, like Brydgett Sefoule and Alyce Steward, in similar fashion did not comment on their financial affairs and refrained from referring to themselves as a 'poor widow' in their legal pleadings.[86] Those who did plead poverty were nevertheless accused of exaggerating their claims by their legal opponents. While Anne Hooton, for example, described herself as 'left a very poor, ignorant, weak and unbefriended woman charged with young Children' after the death of her husband, the complainant in her case claimed that she was, in fact, 'a woman of great wealth and ability'.[87] Since she was capable of paying off her late husband's supposed debt with apparent ease, it is possible that her claims of poverty were exaggerated, if not altogether false.[88] Styling oneself as a poor widow, then, was not an automatic choice: not all widows adopted the persona of the poor widow, but those who did generally chose to accentuate their relative poverty.[89]

Despite the occasional example in which a man referred to his poverty in his pleading, this strategy was largely one employed by women:[90] according to Stretton, men were more inclined to concentrate on their opponent's power, rather than their own weaknesses.[91] It is, of course, true that the Court of Requests was known as the 'poor man's court' and the rethorical options available to widows were largely also available to men – but men did not have recourse to the literary model of the biblical widow(er). The manner in which widows appear to have accentuated their status as weak and vulnerable, in line with St Paul's widow, was quite plainly a gender-specific strategy utilised in the hope of eliciting the sympathy of the court.

The model of the biblical widow was a trope that relied on the highlighting of the power imbalance implicit in the court system. It was therefore the perfect riposte to the image of the litigious widow that was likely to be employed against her, emphasising necessity over choice and conjuring pity to answer the implicit judgement encoded in that stereotype. Choosing this model was a strategic decision which could not only help widows to win their case, but also allowed them to present a specifically designed public persona to the outside world – both in and outside the courtroom. It was a deliberate, autobiographical form of self-fashioning. There were, however, other tropes available to the early modern widow besides this biblical emphasis of their weak and powerless nature, and this was just one of a range of personas that they adopted in their suits.

Until Death Do Us Part

The second type widows could use in their self-definition was the *feme sole* and its counterpart the eternal wife. Both the *feme sole* and the eternal wife are widows who have not remarried after the death of their spouses and perhaps even refuse to do so. The difference between the two is a subtle one: the widowed *feme sole* is a woman who is no longer married, while the eternal wife considers herself effectively still married. The law did not distinguish between them: all widows who had not (yet) remarried lost their *covert* status upon the death of their spouses. Whether a widow depicted herself as one or the other depended not on the type of widow she was, but on the type of widow she *needed to be*, and her self-definition as *feme sole* or eternal wife had serious ramifications for the way in which a widow interacted with the court.

We might expect widows to do rather more than simply celebrate the freedom they now enjoyed and, just as Lady Cowper and others did in their diaries and autobiographies, actively present themselves as *femes soles* in case papers. The records suggest, however, that those few who did assert this particular identity did so only when it was absolutely necessary: when it was the only way in which a widow could continue to enjoy her late husband's property rights. That is, when the law insisted upon it.

Customary law, in particular, could require widows to remain 'sole' if they wanted to continue to enjoy the rights they had while their husband was alive. Manors did not enforce rules prohibiting widows from remarrying as such, but if widowed women wanted to make use of their late husband's real estate – including the house the couple and their children lived in prior to the husband's death – a common condition was that they could only do so when living chaste and alone. Alice Tylcocke is a classic example of this kind of arrangement. Describing herself as 'widow, the late Wife and Relict of William Tylcocke', she was entangled in a suit over land, a cottage and some tenements with Thomas Iuxton after the loss of her husband.[92] According to Tylcocke, she was the rightful legal tenant of this property, on account of an ancient manorial custom. In her bill of complaint, she repeated this customary rule applicable to her manor:

> by the Ancient customs thereof now used, And from the time whereof the memory of man is not to the Contrary hath been Accustomed, That the Widow of every Tenant in fee simple According to the Custom of the said Manor dying seized Shall and may have and enjoy such customary messuages, Cottages, Lands, Tenements and hereditaments from and immediately after the decease of her late husband during her widowhood.

In line with this custom, William Tylcocke was a tenant in fee simple and as his 'then Wife and now his relict and widow', Alice Tylcocke, could now, or so she claimed, legally 'enjoy' the land and cottage for the length of her widowhood. Implicit in the phrase 'during her widowhood' was the assumption that these rights would cease in the event of her remarriage. Tylcocke therefore assumed her husband's tenancy for as long as she remained a *feme sole*. Although she does not use the terminology of the *feme sole*, its significance here is clear: in remaining *sole* she confirms her allegiance to her late husband and maintains her claim to his property. The statement of Alice Bowdon, litigating about a property in Northam, Devon, by contrast very consciously invoked this legal terminology:

> there is a custom which (From the time whereof there is no memory of man to the contrary) hath been that the wife of every such Tenant seized of any the customary lands and tenements of the said manor shall have her widower' estate which is so long as she liveth sole and unmarried although she be not named in the copy.[93]

Bowdon claims that, according to Northam custom, widows were entitled to follow in their late husband's footsteps as tenants, as long as they remained proper widows, meaning that they remained single and chaste ('liveth sole and unmarried'). Even though the woman is not mentioned in the manorial records, her behaviour as a *feme sole* is in line with (what she claims is) the custom. Because her legal power was implicit in her widow's status as *feme sole* and her compliance with this role, these cases demanded that widows actively portray themselves as such. The widowed *feme sole*, a post-mortem version of the *feme covert*, thus remains her husband's property, although he no longer has claim on it. What God has joined together, at least in terms of property rights, only another man can pull asunder.

Stipulations to remain 'sole' are numerous in the court records.[94] Rather than leading to attacks on a widow's chaste and modest behaviour, opponents focus on the terms of the customary law by claiming that the manor in question does not retain such a custom or that the custom has been either misrepresented or misinterpreted. In the case of *Soppe v Weekes* (1594), Margery Soppe stated, in accordance with the usual pattern, that she could enjoy her husband's rights so long as she continued to 'live chaste & unmarried'.[95] Although Soppe implied in her bill of complaint that she indeed lived according to these terms, her legal opponent Christopher Weekes still considered that she had 'no right to enjoy the same copyhold premises during her said widowhood', since

> he verily thinketh to be true, that no widow being the Second wife of any copyholder of the said manor dying tenant of any the copyhold premises, whose husband had an estate by copy of court roll granted unto him and to his former wife by name for term of their lives and the longest liver of them successively according to the custom of the said manor, that then no such second wife should or ought to have & enjoy her widowed estate in the same copyhold lands so taken unto the husband & the wife.

Weekes, then, avoids the tasteless and problematic task of casting aspersions upon a widow's chastity. Rather, he suggests that she misrepresented the custom in question. In this passage he implies that the widow Soppe had stretched the scope of the custom when she claimed that it was also applicable to (unnamed) second wives, not just (named) first wives. The fluid nature of customary law allowed for this kind of interpretation, since custom is by its nature neither written nor static – it is a reflection of what people perceived was normal in the given circumstances, which also made it particularly subject to manipulation. In these types of situations widows necessarily pointed out their status as *femes soles*, just as married women suing for a separation of bed and board did.[96] Rather than explicitly using the terminology of *feme sole*, however, these women more commonly labelled themselves as 'relicts', 'widows' and variants (Tylcocke, for example used the term 'then Wife'); their chaste behaviour was never explicitly stated, but rather implied by these labels.

The very fact that widows could sue in their own name reminds us that these women must have been aware of their renewed legal status. Widows *acted* as *femes soles* simply by starting legal proceedings and they stated their understanding of their legal rights as long as they fulfilled the requirement to live sole and chaste. Their decision not to use the terminology of *feme sole*, but rather of 'widow', 'relict' and 'wife' suggests a subtle grasp of how affiliation works in this context; although their ongoing claim to the land rests on their sole status, their initial claims rest on their previous status as wife.[97] To stress their independent legal status might therefore be counter-productive and was to be avoided. In practice, these women thus form a new and distinct legal category: the widowed *feme sole*. This is related to the trope of the eternal wife.

The eternal wife was a role voluntarily adopted by some widows and forced upon others. Where customary law was not sufficient, a man could control his future widow's behaviour by inserting a clause into his will that limited or completely terminated his wife's rights to her inheritance upon her remarriage. There were several possible motives for a man to restrict his wife's behaviour through such clauses. They could serve to protect a man's children, for example, by limiting a wife's enjoyment of her husband's property to a child's minority. They could be employed to prevent their property (and, perhaps, the inheritance of their children) from falling into the hands of another man (and, potentially, his children by a previous wife), should the widow remarry.[98] Alternatively, husbands driven by sexual jealousy could try to force their wives into sexual loyalty by penalising them for remarriage in their last testaments.[99] As such, husbands could bribe or blackmail their future widows into staying eternal wives, or else face the consequences.[100]

By way of contrast, the early modern clergyman William Gouge was convinced that, for many widows and widowers, 'their love of a former husband or wife departed is so fast fixed in their heart, as they can never again so entirely love any other. They who are so minded are not fit to be joined with another yoke-fellow after they are loosed from one'.[101] This offered widows an acceptable third option alongside remarriage and remaining a relict until death, namely continuing to act as if still married to the dead husband: the widow as 'perpetual wife'.[102] Indeed, both in her 'Elegies' and in the biography of her husband Colonel Hutchinson, Lucy Hutchinson portrays herself as a wife, even when he died either before or very early in the writing process.[103] In *The Life*, Hutchinson writes 'that all that she was, was him, while he was here and all that she is now at best is but his pale shade', while repeatedly using (variations of) the word 'covert' in her 'Elegies', recalling the legal status of a *feme covert*.[104] Katherine Austen described herself to a suitor as 'like pennelope, alwayes employed'. The suitor for her hand in marriage recognised Austen's literary allusion to Penelope, the loyal wife of Odysseus who waited for him to return from the Trojan wars for twenty years while besieged by suitors: 'I ses he her lovers could not abide her for it'.[105] In comparing herself to Penelope, Austen was driven not only by her loyalty to her late husband, but also by the urge to safeguard her eldest son's inheritance.[106] Austen's motive to remain an eternal wife thus overlaps with the intentions of some of the men who used their wills to force their widows into eternal wifedom. The persona of the eternal wife, then, was one that could be strategically adopted by or forced upon a woman, and was not just a sign of a widow's unwavering love for her late husband, much as Gouge may have hoped this was the case.

The possibility that a woman might adopt the persona of the eternal wife becomes especially clear in the texts of Anne Halkett, who used the same strategy in her 'Meditations', but deviated from it in her 'True accountt'. Halkett makes a point of presenting herself as an unmarried, single woman for the larger part of her 'True accountt', which she wrote in *c.*1677/8, when she had already been a widow for some years (her husband died in 1670).[107] Nowhere in the autobiography does she give a reason for wanting to distance herself from her husband, nor does she give the reader the impression that her marriage was anything but happy. Indeed, elsewhere Anne frequently referred to James Halkett as 'the best of husbands' and 'my dearest Husband'.[108] Unlike Lucy Hutchinson and Katherine Austen, Halkett deliberately fashioned herself as a single lady in her 'True accountt'. The reason for this may be found in her tumultuous life during the civil war years. Perhaps she did not want to tarnish her husband's name with her 'scandalous' behaviour or perhaps such behaviour would be especially condemned in a widow. In her 'Meditations', on the other hand, she presented herself as perpetual wife. Halkett remained a widow for twenty-nine years after her husband's death, refusing at least one suitor in marriage. In her 'Meditations', she expressed her resolution to 'euer [. . .] Liue like his Widow'.[109] Halkett thus styled herself according to what best suited the purpose of her different texts, suggesting that the way widowed autobiographers and diarists presented their relationship with and to their late husband not only had to be carefully mediated to satisfy contemporary attitudes towards widowhood, but that it was also dependent on the text's purpose and its perceived audience.

Conversely, and contrary to what we may expect, the legal archives do not give us many cases in which widows discuss the love they felt and perhaps still feel for their late husbands – let alone depict themselves as perpetual spouses. When litigating widows do mention the warm feelings shared between themselves and their husbands, it is more often than not as part of a very different strategy. When Anne Hooton, for instance, found out her late husband had left debts, she claimed that she decided to pay them, 'for the love she bare unto her deceased husband and for the better discharge of her Conscience'.[110] She thus paints her legal opponent's allegation that Hooton is still indebted to him as ridiculous, for she was compelled to pay off her husband's debt on account of the love she felt towards him: to suggest otherwise would be to accuse her of not loving her late spouse. Even though Hooton is already remarried by the time of the lawsuit, by using her warm feelings towards her late husband as evidence of why she must have paid of the debt, she is appealing to the expectations court and society held of a good widow's behaviour. This strategy was, nonetheless, rare, presumably because the eternal wife was trumped by the biblical widow, not least as a poor and needy widow needed more protection than a widow who simply loved her husband so much that she refused to remarry. Moreover, no legal situation necessitated widows to become eternal wives in the legal records.

While the trope of the biblical widow could be invoked by all women who had lost their husbands, there were relatively few legal situations in which widows would want to opt to style themselves as *feme soles* in their legal pleadings, and I have uncovered no legal records in which widows explicitly described themselves as eternal wives. For later seventeenth-century autobiographers and diarists, on the other hand, it was the goal of their text and their perceived audience which determined how they portrayed the relationship between themselves and their late husband. Most importantly, however, widowed life-writers made conscious decisions about their self-representation, carefully considering which version of themselves would serve them best in given circumstances. The (litigious) widow with children, however, might find herself compelled to emphasise her maternal role on entering into litigation.

Mother

Although she would always remain a mother if she had children, a widowed mother was not automatically granted wardship over her children when her husband passed away. If a woman was widow to a man who had been tenant in chief of the crown, a feudal leftover meant that the wardship of his heirs (and, naturally, the land that formed their inheritance), was controlled by the Court of Wards and Liveries, a process designed to avoid the land being taken away from the crown. The allocation of wardships was a lucrative commercial enterprise for the crown, as it sold the wardship over a child and its land to the highest bidder or granted it to someone as a favour. It was also lucrative for the owner of a wardship: wardship of the land gave its guardian the right to reap its fruits, while wardship of the body gave them the right to marry the ward to a marriage partner of their choice, enabling them, for instance, to keep the estate within the family. Like all other parties interested in buying the wardship, a mother would have to acquire the custody over her own child by putting in a bid.[111] The Court of Wards and Liveries could grant a mother wardship over her child, but it was not 'sentiment as to who would most suitably nurture the infant' that won the day, but rather 'rules which governed land tenure'.[112] When the natural mother petitioned for guardianship she received no priority over the other bidders.[113] In fact, few wardships in this period were granted to relatives of the child let alone their mothers, and in those few cases where mothers did find themselves entrusted with the guardianship of their own children it was usually as joint custodians.[114] As such, widows often found themselves losing their children as well as their husbands. This sentiment is expressed by Lady Roussillon in the opening lines of Shakespeare's *All's Well that Ends Well*: 'In delivering my son from me I bury a second husband' (1.1.1–2).

Acquiring the wardship of a child did not require a lawsuit: the interested parties simply petitioned the Master of the Wards, who would judge which of those petitions would be successful. For a petitioning widow there were three possible outcomes: the mother was successful and regained her children; she lost the wardship of her children, but accepted the situation; she was denied legal guardianship but refused to accept the decision. In the latter case, matters stood a good chance of getting severely out of hand. Following the death of Hugh Powell, Katherine Powell refused to accept the awarding of the wardship of his daughter and heir, Anne Powell, to a certain John Gibbons.[115] Unusually, Katherine was Anne's grandmother, rather than her mother – Lucie Powell, Katherine's daughter-in-law, had married Gibbons following Hugh's death. Whether or not Katherine had put in a bid for the wardship is unclear, but it is clear that the wardship of both the girl's lands and her body had fallen into the hands of Gibbons, effectively making Hugh's estate his own. Unwilling to accept this situation, Powell ('being a woman of small experience and knowledge in such matters', as she described herself) ordered a fake copy of a grant of wardship made out in her name with which she promptly opened negotiations for a marriage between her granddaughter Anne and the eldest son of Philip Prosser, Roger – a right that was legally reserved to Gibbons as Anne's guardian. When negotiations faltered and Anne ended up as the wife of Thomas Prosser, the younger and thus less eligible of the sons, Katherine's plan seems to have backfired: if she had envisioned making a prosperous match for her granddaughter, she had failed to do so. Katherine admits to having tried to marry Anne off to Philip Prosser's eldest son, but denies any involvement in bringing together Anne and the less-than-eligible Thomas, which was 'utterly and altogether done and contrived without the privity liking or consent of this defendant'.[116] Regardless of whom Anne ended up marrying, and whose fault this was, her grandmother clearly refused to accept that she no longer had a say in her granddaughter's marital match now that the girl had a new legal guardian.

When a mother lost custody of a child under such circumstances, and refused to accept that the courts had placed her child's future into another's hands, the result was often a charge of abduction. A common way of defending a widow against a charge of kidnapping was to invoke the natural bond between mother and child. This was the defence used by Agnes Griffeth when she was accused of kidnapping her daughter by George Owens, the girl's legal guardian.[117] Griffeth claimed that, when she found her daughter Jenett 'very miserably sick and in small hope to recover' at the house of the girl's guardian, she 'at the pitiful request of her daughter took her away' with her. As her 'natural mother', Griffeth had to step in, to counter the 'lack of Care & attendance' of the girl's legal guardian. As a result of Griffeth's actions, her daughter made a full recovery: 'And ever since the said Agnes hath kept & detain the said Jenett in her custody as lawfully she may And found her such relief as she was best able to do as in nature she is most Bound to do'.[118] Where Griffeth's story is filled with tenderness, the language Owen uses is full of legal terminology: he considers Jenett to be in his 'custody, possession and safe keeping', as he has 'as well the custody of the body of the said Jennett as the wardship of the said lands and tenement'.[119] Rather than invoke the law (not least because in its eyes she was plainly the wrongdoer), Griffeth's defence hinged on the emotional actions of the 'natural mother', thus pitching human nature (and therefore something of the divine) against temporal law. The contrast with Griffeth's emotive defence of her actions is marked: where the legal guardian failed to take care of the girl, the natural mother claimed to know exactly what her child needed. Agnes, along with several other mothers accused of kidnapping in similar circumstances, claimed that the natural bond between mother and child compelled them to intervene when the court-appointed guardian failed to meet their obligations. Their argument was not simply that, when a legal guardian failed, their motherly instincts encouraged them to act against the law: these widows suggested that, when a legal guardian failed in their duty to their ward, this necessarily broke their contract with the law, and that in such circumstances the guardianship should revert to the mother. As such, these women reversed the accusations of kidnapping: the real crime would be to abandon their children.

Those widows who had lost their child not in the wardship system, but through other means, also point to the relationship between parent and child in order to press their claims upon their offspring. One such woman was Margaret ap Mathocke, the widow of John ap John, with whom she had a daughter, Jonett.[120] Ap Mathocke described how she 'most tenderly and Carefully to their great Costs and charges educated and brought up' her child after the death of her husband, first alone and later with the help of her new spouse, John David ap Mathocke. Although the custody of Jonett 'properly belong[s] to' ap Mathocke, as her natural mother, at the age of thirteen the girl was abducted. According to the distraught mother, the abductor, William ap Robert, was 'provided of a covetous and greedy desire to enrich himself' and in order to achieve this he married Jonett as soon as he had taken her out of her mother's 'lawful custody'. As the heiress to her late father's estate, the girl indeed was a most suitable choice for such a man. Ap Mathocke's suit against ap Robert asserted the illegitimacy of ap Robert's actions on the grounds that she, as the girl's guardian according both to 'your majesty's good and godly laws' and 'the law of nature', has not given her consent. Even though ap Mathocke's suit asserted both legal and emotional evidence, she carefully avoids any mention of how ap Robert's actions had affected her own financial situation (as she no longer had charge of her daughter's inheritance), but instead focuses on 'the great disparagement of the said Jonett and utter heaviness and discomfort' of herself.[121] Other widowed mothers fighting over the custody of their children portrayed themselves in similar fashion, regardless of whether they had remarried or remained *femes soles* following the deaths of their husbands. In order to protect their children and in an attempt to justify any behaviour that was technically unlawful, these widows depicted themselves first and foremost as mothers. Motherhood, they argue, gave them special rights and indeed, duties, upon which they needed to act, and the natural bond between mother and child was to be considered ahead of all man-made rules and regulations.

As a widowed mother, the diarist Katherine Austen invoked her status as a mother in order to protect her children's interest. Her refusal to remarry (discussed previously) was partly out of consideration for her children's estates: upon remarriage, her late husband's estate could be subsumed by that of her new husband, who may then choose not to pass it on to her children. Rather than risking this, Austen refrained from remarrying altogether: 'In Answer to one. why not marry to ease me. of my burdens', she writes that 'if my children should find lose in their estates. by Gods blesing, should be able to make a supply. to them in their great disapointments. Which I could never doe by ingaiging my self away from them'.[122] Austen remained both head of her household and the mother of three children, and managed their affairs diligently. As a minor, her eldest son Thomas Austen needed his mother's help to protect his share of his father's estate. The header of the answer to his legal opponent's bill of complaint listed Austen's several roles in the matter: 'The several Answers of Thomas Austen under the age of one and Twenty years that is to say of the age of Sixteen years, one of the defendants to the Bill of Complaint of Sir Allen Apsley, knight, complainant, by Katherin Austen, widow, his Mother and Guardian'.[123] Not only was she a widow, but she was also a mother and legal guardian. Where 'widow' and 'guardian' carried specific legal connotations, however, 'mother' did not. Similar to the mothers accused of abduction, Austen invoked the natural bond between a mother and child to help reinforce her legal status with another, more emotive one. The result of all her endeavours was that, despite her recurrent lamentations of relative poverty, Austen not only succeeded in securing the legacies of her children, but also actively advanced their financial position.[124] In her last will and testament, Austen left her two sons 'all my Lands, houses and Tenements, Together with all my Stock in the Indy Company', as well as her 'Estate in Blackfriars which I leased out to the Scotch Company'.[125] Clearly, the efforts of this widow, mother and guardian to protect her children's interests had met with no little success.

Widows, then, emphasised their roles as mothers in cases pertaining to their children, and *only* in cases to do with their offspring. Whereas those widows adhering to the biblical widow model often referred to their children in order to point out that they had dependents of whom they needed to take care, they refrained from describing themselves as anything other than 'widow'. When a matter directly related to their children, on the other hand, widows often made the strategic and autobiographical choice to label themselves as 'mother'.

Pluralities of a Widow's Identity

The early modern widow thus had recourse to a number of narrative strategies upon entering the law court. The persona she chose to adopt, however, was largely dictated by the kind of suit she brought or was brought against her.[126] While the trope of the biblical widow was both popular and applicable to almost any situation, whether or not the woman in question was in fact weak or poor or far from it, the other types of widow (*feme sole* and mother) would only be invoked in specific circumstances and when the nature of the suit required them to do so. Whereas the writer of an autobiography or diary might fashion themselves as all three types of widow, even simultaneously, the brevity required in court forced widowed litigants to choose one particular assertion of widowhood in their attempt to persuade judge or jury.[127] Writers of larger or multiple pieces of text, such as diaries and autobiographies, could fashion themselves differently in each text – as did Anne Halkett, who wrote from the perspective of a single woman in her 'True accountt', but as a biblical widow in her 'Meditations' – or indeed, within the same text, like Katherine Austen who was biblical widow, eternal wife and mother in her *Book M*. These different versions of the self do not necessarily invalidate each other; widows could switch between roles across a text or between texts whenever they felt it necessary to invoke a different version of the self. As such, widows made use of a strategic form of self-fashioning: never were they merely widows, but they were biblical widows, natural mothers, eternal wives and/or *femes soles*.

There were, of course, those widows who resisted these models altogether. Dame Mary Cheeke, for example, refused to adhere to any of the labels described in this chapter. Rather than styling herself in the light of a biblical widow, *feme sole* or mother, she chose to proudly declare all of her real estate, as opposed to pointing out any financial difficulties, and refrained from describing herself as mother to her three children, adhering, perhaps, to a much more masculine model of self-description. Widows could, and did, tap into any of the existing models, but whether they did so or not depended on how they wanted to portray themselves or how circumstances forced them to.

Crucially, however, these different versions of the self were particularly female models, none of which were available to men. In choosing one of several possibilities, the widow – whether she was a diarist or litigant – was responding to the largely masculine cultural and literary norms of the day and the complicated set of stereotypes surrounding widowhood. She had to negotiate these alongside achieving her main task, vindication. Vindicating themselves in the courts of law, public opinion, the eyes of God or their own consciences was sought through manipulation of the same literary strategies of self-fashioning: because of the strong connotations attached to widowhood, widows made use of similar tropes. The very selection of a trope holds autobiographical value, as it either shows the choice a woman makes regarding her self-identity or demonstrates her lack of choice, both of which can help us to better understand an individual's agency as we follow how they interact with it.[128] Whether they chose to identify as biblical widow, eternal wife, *feme sole*, mother or refused identification with any of these labels, widows actively asserted themselves in direct contrast to the masculine norms of the day.

Notes

1. Katherine Austen, 'Book M', in Sarah C. E. Ross (ed.), *Katherine Austen's* Book M*: British Library, Additional Manuscript 4454* (ACMRS, 2011), p. 106. All citations are taken from this edition, unless otherwise stated.
2. Ann Fanshawe, 'The Memoirs of Ann, Lady Fanshawe', in John Loftis (ed.), *The Memoirs of Anne, Lady Halkett and Ann, Lady Fanshaw* (Clarendon Press, 1979), p. 185.
3. Sarah Cowper, *Diary*, Vol. 4 (1707), p. 133.
4. Ibid., p. 27.
5. Anne Kugler, *Errant Plagiary: The Life and Writing of Lady Sarah Cowper, 1644–1720* (Stanford University Press, 2002), p. 142.
6. Amy Louise Erickson, 'Property and Widowhood in England 1660–1840', in Sandra Cavallo and Lyndan Warner (eds), *Widowhood in Medieval and Early Modern Europe* (Pearson Education Limited, 1999), pp. 145–63.
7. Tim Stretton, *Women Waging Law in Elizabethan England* (Cambridge University Press, 1998), pp. 21–2, 109.
8. T. E., *The Lawes Resolutions of Womens Rights* (London, 1632), STC 7437, p. 232.
9. Stretton, *Women Waging Law*, p. 109.
10. Amy Louise Erickson, *Women and Property in Early Modern England* (Routledge, 1993), p. 154. For more on remarrying widows, see for instance Vivien Brodsky, 'Widows in Late Elizabethan London: Remarriage, Economic Opportunity and Family Orientations', in Lloyd Bonfield, Richard M. Smith and Keith Wrightson (eds), *The World We Have Gained: Histories of Population and Social Structure* (Basil Blackwell, 1986), pp. 122–54; Todd, 'The Remarrying Widow', pp. 54–92.
11. Stretton, *Women Waging Law*, pp. 108–9.
12. Asuka Kimura's doctoral thesis offers an extremely useful overview of plays featuring widows between 1538 and 1642, see: 'The Representation of Widows and Widowhood in English Drama, 1576–1642' (UCL, 2016).
13. Todd, 'The Remarrying Widow', pp. 54–92, at 55.
14. Eleanor Hubbard, on the other hand, considers that widows 'were not troublesome anomalies, but legitimate household governors', arguing that approximately 80 per cent of London's widows lived independently and as such, widows clearly posed no problem to patriarchy. That women performed the role of head of household does not, however, necessarily mean that others did not feel uneasy about this. It may perhaps only strengthen Todd's argument: the large number of widows living solitary gave rise to anxiety. See Eleanor Hubbard, *City Women: Money, Sex and the Social Order in Early Modern London* (Oxford University Press, 2012), pp. 261–2.
15. Renu Juneja, 'The Widow as Paradox and Paradigm in Middleton's Plays', *The Journal of General Education*, 34(1) (1982): 3–19, at 4–5.
16. Elizabeth Foyster, 'Marrying the Experienced Widow in Early Modern England: The Male Perspective', in Cavallo and Warner (eds), *Widowhood*, pp. 108–24, at 111.

17. George Chapman, *The Widow's Tears*, ed. by Akihiro Yamada (Methuen, 1975), 1.1.125.
18. Ibid., 1.1.141–2.
19. Austen, 'Book M', p. 166.
20. Nicholas Culpeper, *A Directory for Midwives: or, a Guide for Women, in Their Conception, Bearing, and Suckling Their Children, etc.* (1651; London, 1693), C7495, p. 278.
21. James Sharpe, *Instruments of Darkness: Witchcraft in Early Modern England* (University of Pennsylvania Press, 1996), p. 176; Lyndal Roper, *Oedipus & the Devil: Witchcraft, Sexuality and Religion in Early Modern Europe* (Routledge, 1994), p. 211; Foyster, 'Marrying the Experienced Widow', pp. 108–24, at 109. Una McIlvenna, *Singing the News of Death: Execution Ballads in Europe 1500–1900* (Oxford University Press, 2022), p. 213. In the words of *The Witch of Edmonton*'s Elizabeth Sawyer: 'an old woman / Ill-favoured grown with years, if she be poor, / Must be called bawd or witch' (Thomas Dekker, John Ford and William Rowley, *The Witch of Edmonton*, ed. by Lucy Munro (The Arden Shakespeare, 2019), 4.1.140–1).
22. Pamela S. Hammons, 'Introduction', in Katherine Austen, 'Book M', in Pamela S. Hammons (ed.), *Book M: A London Widow's Life Writings, Katherine Austen* (Iter, 2013), pp. 1–37, at 1.
23. TNA, REQ 2/44/15, *Gryssell Drables v John Drables and William Cocke*, answer of John Drables (1600).
24. Thomas Middleton, 'The Widow', in Gary Taylor and John Lavagnino (eds), *Thomas Middleton: The Collected Works* (Clarendon Press, 2010), 2.1.98, 2.1.101.
25. Ibid., 4.1.60.
26. William Wycherley, 'The Plain Dealer', in Peter Dixon (ed.), *The Country Wife and Other Plays* (Oxford University Press, 1996), pp. 283–399, at 289; 1.1.391–410.
27. Ibid., 1.1.412–429.
28. TNA, REQ 2/42/95, *Agnes Maddilowe v Robert Barnes* (1597).
29. TNA, REQ 2/42/49, *Alice Bowdon v Alexander Beaple* (1566).
30. Tim Stretton, 'Widows at Law in Tudor and Stuart England', in Cavallo and Warner (eds), *Widowhood*, pp. 193–208, at 205.
31. TNA, REQ 2/47/16, *Edward Bassett v Marye Daughan*, bill of Edward Bassett (1587).
32. Richard T. Spence, 'Clifford, Anne, countess of Pembroke, Dorset, and Montgomery (1590–1676)', *Oxford Dictionary of National Biography* (25 September 2014). Accessed 18 March 2024.
33. Nancy E. Wright, 'Accounting for a Life: The Household Accounts of Lady Anne Clifford', in Ronald Bedford, Lloyd Davis and Philippa Kelly, *Early Modern Autobiography: Theories, Genres, Practices* (University of Michigan Press, 2006), pp. 234–51, at 243.
34. Richard T. Spence, *Lady Anne Clifford: Countess of Pembroke, Dorset and Montgomery (1590–1676)* (Sutton Publishing, 1997), pp. 114–35.

35. Ibid., pp. 122–4.
36. Ibid., p. 114.
37. Austen, 'Book M', p. 164.
38. She writes that she is committed to her case 'what misery soever it brought me to' and 'whatsoever became of me and mine', demonstrating that although she is involved in legal proceedings, this is not because she enjoys spending her time in court. Instead, she desires 'God to send a good end to these troublesome businesses' (Anne Clifford, *Anne Clifford's Autobiographical Writing, 1590–1676*, ed. by Jessica L. Malay (Manchester University Press, 2018), pp. 32; 58; 51.
39. Spence, *Lady Anne Clifford*, p. 116.
40. Cheeke's various suits are also discussed in Stretton, *Women Waging Law*, pp. 118–19; 126; 202–3.
41. TNA, REQ 2/47/36, *Mary Cheeke v Christopher Symcocks*, answer of Christopher Symcocks (1594).
42. TNA, REQ 2/39/96, *Elizabeth Bristowe v Henry Bristowe*, bill of Elizabeth Bristowe (1582).
43. Ibid., answer of Henry Bristowe (1582).
44. TNA, REQ 2/42/49, *Alice Bowdon v Alexander Beaple*, bill of Alice Bowdon (1566).
45. TNA, REQ 2/43/95, *Fridefreed Norwood v Thomas Smith, John Hanwell and William Saunders*, bill of Fridefreed Norwood (1593).
46. TNA, REQ 2/43/91, *Walter and Anne Knyght v Wylliam Dryver*, bill of Walter and Anne Knyght (1597).
47. TNA, REQ 2/50/22, *Margarett Eaton v Thomas Hackett*, bill of Margarett Eaton (1597).
48. TNA, REQ 2/55/29, *Dame Elizabeth Wallwyn v Elye Wallwynn*, bill of Elizabeth Wallwyn (1590).
49. TNA, REQ 2/140/36, *John Clerke v Alice Cowper*, answer of Alice Cowper (1594).
50. Ibid., answer of Alice Cowper (1594). Katherine Austen similarly stressed the honest nature of her suit: 'Our Aduar[s]aries doe see our cause is so apparently right. as I hope ^and yet^ they will <. . . .> essay to vex us more'. Austen here not only emphasised the rightfulness of her own cause, she simultaneously discredited her legal opponents by stating they knew she was right, but engaged in vexatious litigation anyway. However, Austen could rely on 'an Allmighty God (and a Iust Cause.) who I trust will defend me' (Austen, 'Book M', pp. 111, 115).
51. Anne Halkett, 'Ocational Meditations and Select Contemplations, 1668–1670/1', p. 37, in Suzanne Trill (ed.), *Lady Anne Halkett: Selected Self-Writings* (Ashgate, 2007).
52. Ibid., p. 35.
53. Suzanne Trill, 'Beyond Romance? Re-Reading the "Lives" of Anne, Lady Halkett (1621/2?–1699)', *Literature Compass*, 6(2) (2009): 446–59, at 454; Susan Wiseman, '"The most considerable of my troubles": Anne Halkett

and the Writing of Civil War Conspiracy', in Jo Wallwork and Paul Salzman (eds), *Women Writing, 1550–1750* (Meridian, 2001), pp. 25–45, at 29.
54. See, for instance, Psalm 68:5; Exodus 22:22; James 1:27; Isaiah 1:17; Malachi 3:5; Zechariah 7:10.
55. Halkett, 'Ocational Meditations and Select Contemplations, 1668–1670/1', p. 37, in Trill (ed.), *Lady Anne Halkett.*
56. Anne Halkett, 'The Widows Mite, & Occationall Meditations, 1673–41', pp. 48–9, in Suzanne Trill (ed.), *Lady Anne Halkett: Selected Self-Writings* (Ashgate, 2007).
57. Ibid., p. 49.
58. Suzanne Trill, 'Introduction', in Trill (ed.), *Lady Anne Halkett*, p. xviii.
59. Anne Halkett, 'The Autobiography of Anne, Lady Halkett, 1677–78', p. 131, in Trill (ed.), *Lady Anne Halkett.*
60. Fanshawe, 'The Memoirs of Ann, Lady Fanshawe', p. 185.
61. Austen, 'Book M', p. 116.
62. Ibid., p. 108.
63. Fanshawe, 'The Memoirs of Ann, Lady Fanshawe', p. 185.
64. TNA, REQ 2/138/62, *Ales Bygge/Alice Bigge v Anthony Pycke* (1577).
65. TNA, REQ 2/141/18, *Johane Coppe v Smith* (first name unknown) (1596).
66. TNA, REQ 2/188/6, *Margaret Carter v Robert Hogge and Rowland Bates*, bill of Margaret Carter (1595).
67. Austen, 'Book M', p. 117.
68. Ibid., p. 108.
69. TNA, REQ 2/50/27, *Thomas Bownest v Elizabeth Bedell*, answer of Elizabeth Bedell (1600).
70. TNA, REQ 2/48/25, *Andrewe Huntington v Maryan Smythe*, answer of Maryan Smythe (1591).
71. TNA, REQ 2/140/36, *Clerke v Cowper*, answer of Alice (1594).
72. Laura Flannigan, 'Litigants in the English "Court of Poor Men's Causes," or Court of Requests, 1515–25', *Law and History Review*, 38(2) (2020): 303–37, at 313, 329; Stretton, 'Widows at Law', 206–7; Stretton, *Women Waging Law*, 185–7.
73. TNA, REQ 2/44/59, *Margerie Themilthorpe v Sr John Ecerton*, bill of Margerie Themilthorpe (1600).
74. TNA, REQ 2/43/51, *Anne Davie v Andrewe Davie*, bill of Anne Davie (1588).
75. Fanshawe, 'The Memoirs of Ann, Lady Fanshawe', p. 185.
76. TNA, REQ 2/56/87, *Agnes Bridges v John Shynner and Martin Obey*, bill of Agnes Bridges (1578).
77. TNA, REQ 2/188/6, *Margaret Carter v Robert Hogge and Rowland Bates*, bill of Margaret Carter (1595).
78. TNA, REQ 2/41/99, *Elizabeth Thomas v Clement Finche*, bill of Elizabeth Thomas (1575).
79. Flannigan has noted that this reference to relative poverty was made more often by litigants in the Court of Requests (Flannigan, 'Litigants', 331–4).

80. Julius Caesar, *The ancient state, authoritie, and proceedings of the Court of Requests* (1596) STC (2nd ed.) / 4341, unnumbered page.
81. TNA, REQ 2/44/51, *Johan Fowles v John Sencler* (1559).
82. TNA, REQ 2/42/76, *Margaret and Thomas Pralyng v Robert Lloyd* (1594).
83. Austen, 'Book M', p. 115.
84. Ibid., p. 112.
85. TNA REQ 2/47/36, 2/57/13, *Mary Cheeke v Christopher Symcocks* (1593); REQ 2/188/23, 2/44/56, *Mary Cheeke v John Whittinge* (1594); REQ 2/288/31, 2/157/91, *John Whyttyng v Mary Chicke* (1594).
86. TNA, REQ 2/40/17, *Brydgett Sefoule v John and Elizabeth Godbould* (1594); TNA REQ 2/42/43, *Alyce Steward v William Stowe, Thomas Thorold and Robert Watson* (undated); TNA REQ 2/44/1, *Margaret Nodes v William Bucknell* (1569).
87. TNA, REQ 2/50/26, *Thomas Williams v Anne and John Hooton* (1598).
88. Katherine Austen, too, seems to have exaggerated her claims of poverty in her diary. Her will reveals her material wealth at the time of her death and in her diary, too, Austen at times diverges from her usual lamentations of poverty, as is the case when she writes: 'Neither is it riches I want: Heauen has gaue already most bou[n]tiful'. Although the riches she refers to may be heavenly, rather than earthly, such a lack of regard for her material assets suggests her comfortable financial position. At other times, however, Austen claims she must borrow to keep afloat: 'Let me borrow too and keep up my repute. and freely pay the encombents and taxes & debtes I am engaidged' (Austen, 'Book M', pp. 94; 164). See also Raymond A. Anselment, 'Katherine Austen and the Widow's Might', *Journal of Early Modern Cultural Studies*, 5(1) (2005): 5–25; Hammons, 'Introduction', p. 21.
89. This was different for witnesses, as Alexandra Shepard's study of the various ways in which witnesses before the church courts described themselves as poor has revealed. Her study shows that those describing themselves as poor were deemed less authoritative and of less significance than those who were worth more, and, when it came to offering false depositions, considered more blameworthy than a richer person who may have elicited such false testimony (Shepard, *Accounting for Oneself: Worth, Status, and the Social Order in Early Modern England* (Oxford University Press, 2015), chapter 4). Because of the negative stigma attached to poverty, the poor appeared less often as witnesses than their counterparts of higher social status before the medieval church courts (Bronach C. Kane, *Popular Memory and Gender in Medieval England: Men, Women, and Testimony in the Church Courts, c.1200–1500* (The Boydell Press, 2019), p. 27).
90. For a man's pleading drawing on his poor financial state, see, for instance, TNA, REQ 2/42/38, *John Doe v Elizabeth, William and Clement Bacon* (1590); TNA, REQ 2/46/45, *John Judd v Elizabeth and Frauncis Donne* (1603).
91. Stretton, *Women Waging Law*, p. 184.
92. TNA, REQ 2/41/36, *Alice Tilcocke and her son William Tilcocke v Thomas Iuxton* (1579).

93. TNA, REQ 2/42/49, *Alice Bowdon v Alexander Beaple* (1566).
94. We find them, for example, in the following cases: TNA, REQ 2/42/49, *Bowdon v Beaple* (1566); TNA, REQ 2/210/118, *Agnes Grove v Wylliam Gould and John Peverell* (1571); TNA REQ 2/35/50, *Agnes Grove v John Thynne* (1573); TNA, REQ 2/41/36, *Tilcocke v Iuxton* (1579); TNA REQ 2/168/19, *William Allambrigge v Anne Allambrigge* (1586); TNA, REQ 2/56/34, *Margery Soppe v Christopher Weekes* (1594); TNA REQ 2/187/49, *Johan Cosynes v Richard Morgan and John Brodribbe* (1560).
95. TNA, REQ 2/56/34, *Soppe v Weekes*, bill of Margery Soppe (1594).
96. See chapter 2 ('Courtship and Marriage') for more on this.
97. For examples of married women acting as *femes soles*, but claiming the protection of a *feme covert*, see Cordelia Beattie, '"Living as a Single Person": Marital Status, Performance and the Law in Late Medieval England', *Women's History Review*, 17 (3) (2008): 327–40.
98. Erickson, *Women and Property*, p. 166.
99. Todd, 'The Remarrying Widow', pp. 54–92, at 73. See also Vivien Brodsky, 'Widows in Late Elizabethan London: Remarriage, Economic Opportunity and Family Orientations', in Lloyd Bonfield, Richard M. Smith and Keith Wrightson (eds), *The World We Have Gained: Histories of Population and Social Structure* (Basil Blackwell, 1986), pp. 122–54, at 144.
100. Vivien Brodsky, 'Widows in Late Elizabethan London', p. 144.
101. William Gouge, *Of Domesticall Duties* (London, 1622), STC 12119, p. 226.
102. Barbara J. Todd, 'The Virtuous Widow in Protestant England', in Cavallo and Warner (eds), *Widowhood*, pp. 66–83, at 67.
103. John Hutchinson died in 1664. For the dating of the 'Elegies' see: David Norbrook, 'Lucy Hutchinson's 'Elegies' and the Situation of the Republican Woman Writer', *English Literary Renaissance*, 27(3) (1993): 468–521, at 470. The biography was written *c.*1664–71.
104. See Pamela S. Hammons, *Gender, Sexuality, and Material Objects in English Renaissance Verse* (Ashgate, 2010), p. 178; 'Another on The Sun Shine', ll. 6, 12.
105. Austen, 'Book M', p. 148. See Hammons' introduction, pp. 19–20, for a more thorough analysis of the simile between Austen and Penelope.
106. Sarah C. E. Ross, '"Like Penelope, always employed": Reading, Life-Writing and the Early Modern Female Self in Katherine Austen's *Book M*', *Literature Compass*, 9(4) (2012): 306–16, at 313.
107. Because the first folio of the text is missing, it is unclear under which name the author wrote her 'True accountt': Anne Murray, Anne Halkett or simply Anne.
108. Anne Halkett, 'Occationall Meditations, 1660–63', pp. 22, 23, in Suzanne Trill (ed.), *Lady Anne Halkett: Selected Self-Writings* (Ashgate, 2007).
109. Ibid., p. 38.
110. TNA, REQ 2/50/26, *Thomas Williams v Anne and John Hooton* (1598).
111. The wardship could be split between that of the body of the child and the land or could be bought in its entirety; see H. E. Bell, *An Introduction to the History and Records of the Court of Wards and Liveries* (Cambridge University Press, 1953), pp. 115–19.

112. Sue Sheridan Walker, 'Widow and Ward: The Feudal Law of Child Custody in Medieval England', in Susan Mosher Stuard (ed.), *Women in Medieval Society* (University of Pennsylvania Press, 1976), pp. 159–72, at 160.
113. Joel Hurstfield, *The Queen's Wards: Wardship and Marriage under Elizabeth I*, 2nd edition (1953; Frank Cass, 1973), p. 124.
114. Hurstfield, *The Queen's Wards*, p. 124; Garthine Walker, '"Strange Kind of Stealing": Abduction in Early Modern Wales', in Michael Roberts and Simone Clarke (eds), *Women and Gender in Early Modern Wales* (University of Wales Press, 2000), pp. 50–74, at 59. According to Hurstfield, during Elizabeth's reign, at most one out of seven recipients of a wardship would be the maternal mother (p. 124).
115. TNA, STAC 7/4/27, *Philip Prosser v Katherine Powell* (1593).
116. Ibid., answer of Katherine Phillips (1593).
117. TNA, STAC 5/O4/7, *George Owens v Agnes Griffeth and James ap Kynon* (1580).
118. Ibid., answer of Agnes Griffeth and James ap Kynon (1580).
119. Ibid., bill of George Owens (1580).
120. TNA, STAC 5/M5/37, *Margaret and John David ap Mathocke v William ap Robert* (1598).
121. Ibid., bill of complaint of Margaret and her husband John David ap Mathocke (1598).
122. Austen, 'Book M', pp. 117–18.
123. TNA, C 5/41/3, *Sir Allen Apsley v Thomas Austen (and others)* (1662).
124. Sarah C. E. Ross, 'Introduction', in Katherine Austen, *Book M: British Library, Additional Manuscript 4454*, ed. by Sarah C. E. Ross (ACMRS, 2011), pp. 1–47, at 14. Susan Wiseman has shown how Austen discusses her legal struggles in biblical language (Wiseman, 'The Contemplative Woman's Recreation? Katherine Austen and the Estate Poem', in Susan Wiseman (ed.), *Early Modern Women and the Poem* (Manchester University Press, 2013), pp. 220–43.
125. TNA, PROB 11/375/79.
126. Rebecca Mason has recently demonstrated that early modern Scottish women, too, described themselves differently in the Scottish burgh and commissary court records, depending on the nature of their lawsuit (Mason, 'Women, Marital Status, and Law: The Marital Spectrum in Seventeenth-Century Glasgow', *Journal of British Studies*, 58 (2019): 787–804).
127. Dosia Reichardt has noticed something similar in prison writing of the time: according to her, '[p]rison life writing inevitably circles around protestations of innocence that depend on the presentation of a stable, predictable self. Evidence of protean identity, the malleability that often adds interest to a narrative, undermines claims to an unwavering faith or loyalty' (Reichardt, 'The Constitution of Narrative Identity in Seventeenth-Century Prison Writing', in Ronald Bedford, Lloyd Davis and Philippa Kelly (eds), *Early Modern Autobiography: Theories, Genres, Practices* (University of Michigan Press, 2006), pp. 115–30, at 121).

128. For more on the autobiographical value of choosing one model or script over another, see also Lynne Magnusson, 'A Rhetoric of Requests: Genre and Linguistic Scripts in Elizabethan Women's Suitors' Letters', in James Daybell (ed.), *Women and Politics in Early Modern England, 1450–1700* (Ashgate, 2004), pp. 51–66.

Chapter 5

Afterlives: Case Studies in the Production of Alternative Truths

One of the functions of legal proceedings is to offer dispute resolution. In order to do so, liabilities must be determined, guilt must be ascertained and compensation offered or punishment meted out. This process brings about a certain finality: there was a problem which has now been resolved, according to law. But this, of course, is neither the beginning nor the end of the story. Just because a legal judgement has been reached does not mean both parties accept the verdict, nor does it mean that other interested parties feel that the proceeding's outcome is just. In some instances, the 'truth' seems impossible to determine when it is merely the word of one person against that of another. In these cases, counter-narratives are presented alongside each other, each offering different accounts of the 'facts' of the matter. While the urge to present a counter-narrative or rewrite a situation entirely is the force that initiates legal proceedings, it does not necessarily end when the trial is over, even if judgement is passed. The proliferation of truths can shift into other (sometimes multiple) genres, straddling both the legal and literary spheres.

One example of a woman determined to offer an alternative version of events in the face of opposition is Lady Mary Fenwick (*c.*1646/50–1708). Mary Fenwick (née Howard) married the army officer Sir John Fenwick (*c.*1644–97) in 1663. John Fenwick was a Jacobite conspirator who actively strove to restore James II to the throne. He was appointed as one of a group named the 'select Number' by James himself in order to keep the deposed king in the loop regarding the state of political and military intelligence.[1] Fenwick was, by all accounts, not a particularly successful Jacobite conspirator. Although he vehemently opposed plans to kill William III, he was arrested and imprisoned in 1696 upon suspicion of conspiring to assassinate the king. Fenwick offered to share some vital information with William himself in return for a pardon, but his intelligence, which he gave in two written confession papers, failed to satisfy the king, and he was subsequently arraigned. While two witnesses were required to commence a capital case such as this one, one of those named had escaped (allegedly with the help of Lady Mary).[2] This, however, did not save Fenwick from prosecution: a bill of attainder was proposed and accepted. It was passed on 12 January 1697, allowing for the alleged conspirator to be executed without trial. The official legal records thus record his guilt in unequivocal terms: he was a traitor.

Fenwick's wife refused to stand idly by and allow her husband to be written into the records as an enemy of the state, and she actively sought to correct this portrayal despite the odds weighing heavily against her success. She petitioned the House of Commons for clemency during his imprisonment and the correspondence between the two spouses reveals her efforts to mediate and intervene on her husband's behalf.[3] Fenwick's subsequent execution failed to dent her resolve and she spent her remaining years commemorating him and rewriting his story in a biography. This biography is sadly incomplete, though it is unclear whether she simply failed to finish it or whether its final part has since disappeared.[4] Those folios that have survived depict Sir John Fenwick as a strong military leader and a noble man, failing to mention the debauchery for which he was notorious.[5] Mary Fenwick appears, however, to have at the very least been intent on writing about her husband's last days, as Thomas Petriburg, the last person to visit John Fenwick in prison, agreed to share the memories of his visit with Mary, 'knowing your Ladyship has Nobler ends to serve in gathering up the fragments of the last & best part of his life'.[6]

As well as penning a somewhat partial biography, Lady Fenwick also erected a monument for him in York, thus 'wr[i]t[ing] history for posterity' to shape the way her husband would be remembered.[7] She portrayed herself as a grieving widow, dressed in black mourning clothes, holding a miniature portrait of her late husband in her hand and sitting in front of an urn. She spent her final years labouring to pay off her husband's debts and trying to undo the damage done by the bill of attainder, instead memorialising him by celebrating his military successes, his loyalty to James II and his happy, loving marriage. Her efforts transformed the records of Sir John Fenwick's arraignment into but one part of an interconnected series of texts and objects: while Fenwick's own last words, in the form of his confession, led to his arraignment, his widow's words were all designed, in effect, to rewrite those of her husband. The documents relating to the Fenwick case exist in a state of perpetually competitive dialogue, so much so that it is impossible to determine which, if any, provides us with the 'true' version of events. If anything, their disputes rather lead us to mistrust each of them. The proliferation

Figure 5.1 The Lady Mary Fenwick, 1737. The British Museum.

of narratives does not stop here. Lady Mary Fenwick's own involvement in several Jacobite intrigues combined with her various attempts to vindicate her husband eventually spilled onto the stage: Thomas D'Urfey allegedly based the character Lady Addleplot, who appeared in his play *Love for Money* (1691), on her.[8] By the end of the seventeenth century, the story had thus taken on a fictional afterlife: a literary corrective to Lady Fenwick's obvious bias and her grandiose desire to control her husband's story.

As the case of Lady Mary Fenwick demonstrates, a legal judgement did not necessarily mark the endpoint of a story. The existence of contesting narratives could not only lead to a trial in one party's attempt to get the judge to confirm their side of the story, but a legal judgement could also act as the motivation for the production of further narratives. Legal conflicts could thus potentially exist far beyond their time in court and live on through the counter-narratives they triggered; by being positioned alongside these competing narratives, trial records become part of a larger web of interrelated texts. This allowed women to (re)fashion history and lives, whether their own or, as in the case of Mary Fenwick, that of their husband's, and present such counter-narratives to a potentially even larger audience.

This potential for rewriting the official court records had a downside, of course, as it could also lead to women's stories as told in court becoming eclipsed by more successful counter-narratives. The ramifications of this are explored in two case studies. The first case examines the interconnected (counter)narratives of which *A True Report of the Life and Martyrdom of Mrs. Margaret Clitherow* has become the dominant version, despite Catholic martyr Margaret Clitherow's own reticence. The second focuses on how Elizabeth Sawyer's witchcraft trial took on an afterlife of its own when it was rewritten in popular, printed accounts – a pamphlet, several (no longer extant) ballads and a play, *The Witch of Edmonton* – thereby gaining a national reputation, even though Sawyer's voice itself is lost in the process. In both cases the 'truth' seems impossible to determine, partly because the women whose stories are being narrated hold their tongue and partly because their trial records are no longer extant. Even silence, however, when actively asserted, can be seen as life-writing, and not being able to assess veracity is no barrier to treating texts as life-writing: by turning to more obviously literary genres, the fictional nature of all life-writing, including that which is done at the instigation of a court of law, can be highlighted.

Conflicting Stories: Margaret Clitherow's Trial Narrative

The legal records of the executed Catholic martyr Margaret Clitherow (1552/3–86) are no longer extant: all that remains is a literary account of her legal process. In the absence of the original legal records, any alternative versions created to counter the official records become a substitute for those official legal documents. If the different versions of events told in the courtroom have to be doubted in terms of their veracity, then this is certainly the case with narratives created outside the courtroom and with yet another readership or audience in mind. While the purpose of the stories contained in the case papers is usually clear (namely, to convince the judge), we can be less sure about the aims and interests of outsiders who appropriate a story. This uncertainty is even greater when the subject of a retelling leaves no personal records of their life, as is the case with Margaret Clitherow. Indeed, Clitherow is famous for her silence: her refusal to plead meant that she was condemned to *peine forte et dure* (i.e. to be pressed to death). Her silence was equally valuable to friend or foe because of its ambiguity: it was appropriated both by the authorities who prosecuted her as a sign of her guilt and by fellow Catholic recusants as a statement of her endurance and faith. However, while the authorities relied on the legal process to record its judgement, Clitherow's Catholic biographer made use of a literary form that disseminates the story as hagiography. In this process, however, Clitherow's deliberate silence is being interpreted and filled, culminating in the production of a biography of the unwilling Clitherow: her 'text', in the form of her silence, is appropriated to further the Catholic recusants' agenda. It is their version that comes to obliterate all other accounts.

Although Elizabeth I allegedly claimed that she would not open windows into men's souls, her apparent religious tolerance waned in the face of threats to the stability and peace of the country.[9] Margaret Clitherow, whose public nonconformity and staunch Catholic viewpoints directly challenged the state faith, was the personification of one such threat. The narrative of Clitherow's life and death theoretically exists in multiple versions. Firstly, there is the ur-narrative, the events as they really happened. Secondly, there is the legal narrative from the perspective of the Protestant state as it attempted to enforce religious conformity and thus documented the arrest and arraignment of a heretic for crimes against the state. Although there are some entries that document Clitherow's various misdemeanours, the official records regarding her arraignment are no longer extant, as none of the Assize records of the northern circuit prior to 1607 have survived. Finally, there is a third narrative: the version penned by Father John Mush (1552–1612), *A True Report of the Life and Martyrdom of Mrs. Margaret Clitherow*.[10] This hagiographic narrative of Clitherow's life and arraignment is written from the viewpoint of the recusant community that regarded Clitherow's acts as heroic, her arrest as persecution and her death as martyrdom. The text not only served to vindicate its subject, but also functioned as an example to its like-minded circle of readers. Clitherow's story therefore comes to us neither in her own voice, nor that of the court records. The Margaret Clitherow bequeathed to us is, instead, Mush's Clitherow, one designed as a counter-narrative to the official version of events as presented by the state. It has, by default, become the dominant narrative.

Mush's account offers the life story of Margaret Clitherow. She was born in York in 1552/3, daughter of Thomas Middleton and Jane Turner. She married John Clitherow in 1571, when she was around eighteen years old. Some two or three years after her marriage Clitherow converted to Catholicism and 'became desirous to learn the Christian duty in truth and sincerity'.[11] Indeed, her desire to be a good Catholic was so strong that she spent much of the twelve years that followed her conversion in prison. She was tried before York's Quarter Sessions in 1583 for failing to attend church services,[12] and on 14 March 1586 went before the Assizes for harbouring priests (something that had only recently been made illegal, in the 1585 Act Against Jesuits and Seminary Priests).[13] When asked how she would plead to the latter accusations, Clitherow refused to answer. Several attempts by the judges to force her to comply that day failed, as they did the next day. Without Clitherow's cooperation, no trial could commence, and the judges found themselves forced to subject her to *peine forte et dure* on 15 March. This particular punishment was reserved for those defendants who repeatedly refused to plead to the charges against them and thereby refrained from abiding by court procedure.[14] Clitherow spent several more days in prison awaiting her punishment, which eventually took place on 25 March: Clitherow was pressed to death and thus died indicted, but not convicted, of the charges against her.

In his *True Report*, Mush pits his version of events against the (now missing) official state records. In so doing, he asserts a binary opposition between the views of the authorities and those of the recusant community, views which, according to Mush, are mutually exclusive. From what Mush shares with his readers, the sheriffs of York clearly viewed Clitherow and her staunch Catholicism to be such a danger that they were willing to take the risk of arraigning her. A trial was, of course, a public affair, as would be the (probable) subsequent execution, and a recusant could easily use the platforms of dock and scaffold to reach a wider audience: executions were public spectacles and condemned recusants could (and did) see them as an opportunity for some last-minute proselytising.[15] While Clitherow was in custody, the sheriffs of York did not stop at merely emphasising her religious non-conformity; they also attacked her on a personal level: she was accused of infidelity to her husband as well as the abandonment of her children for the sake of her cause. The narrative that emanated from her Catholic supporters through the pen of John Mush was rather more sympathetic. Indeed, for them she was the epitome of a good Catholic, as well as the perfect mother, wife and neighbour. In the days after Clitherow's execution the Protestants 'railed against her out of their pulpits' and suggested 'that she died desperately'; during that same time Mush began to create his hagiographical account of her life, which would memorialise her as a martyr.[16] Both sides sought to make an example of Clitherow, albeit in very different ways: while the authorities may have hoped that arresting Clitherow would force her to amend her behaviour and discourage others from following her lead, Mush, on the other hand, promoted Clitherow's recusant beliefs and her intransigence in asserting them to his readership, in the hope of stimulating them to follow suit.

In his efforts to show Clitherow in the best light possible, Mush makes use of the same strategies we have seen women use in their own pleadings, including the shifting of blame and the alignment with the trope of the obedient and eternal wife. Mush's account systematically turns the accusations against Margaret Clitherow around: he tries to make it clear that it was not Clitherow who jeopardised her relationship with her husband, but the authorities. Despite her frequent stays in gaol, Mush stresses that Clitherow was a dutiful wife and mother. He describes Clitherow as 'worthy to be preferred before [her neighbours] in every point wherein the commendation of a good housewife standeth' and claims that John Clitherow publicly announced that 'he could wish no better wife than she was'.[17] Mush asserts that it was the authorities who 'separated her from house, children, and husband', not just once, but 'divers times [she was] separated from her husband and children, cast into prison' by external forces.[18] When Clitherow was arraigned and incarcerated for harbouring priests, the authorities equally ensured that Margaret would be separated from her family: '[o]nce the martyr was permitted to speak with her husband in the audience of the gaoler and other more, but she never saw him after, notwithstanding all which both their friends could labour for it, unless she would yield to do something against her conscience'.[19] Despite, or perhaps because of, the lack of direct contact allowed between them, John was very much on Margaret's mind both at the arraignment and during the time of her imprisonment. 'As for my husband,' Mush records her having said, 'know you that I love him next unto God in this world, and I have care over my children as a mother ought to have'.[20] When the judges urge her to admit to having offended her husband, Clitherow said: '"I trust my husband will not accuse me that I have offended him at any time, unless in such small matters as are commonly incident to man and wife; and I beseech you," said she, "let me speak with him before I die."'[21] Her request to see her husband was once more refused. Mush thus presents Clitherow as the perfect obedient wife. When the state temporarily widowed her by refusing to let her see her husband, Clitherow played the eternal wife. Much as many women had done before him, Mush thus shifts blame from Clitherow to the authorities, while claiming her status as a dutiful wife.

Throughout his hagiography, Mush continues to play with these kinds of tropes. This is particularly the case in his description of the marriage between Margaret and John Clitherow. Although Margaret's conversion took place during their marriage, it was not John who convinced his wife to convert. On the contrary, according to Mush, John had said that his wife had but 'two great faults, as he thought, and those were, because she fasted too much, and would not go with him to the church'.[22] However, while he may not have liked his wife's religious viewpoints, John seems to have done nothing to stop her from exercising her faith. He let her send away their son to France to receive a Catholic education and he turned a blind eye when she prepared two chambers for religious service, one 'adjoining' their house and one at a distance from it. In these rooms, Margaret could retire and pray 'without sight or knowledge of any neighbours'.[23] While her neighbours may not have noticed Margaret's religious endeavours, it is more difficult to believe that her husband was not apprised of the situation. Mush, however, states that Margaret deliberately left her husband in the dark regarding her non-conforming actions within their own household in order to protect him: it was her 'husband's most safety not to know these things unless he were resolved to serve God notwithstanding any danger'.[24] It is obvious why this left Margaret open to attack: by defying her husband's wishes and turning their household into a centre of Catholic service behind his back she was behaving contrary to the ideal of the perfect housewife. Mush takes an alternative stance: by protesting his innocence and thus protecting him from prosecution, Margaret shows her husband ultimate loyalty, while at the same time remaining true to her heavenly husband. As we have seen, a wife's behaviour could have a great effect on her husband's reputation, and Mush manipulated this fact quite deftly.

The reality of the events that befell Clitherow – what we might call the ur-account – presumably lies somewhere in the middle, but Mush's account claims to be nothing but the truth:

> I will not, by God's grace and assistance, make relation of anything more than that which I saw and well knew in her myself by some years of our conversation together, for which season I was privy to her whole heart as much as any. And as for those things which happened at her apprehension, imprisonment, arraignment, judgment, and death, I will report no more than that which I have received from the mouth of divers honest and credible persons, which were present witnesses and beholders of every action.[25]

Mush's assertion that he is a credible narrator must, of course, be taken with a pinch of salt.[26] His claims of truthfulness are simply another strategy frequently used in court cases, and his attempts at even-handedness, by highlighting the accusations made against Clitherow before countering them, too, are something that we have seen before. In its very survival, and perhaps even the fact that scholars are not unanimous in their judgements of its veracity, *A True Report* is the embodiment of the successful counter-narrative, in that it has vanquished its foe (even if it has done so by default). In accordance with its own title, as the only extant version, *A True Report* now comes to be regarded as 'true'.

The success of Mush's narrative can largely be attributed to its lack of competitors, as well as its dissemination and materiality. Longley has traced seven different manuscript copies of the text: five of the entire text and another two that only comprise chapters eighteen to twenty.[27] That seven copies of the original output survive suggests that the manuscripts were copied in abundance: loss rates of manuscripts in circulation are generally presumed to be high, with estimates for the ratio of extant texts to total number of produced manuscripts varying between one in 600 to one in 10,000 for texts in small formats.[28] Different manuscript versions of the text, the two incomplete parts (one narrating her life, the other her death) and the full story, were in circulation towards the end of the sixteenth century.[29] Alongside these manuscripts is an image of Clitherow's execution included by Richard Verstegan in his *Theatrum crudelitatum haereticorum nostril temporis*, dating August 1587.[30] Manuscript was the preferred choice of communication for those people who wanted to convey their message to an exclusive readership, particularly when a manuscript, and thus its circulation, was clandestine.[31] Printed works could, however, reach a far wider audience and Mush's story was presumably committed to print as soon as it was considered safe to do so. In the early seventeenth century an abbreviated account of Clitherow's life, imprisonment, arraignment and execution was published as *An Abstracte of the Life and Martirdome of Mistres Margaret Clitherow* (Mechlin, 1619).[32] Although a complete version of the entire text was not published until the nineteenth century, Mush's response to the official legal proceedings and records was circulated in both manuscript and print, over a long period of time, reaching a wide, perhaps even international readership.

The dissemination of legal documents provides a stark contrast to this narrative of circulation. The law courts were mass producers of manuscripts and all of the texts that came into creation in support of legal proceedings were written down on parchment, vellum or paper. After the reading out of a judgement, the case papers would be stored, often not to be looked at again for centuries. These texts were thus originally public, but were then written into (unwitting) privacy. The documents were not meant to be circulated and as such, they usually existed only in single copies. It is possible to find two versions of the same legal record in the archives, but in my experience, these are then often stored together, suggesting that the different copies were not meant to be circulated – if so, they would not still be in the court's archive.[33] That is not to say that litigants could not consult records and make copies of them against payment;[34] the courts themselves did not produce these manuscripts with a view to circulate them.

Politics could also influence the records' chances of survival. After the abolishment of the Court of Star Chamber during the civil wars, for example, its records were moved to a less prominent place, where many of them were exposed to water and vermin.[35] As a result of this, a large part of these records has been lost or destroyed. As such, these legal records are in no position to compete with printed literary texts in the directing of the public understanding of such cases. Even if we still had access to the original records pertaining to the Clitherow case, it is debatable whether those would have told us much more than these basic facts: many of the recorded answers given by the alleged heretics to the questions of their interrogators in heresy trials are so schematic and truncated that they give us little information.[36] In these types of cases it is the trial narratives created by the prisoners themselves that form 'a kind of textual "answer"' and that give the accused the opportunity to fill in the gaps present in the official records.[37] No letter, account book or note penned by Clitherow survives, let alone a trial narrative. She thus refused to tell her story not only in court, but outside of it. This is not surprising: Mush emphatically informs his readers that Clitherow could read English, but he does not mention any writing skills.[38] Since having such a passive form of literacy was far from uncommon in early modern England, it is not unlikely that Clitherow could not write.

As the only account available, *A True Report* is, in effect, the textual answer Margaret Clitherow would not give to the court, and in combining the literary genres of the trial narrative and the hagiography, it 'conforms to standard generic conventions of the saint's life'.[39] Mush's continual praise of Clitherow's exemplary behaviour throughout the text fits with this tradition, as does his elaborate description of her suffering under the hands of the Protestant officials who tried to get her to conform to their ideas. Clitherow is clearly presented as an exemplar, her life a blueprint for others to model theirs upon. Notably, the example she sets – by being portrayed as an uneducated, illiterate laywoman who converted to Catholicism later in life – is an achievable, yet nonetheless inspiring one. That the text comprises two distinct parts, with chapters one to seventeen focusing on the life of the martyr and chapters eighteen to twenty on her arrest, trial and execution, also conforms to the generic standard of the traditional medieval hagiography. The scholarly consensus is that the two parts were written by different authors;[40] Clitherow's fellow prisoner William Hutton seems the most likely candidate for the role of author of the later chapters.[41] This two-part structure would be a familiar format for its intended audience.[42]

In framing itself as a hagiographical trial narrative, the manuscript not only does battle with the government's office, it also relates itself against a literary tradition of these types of text. Indeed, Genelle Gertz has traced in detail how Clitherow's account 'can be read as a Catholic alternative to the recently published trials' of Protestant women, such as Anne Askew, Alice Driver, Elizabeth Young and Agnes Prest.[43] Where these Protestant women put on trial during the reigns of Henry and Mary used their trials to showcase their ideas and beliefs, Clitherow took a markedly different approach by resorting to 'tactics of silence'.[44] Askew, of course, makes claims of silence, but only in order to preach and encourage conversation.[45] Asked why she 'had so few words', she answered that 'God hath given me the gift of knowledge, but not of utterance. And Salomon saith that a woman of few words, is a gift of God'.[46] Askew merely feigns silence and chastises her examiners for not adhering to the word of God by urging her to speak more. Clitherow, on the other hand, gives short answers that actually close off dialogue and as such rejects the Protestant standard of trial as a testing of religious belief.[47] During her imprisonment she is accused of following 'blind guides', and her examiner asks: '[i]s there any of them that hath any learning, I would fain know?' Clitherow answers: '[p]eruse their works, and you shall see', thereby refusing to be tempted into a debate about scriptures.[48]

Clitherow's reticence causes her to avoid trial altogether. As such, *A True Report* not only offers a counter-narrative to the story promoted by Clitherow's opponents, it is also an alternative to the Protestant trial narratives produced in the decades before Clitherow's arraignment. By insisting on Clitherow's silence, Mush pits his text against Askew and the others. In so doing, Mush tacitly accuses the Protestant women of failing to be silent, and therefore good, women; his reticent Clitherow sets the right example. Both Bale's version of Askew's *Examinations* and Foxe's version in his 'Book of Martyrs' were easily accessible to an audience, and Mush would certainly have been familiar with them.[49] It is possible, then, that Mush's text imitated the 'proven textual tactic[s]' of Askew's narrative, as Anne Dillon has suggested, while at the same time holding them in the negative image.[50] Clitherow's and Askew's (auto) biographies certainly seem to be in dialogue, at least implicitly, and this suggests a form of literariness in which the author, Mush, actively responds to an existing tradition.[51] His use of tropes similar to the ones used by female litigants suggests much the same.

Just as Mush responds to this tradition, so does Clitherow. Where Askew was very vocal during her trial and penned her own account of it, Clitherow not only avoided creating her own trial account, she also avoids a trial by choosing to be reticent. Just as *A True Report* competes with the Protestant trial narratives, so does Clitherow, in her silence, pit herself against her accusers. Not only did she refuse to plead, she also refused to confirm she was pregnant, when doing so would at the very least have delayed the execution of her punishment. When asked on multiple occasions whether she was with child, she 'would never affirm it of any certainty', forcing the authorities to make a martyr out of her.[52] Clitherow rendered herself beyond innocent or guilty, and is punished only for her silence, not for any heresy. Her punishment is thus, quite literally, for nothing. Her tactic of silence, however, is not reserved only for her condemnation; Mush represents it as a response to which Clitherow resorted throughout her life:

> When she had been reproved of anything, she would mildly have answered to have satisfied them; and if it would not serve, then, without all contention, keep silence, and return to the comfort of her inward mind and conscience, referring all to God, rather more willing to acknowledge a fault, although she were innocent, than to defend or excuse herself when she was any way reprehended[.][53]

When faced with reproach, then, Clitherow resorted to silence. Although silence and obedience were the norm for women in the early modern period, Clitherow's silence can be seen as a form of disobedience. Women could thus also provoke male fears and anxieties by remaining quiet, and as such, '[f]eminine silence can be constructed as a space of subjective agency which threatens masculine authority'.[54] Moreover, this silence bypasses the judgements of men in a direct appeal to God. Clitherow's silence should thus be interpreted as a form of subversion.

An early modern woman's position and reputation depended largely on how she was defined and described by others.[55] Clitherow was asserted by both Mush and the authorities in mutually exclusive terms (though we only have Mush's word for this). Dutiful housewife or negligent wife and mother, railing heretic or faithful martyr, Clitherow's life can be interpreted in various ways.[56] A modern, unbiased audience may struggle to decide which version of events to find more credible, but the question is whether it is necessary to make a choice. The way trials are structured necessarily invites dualistic modes of discourse. Normally, the jury would pick one of these perspectives as the authoritative account for sentencing, but in Clitherow's case, the matter never reached the trial stage. Instead of a heretic *or* a martyr, then, Clitherow became both. By allowing herself to be killed by *peine forte et dure*, Clitherow turns into the embodiment of the various versions of events, as captured in Mush's account: she manifests each of the conflicting narratives at once, by neither confirming nor denying any one of them. It is Clitherow's silence that allows multiple versions of truth to co-exist – even if one of those has come to dominate all others. Clitherow's reticence makes it possible for Mush to fill the vacuum that she leaves in refusing to assert her own life story. Clitherow's case illustrates the importance of a woman's vocally asserting her life story, as avoiding doing so gave others the opportunity to do so in her stead. While silence can be a form of asserting the self, it is a form prone to being overwritten by other, more vocal narratives.

Elizabeth Sawyer: The Witch of Edmonton

Various narratives are in competition in the case of Elizabeth Sawyer, a woman condemned of an act of witchcraft which resulted in the death of her neighbour, a crime to which she allegedly confessed. She was convicted and hanged as a witch in April 1621. No formal records of the legal proceedings survive, yet her story was well documented. Several ballads were composed narrating Sawyer's diabolical acts, and the chaplain of Newgate prison, Henry Goodcole (*bap.* 1586, *d.* 1641), produced a pamphlet (1621) that discussed both the proceedings and Sawyer's confession at the scaffold. Later in the same year, the playwrights John Ford, Thomas Dekker and William Rowley collaborated on a rewrite of the story entitled *The Witch of Edmonton*, first published in 1658, but performed at court as early as 29 December 1621.[57] Just one year after Sawyer's execution, then, several versions of her story were circulating, each focusing on a different aspect of the narrative and each presented in a different literary form. None of these versions, however, can be justly said to contain Sawyer's side of the story. Rather, each of them appropriates Sawyer's case for their own benefit and in doing so, Sawyer's own narrative becomes wholly eclipsed.

Although the danger witchcraft posed stood undisputed in the minds of early modern English men and women, they also realised that it was an extremely difficult crime to prove.[58] Without the alleged witch's confession, how could her *maleficium* – which was by definition the result of some unknown power and often performed without witnesses – be proven in the eyes of the law? Any causal relationship would be extremely difficult to pinpoint. The statutes did not provide any help on this front and widespread heated public debate also failed to offer a clear and uniform solution to the problem.[59] As a result, several methods of establishing guilt were used alongside one another. As clear, direct evidence was rarely available (for perhaps obvious reasons), a suspect would generally find themselves convicted of witchcraft on the basis of circumstantial evidence. This ranged from physical signs, like the identification of Elizabeth Sawyer's 'thing like a Teat',[60] to supernatural signs, such as the conjuration of familiars or passing the swimming test. The swimming test embodies the evidentiary problem: when the alleged witch sank after being thrown into the water, she would be deemed innocent, but ran the risk of drowning in the process; floating indicated guilt, so any initial relief the suspect might have felt at not drowning would be short lived, as she then faced execution by hanging.

Proving that a woman – or, in rare cases, a man[61] – was a witch thus posed problems. But the reverse was also true: it was virtually impossible to prove oneself not to be a witch following a public accusation. Once rumours started being spread regarding the alleged use of *maleficium*, the suspect was in a precarious situation: the nature of the crime made alibis worthless, as acts of witchcraft could be performed at a distance and long before their actual results were felt. As such, suspicion alone could suffice to criminalise the alleged witch. In the words of *The Witch of Edmonton*'s version of Elizabeth Sawyer: ''Tis all one / To be a witch as to be counted one'.[62] Ultimately juries had to choose one of several competing narratives and in each scenario innocent parties could lose their lives: acquitting a witch based on a lack of evidence meant that her neighbours and fellow citizens were in potential danger, whereas the alternative scenario, the conviction of the alleged witch based on circumstantial proof, meant an innocent woman might be executed.

That the early modern period witnessed a rise in concerns about witches and witchcraft can be seen in the implementation of several witchcraft laws in the period: the 1542 statute introduced witchcraft as a crime, and in 1563 Elizabeth I determined that in certain cases witchcraft was punishable by death.[63] A 1604 statute made it punishable to enter into a diabolical contract.[64] Real fear may have been at the heart of many witchcraft cases, but accusations of witchcraft would also be uttered to deal with old grudges and little quarrels. Dealing with witchcraft was a social enterprise: while witchcraft itself might undermine a community, as one of the group attacked the others, entire neighbourhoods would unite in the tracking down of witches, and once a suspected witch had been found, it was her neighbours and fellow citizens who would testify against her. So it was the case with Elizabeth Sawyer: her neighbours allegedly had a '[g]reat, and long suspicion' that Sawyer was dabbling in witchcraft, and a local justice of the peace in neighbouring Tottenham, Arthur Robinson, was said to be 'watchful over her, and her ways'.[65] It was this communal fear and vigilance that led to the eventual arrest and arraignment of 'the witch of Edmonton', following the suspicious deaths of cattle, children and Sawyer's neighbour Agnes Ratcliefe. The enormous anxiety regarding witchcraft, exacerbated by James I's obsession with the subject, meant that witchcraft cases had the potential to receive widespread and intense attention. As one of only a handful of such prosecutions in London, Sawyer's case seemed to have been exceptionally (and perhaps even disproportionately) interesting to a wide audience, spawning numerous different accounts, in a wide variety of genres.

Several ballads on Sawyer's case were in circulation around the time of her arraignment, trial and subsequent execution. The ballad form was 'the country's most widely and frequently distributed news form until the later seventeenth century' and allowed news stories to be spread widely both quickly and cheaply.[66] As they were news-dependent, they were also ephemeral, and so few of these ballads have survived. One example is *A new ballad of the life and deaths of three witches arrayned and executed at Chelmsford 5 July 1589 (To the tune of 'Bragandary Down', & etc* (London, 1589).[67] In the absence of the original witch of Edmonton ballads, *A new ballad* can give an impression of what these no longer extant ballads may have contained in terms of content and tone. The opening verse is illustrative of the rest of the ballad:[68]

> List Christians all unto my Song
> 'Twill move your Hearts to Grace,
> That Dreadful Witchcraft hath been done,
> Of late about this place;
> But Three that cried the Devil's Name
> With those who did them follow,
> Now to Justice are brought home
> To Swing upon our Gallow.

This anonymous ballad has a highly moralising tone. Aimed at good Christians, it narrates the story of three 'Dreadful' witches who allegedly terrorised the town of Chelmsford. The author uses a fair amount of contrast in order to highlight the difference between good and bad: Grace, or the reward of good Christians, is juxtaposed with gallows, the punishment for witchcraft; God's light and reason are contrasted with the devil's witchcraft and treason; and now that the 'rule of Imps and Spells and Dread' has ended, calm and peace have returned to the town of Chelmsford. As such, it is clear how the audience is meant to interpret the ballad: the evil witches have been defeated through God's intervention and all of Chelmsford rejoices. The melody to which the ballad was meant to be sung, too, would have signalled to the reader that the topic of the ballad was a grave one. The tune of 'Bragandary Down' was usually saved for the rendition of unnatural events, such as murder, tales of the demonically possessed and the supernatural.[69]

But ballads were not written simply for edification; they also aimed to entertain and titillate. Therefore, they relied on their audiences' desire to laugh, or gape in mock-horror, at the behaviour of the ballads' subjects.[70] Those ballads that sang Elizabeth Sawyer's case may no longer be extant, but they were reported to contain stories about 'a Ferret and an Owl daily sporting before her, of the bewitched woman braining her self, [and] of the Spirits attending in the Prison'.[71] The facts surrounding her arrest were supplemented by what we can only assume were creative additions to amuse and horrify the public.

Goodcole, as chaplain of Newgate prison and producer of a series of 'criminal biographies' including *The Wonderfull Discouerie*, objected to these fictionalisations.[72] He claimed that entertainment played no role in his pamphlet about Elizabeth Sawyer and that its purpose was rather to 'meddle herewith nothing but matter of fact'. Goodcole explicitly juxtaposed his pamphlet with the 'base and false Ballads, which were sung at the time of our returning from the Witches' execution' for this very reason: in the ballads 'I was ashamed to see and hear such ridiculous fictions [. . .], all which I knew to be fitter for an Ale-bench than for a relation of proceeding in Court of Justice'.[73] The pamphlet therefore seeks, and fails, to remove the ballads from making any claim to a counter-narrative: it is only because of his reference to them that we know something about the ballads' contents.[74]

The story of Elizabeth Sawyer's life with which Goodcole hoped to replace the ballads focuses on her crimes and trial. His position at Newgate gave him access to prisoners and the condemned, which enabled him to hold a conversation with Sawyer, a verbatim account of which is supplemented to the trial account. Goodcole narrates how the devil first gained access to Sawyer: '[t]hat tongue which by cursing, swearing, blaspheming, and imprecating, as afterward she confessed, was the occasioning cause, of the Devil's access unto her'.[75] When unexplained deaths occurred in Edmonton, Sawyer was quickly suspected of witchcraft and put on trial. It is again Sawyer's tongue which brings about her downfall, this time of her earthly body, as the pamphleteer relates how during the proceedings Sawyer was 'not able to speak a sensible or ready word for her defense' and instead burst out cursing.[76] Her tongue is therefore described as 'the means of her own destruction',[77] and those present at the trial were certainly astonished and shocked by her foul language. The verbatim account of Goodcole's conversation with the imprisoned Sawyer, too, shows her being condemned by her own tongue. Following the question of whether her confession is true, for instance, the answer follows: '[y]es, it is all truth, as I shall make answer unto almighty God', vocalising her confession to God.[78] In his 'Conclusion', addressed to 'Dear Christians', Goodcole reinforces his message one more time, instructing his readership to refrain from swearing, 'for here you may see the fruits thereof, that it is a plain way to bring you to the Devil'.[79] In her final confession at her execution, Sawyer admits all crimes. Goodcole thus allows us to hear, from the witch's mouth herself ('with my own mouth I spake it to him'), that she has damned herself.[80]

Goodcole describes his account of Sawyer's trial and their subsequent conversation as a 'true declaration' and a 'true Relation', statements of superiority like we have seen used by Mush in his account of Margaret Clitherow's trial and tribulations.[81] Authors referred to their texts as 'true relations' in particular when they feared that readers might consider their narrative incredible.[82] Having dismissed the ballads as fictions, Goodcole may have wanted to stop his readership from thinking the same thing about his own text or wished to support his opinion through assertions of authority and reliability. Using standard paratextual rhetoric, the packaging and marketing of the pamphlet indicate its readership should trust its author and contents. The presentation in dialogue of his interrogation of Sawyer suggests the pamphleteer is giving a verbatim account of her voice, noting each question he asked her followed by her answer written down in the first person.[83] Goodcole also strives to give the sense that he is an insider with access to both the prisoner and the members of the legal system and should therefore be trusted. The pamphlet's title asserts that it is 'Published by Authority' and it emphasises Goodcole's status: 'Henry Goodcole Minister of the Word of God, and her continual Visitor in the Gaol of Newgate'.[84]

But Goodcole's attempts at offering an unbiased account are overridden by his interest in edifying the people. Goodcole sought to warn his readers away from their sinful lives, and each of his pamphlets thus focused 'on a particular sin and its apt punishment'.[85] In *The Adulteresses Funeral Day* he addressed domestic violence and in *Heavens Speedie Cry Sent after Lust and Murther* he warned against the dangers of lust. The message Goodcole wants his readers to take away from *The Wonderfull Discouerie* is that they should not swear. As such, sins of the tongue in the form of cursing and blaspheming are the main subject of Goodcole's pamphlet, and Sawyer's story and confession are in service of his narrative – hence the insistence on Sawyer's tongue as the instrument of her destruction. Although Goodcole's desire to moralise may not necessarily undo his claims of relating a truthful account, it is clear that he employs Sawyer's story for a specific moral purpose. And she is not the only one treated by Goodcole in this way: none of Goodcole's pamphlets display much sympathy for their subjects, which makes it 'hard not to see Goodcole as effectually capitalizing on their misfortunes'.[86] Goodcole's relentless moralising undermines his assertions that he offers an unbiased rendition of events.

Alongside edifying his readers, Goodcole also seems interested in titillating his audience – much like the ballads he tries so hard to dismiss.[87] Sawyer is found 'to be guilty, by diabolical help, of the death of *Agnes Ratcliefe* only' (Goodcole's use of italics).[88] However, when the pamphleteer asks Sawyer, '[*w*]*hether did you procure the death of* Agnes Ratcliefe *for which you were found guilty by the Jury?*', she answers: '[n]o, I did not by my means procure against her the least hurt'.[89] This seemingly satisfies Goodcole, as no further questions are asked. This is in marked contrast with his interest in Sawyer's 'thing in the form of a Teat'. After it is first mentioned in their conversation, Goodcole finds it necessary to ask three follow-up questions to ascertain what exactly the process of sucking the 'Teat' entailed.[90] He wants to know where on Sawyer's body the 'Teat' is located and who chose that spot; whether Sawyer took off her coat to enable the sucking; and how long one sucking session would last and whether such sessions were painful. Goodcole thus takes Sawyer's story and appropriates it for his own purpose.

That purpose is to make Sawyer into an example of how *not* to behave. As such, *The Wonderfull Discouerie* is linked to, and simultaneously stands in marked contrast with John Mush's *A True Report of the Life and Martyrdom of Mrs. Margaret Clitherow*. Both male authors write about a woman's life, appropriating her voice. But where Mush speaks for Clitherow, Goodcole condemns Sawyer's words. And where Margaret Clitherow is turned into an example of piety and virtuousness, Sawyer is demonised. As a martyr, it is perhaps because Clitherow is presented in a favourable, even hagiographical light, that it is easy to assume that Mush conveyed Clitherow's wishes when 'narrating' her story. Goodcole, on the other hand, makes it clear that Sawyer is a less than willing participant in his interview of her, as he had to elicit her confession 'with great labour'.[91] The Goodcole-Sawyer relationship is thus presented as an inversion of the one between Mush and Clitherow, and yet the two are not so different: both Goodcole and Mush present the reader with highly partial texts written by men with specific religious agendas. Furthermore, the subjects of both texts, being deceased, are not in a position to contradict them. Indeed, neither woman – whether martyr or witch – chose to speak and freely share her story with an audience, and they are thus both unwilling participants in the fashioning of their life stories.

Goodcole's 'general practice' of exploiting the faults of others in his pamphlets, Kinney has argued, 'may have inspired Dekker and Ford to retell the story of Mother Sawyer just as much as the notoriety of her case'.[92] *The Witch of Edmonton* was written in the months after the Sawyer affair and first performed on 29 December of the same year, when the case would presumably still be relatively fresh in people's minds.[93] It was advertised as 'A known true STORY' on its title page, thereby capitalising on the massive interest in the case. The playwrights clearly used Goodcole's pamphlet as a model for their drama.[94] The pamphlet and the play both cover the same narrative period, starting with the suspicions her neighbours have against her and ending with her execution. Each narrative features Sawyer's familiar in the form of a black dog named Tom. And in both cases it is Sawyer's cursing that invites the devil into her life.[95] Sawyer gives the dog access to her soul and body and allows the dog to suck her blood. In each version, the dog teaches Sawyer a Latin phrase which she can use to conjure the dog: '[s]anctibicetur nomen tuum'.[96] Even the 'slight and ridiculous' test described by Goodcole that her neighbours used to unmask Sawyer as a witch features in the play.[97] As such, the playwrights drew heavily on their source material, appropriating Goodcole's appropriation of Sawyer's story.

But the play also differs notably from the pamphlet: various changes are made to 'heighten the dramatic quality' of the dramatists' source.[98] Although the play's title suggests Elizabeth Sawyer is the sole focus of the drama, the account of her witchcraft is merely one of three plots in the play. Sawyer is not mentioned, nor does she make an appearance on the stage, until act two. Alongside Sawyer's trials and tribulations, the audience is presented with the stories of the bigamist Frank and the clown Cuddy. As a result, the plot involving Sawyer moves at great speed: it turns from the suspicions of her neighbours straight to the execution scene. Although Goodcole's account of Sawyer's trial is marginal, he acknowledges its existence. Dekker, Ford and Rowley, conversely, neglect to mention it altogether. The play is therefore less of a trial narrative and more of an exploration of communal life as well as a depiction of the demonic. Moreover, it is an acceptance of the truth that to be thought of as a witch was tantamount to being one.

Perhaps the most important difference between the pamphlet and the play, however, is the manner in which Sawyer is depicted. Goodcole's interview with Sawyer makes it clear that Sawyer invoked the devil into her life through her cursing and swearing. In other words, Sawyer was already dabbling in sin before turning to witchcraft. Conversely, the Sawyer of the play only turned to witchcraft after she had unjustly been accused of it. Her neighbours are already convinced that she is a witch, and it is this that makes her become one: '[s]ome call me 'witch', / And being ignorant of myself they go / About to teach me how to be one'.[99] This may remind us of Caliban, who counters Prospero's accusations of savagery and brutality by saying 'You taught me language, and my profit on't / Is I know how to curse. The red plague rid you / For learning me your language' (1.2.365–7). It is the psychological cruelty of the community Sawyer lives in that drives her to demonism. This is also related to the (lack of) anchoring Sawyer has in Edmonton's society, an issue which is represented differently in the two texts. Goodcole refers to Sawyer's husband and children in his pamphlet, as well as to her occupation of selling brooms.[100] She is thus rooted in society, however marginally. The playwrights, on the other hand, suggest Sawyer lacks family and friends and has no job, which isolates her from the rest of the Edmonton community. Heading her own household, Sawyer would have faced social ridicule.[101] In Sawyer's own words: 'an old woman / Ill-favoured grown with years, if she be poor, / Must be called bawd or witch'.[102]

Sawyer is thus a locus of conflict between two opposite forces: Goodcole's desire for edification and Dekker, Ford and Rowley's aim to entertain. The witch from the play is depicted as a pitiable character: in her first lines of the play, Sawyer describes herself as 'poor, deformed and ignorant'.[103] The alleged witch is ostracised by society and turns to the devil because she has no one else to turn to. Her reasoning is sensible and easy to follow ('If every poor old woman be trod on thus by slaves, reviled, kicked, beaten, as I am daily, she to be revenged had need turn witch') and her overall speech is eloquent, apart from a few bouts of swearing ('Rots and foul maladies eat up thee and thine').[104] Sawyer asks herself why she is 'made a common sink / For all the filth and rubbish of men's tongues / To fall and run into'.[105] For Dekker, Ford and Rowley, it is thus the tongues of others that are the cause of Sawyer's damnation. For Goodcole, Sawyer is damned by her own tongue, which leads her to invite the devil into her life, makes her utter only oaths and curses instead of defending herself in court and causes her to confess on the scaffold and ask for forgiveness for her 'grievous sins'.[106] The play's witch, however, refuses to publicly admit her alleged wrongdoings, nor does she ask for forgiveness. Instead, she wonders why every crime (even those she had no hand in) must be attributed to her: 'is every devil mine?'[107] Although in her final speech Sawyer 'repent[s] all former evil', it is not clear what, exactly, she is sorry for.[108] These different portrayals make Elizabeth Sawyer an elusive character, despite the various attempts at narrating part of her life: while in each case Sawyer is damned, guilt is attributed to different tongues. The driving forces behind the two texts are characterised by the different assertions of guilt apportioned to Sawyer in them.

Each successive version of Elizabeth Sawyer's story is shaped in reaction to existing accounts: the pamphlets sensationalise the case of the presumed witch; Goodcole claims to correct these falseties with a 'true' account of his interview with the witch and her subsequent confession; and Dekker, Ford and Rowley, while using Goodcole's pamphlet as the source text for their play, seek to engage the sympathy of the audience for a complex character forced into witchcraft by her cruel community. While each counter-narrative competes with the others, none of them dominates. In responding to their competitors, Goodcole, Dekker, Ford and Rowley thus do what early modern women themselves did: they take the text of others and twist it to their own purposes. The battle for the most convincing representation of a woman's self is moved from the courts of law to the courtroom of the early modern stage. Unfortunately, the authors of the texts did not heed the advice of the Justice in *The Witch of Edmonton*: 'Take heed, sirs, what you do. Unless your proofs come better armed, instead of turning her into a witch you'll prove yourselves stark fools'.[109]

Alternative Realities

When Margaret Cavendish (1623–73) wrote her autobiography, she did so 'not to please but to tell the truth, lest after-ages should mistake'.[110] Her autobiographical account was thus intended to take control over how later readerships would view her. Even if there would be conflicting narratives, Cavendish had constructed her own, authoritative version, asserted as truthful just like Goodcole's. Not all women were capable of, or interested in controlling their own afterlives in quite the same way, however. Courts of law offered the illiterate the opportunity to leave traces of their lives in the court record, but by the flipside of the same coin, it could force people to defend themselves. In many cases, we can never know whether women used the courtroom to set the record straight, for that very same record has often failed to survive, as we have seen in the cases of Clitherow and Sawyer. If women refused to leave an account, or this account is no longer available, they run the risk of others filling that void.

This risk is especially tangible in cases where women's legal accounts were asked not only to compete with their legal opponent's version of events. The proliferation of truths that often compete in legal proceedings is sometimes marked by a shift into other (sometimes multiple) genres. It is in this shift that we see the full impact of legal texts on the literary sphere, and vice versa, in the early modern period. The trials of Margaret Clitherow and Elizabeth Sawyer (or lack thereof, in the case of Clitherow) inspired the production of alternative versions outside of the courtroom – literature comes to replace the legal account. Although both Mush and Goodcole give the impression of presenting a straightforward account of their subjects' trials, these texts cannot be taken at face value. These men place their own tongues in the mouths of the woman they are describing, appropriating her voice and filling in the silence she left behind her (whether deliberately, in the case of Clitherow, or unwittingly, as her trial record is now lost, in the case of Sawyer). Clitherow and Sawyer's voices (or lack thereof) become eclipsed by more powerful, seemingly authoritative, or better circulated narratives of these women's plight.

Much of this has to do with the posthumous publications of Clitherow's and Sawyer's accounts. *A True Report*, *The Wonderfull Discouerie*, the various ballads and *The Witch of Edmonton* were all produced after the deaths of their subjects. For case papers, such as bills of complaint, there is clearly some kind of direct collaboration between a female client and her male lawyer: she would, after all, have to feel comfortable relating a similar story in the courtroom should she be asked to do so. Crucially – and in direct contrast to the cases of Margaret Clitherow and Elizabeth Sawyer – she *could* be asked to do so. Any story penned by her legal counsel would thus have to have the litigant's blessing. In the case of Clitherow and Sawyer, however, their deaths gave their biographers all the freedom they needed to present these women in whichever way they wanted: these authors would face no opposition from their texts' subjects. As such, these writers had the freedom to blur the legal and literary spheres in their texts and use these texts for their own purposes – exactly as the women themselves might have done. In so doing, these authors highlight the fictional quality of all life-writing, even when it takes place in or for a court of law. Early modern women's life-writing, regardless of its form or shape, is created by a cross-fertilisation of three factors: 'truth', namely the things that actually happened (to which we have little to no access); 'need', how these women needed to present themselves; and 'forum', the strictures operating in a particular genre, whether legal defence, (auto)biography or hagiography. The stories of Margaret Clitherow and Elizabeth Sawyer were all fictionalised in one way or another. We do not know to what degree (partly because in each case vital context is missing: a true verdict), but that, in many ways, is beside the point. What matters is that a part of their life is asserted, whether it has been pronounced trippingly on the tongue, or merely mouthed, as if by the town crier.

Notes

1. BL Add. MS 47608, f. 120.
2. Paul Hopkins, 'Fenwick, Sir John, third baronet (c.1644–1697)', *Oxford Dictionary of National Biography* (23 September 2004). Accessed 18 March 2024.
3. BL Add. MS 47608, f. 154; ff. 1–78.
4. Ibid., ff. 162v–179v.
5. Hopkins, 'Fenwick'.
6. BL Add. MS 47608, f. 92r.
7. Peter Sherlock, 'Monuments and Memory', in Patricia Phillippy (ed.), *A History of Early Modern Women's Writing* (Cambridge University Press, 2018), pp. 292–311, at 292.
8. Thomas Bruce, *Memoirs of Thomas, Earl of Ailesbury*, ed. by W. E. Buckley, Vol. 2, Roxburghe Club 122 (1890), pp. 390–1.
9. Jeffrie G. Murphy, *Punishment and the Moral Emotions: Essays in Law, Morality, and Religion* (Oxford University Press, 2012), p. 151. According to Kenneth L. Campbell, it was Francis Bacon who used the phrase to describe Elizabeth's religious policy, see Campbell, *Windows into Men's Souls: Religious Nonconformity in Tudor and Early Stuart England* (Lexington Books, 2012), p. 4.
10. All references to *A True Report* are taken from John Morris's edition: John Mush, 'A True Report of the Life and Martyrdom of Mrs. Margaret Clitherow', in John Morris (ed.), *The Troubles of Our Catholic Forefathers, Related by Themselves*, Vol. 3 (Burns and Oates, 1877), pp. 360–440.
11. Mush, 'True Report', p. 368.
12. York Explore Library and Archive, Y/ORD/1/1/3, York Quarter Sessions Minute Book, 1571–1583 (8 March 1583), p. 739; Katherine M. Longley, 'The "Trial" of Margaret Clitherow', *Ampleforth Journal,* 75 (1970): 335–64, at 357.
13. Mush, 'True Report', pp. 412–13; Statute 27 Eliz I c 2.
14. This grim sentence was the result of an unfortunate misunderstanding: the original punishment for refusing to plead was *prison forte et dure*, which would entail a long spell in prison on a restricted diet, but a misreading turned *prison* into *peine forte et dure*, which meant that the defendant

was placed under heavy weights, often resulting in death (J. H. Baker, *An Introduction to English Legal History*, 4rd ed (Oxford University Press, 2007), pp. 508–9). For a more thorough discussion of *peine forte et dure*, see Judith Hudson, *Crime and Consequence in Early Modern Literature and Law* (Edinburgh University Press, 2021), pp. 158–62.

15. Peter Lake and Michael Questier, 'Agency, Appropriation and Rhetoric under the Gallows: Puritans, Romanists and the State in Early Modern England', *Past & Present*, 153 (1996): 64–107; Joad Raymond, *Pamphlets and Pamphleteering in Early Modern Britain* (Cambridge University Press, 2003), p. 120. See also Thomas S. Freeman, '"Imitatio Christi with a Vengeance"': The Politicisation of Martyrdom in Early-Modern England', in Thomas S. Freeman and Thomas F. Mayer (eds), *Martyrs and Martyrdom in England c.1400–1700* (The Boydell Press, 2007), pp. 35–69, at 37–9. Freeman has argued that a martyr's behaviour at their execution was carefully scrutinised by both their opponents and supporters, with each group interpreting this behaviour differently and to their own advantage.
16. Mush, 'True Report', p. 433.
17. Ibid., pp. 374–5, 407.
18. Ibid., pp. 372, 369.
19. Ibid., p. 412.
20. Ibid., p. 426.
21. Ibid., pp. 427–8.
22. Ibid., p. 407.
23. Ibid., p. 388.
24. Ibid., p. 381.
25. Ibid., p. 368.
26. According to Peter Lake and Michael Questier, Mush's account of Clitherow is 'deeply polemical and most of its facts cannot be verified' (*The Trials*, p. 6); Claire Cross has described Mush's own agenda for turning Clitherow into a martyr (Claire Cross, 'An Elizabethan Martyrologist and his Martyr: John Mush and Margaret Clitherow', in Diana Wood (ed.), *Martyrs and Martyrologies* (Blackwell Publishers, 1993), pp. 271–81). Katherine Longley, on the other hand, seems to take Mush's account at face value (Longley, 'The "Trial"').
27. See Longley, 'The "Trial"', footnote 64; and Appendix 1 of Longley's *Saint Margaret Clitherow*.
28. Steven W. May and Heather Wolfe, 'Manuscripts in Tudor England', in Kent Cartwright (ed.), *A Companion to Tudor Literature* (Wiley-Blackwell, 2010), pp. 125–39, at 133. Manuscript loss studies based on unseen species models may more accurately estimate the total number of produced manuscripts (Mike Kestemont et al., 'Forgotten Books: The Application of Unseen Species Models to the Survival of Culture', *Science*, 375 (2022): 765–9).
29. Dillon, *The Construction*, p. 280.
30. Richard Verstegan, *Theatrum Crudelitatum Haereticorum Nostri Temporis* (Antwerp, 1587), p. 77.

31. Julia Crick and Alexandra Walsham, 'Introduction', in Julia Crick and Alexandra Walsham (eds), *The Uses of Script and Print, 1300–1700* (Cambridge University Press, 2004), pp. 1–28, at 8.
32. Facsimile published in D. M. Rogers (ed.), *English Recusant Literature, 1558–1640*, Vol. 393 (Scolar Press, 1979). Thomas S. Freeman traces a similar circulation and publication pattern of the works of Protestant prisoners in his 'The Scribal Culture of the Marian Martyrs', in Crick and Walsham (eds), *Script and Print*, pp. 235–54.
33. Chancery bills, for example, are to be found in sets of two: with one version penned in secretary hand and another engrossed in court hand.
34. For more on access to public records and papers, see Kate Peters, '"Friction in the Archives": Access and the Politics of Record-Keeping in Revolutionary England', in Kate Peters, Alexandra Walsham and Liesbeth Corens (eds), *Archives and Information in the Early Modern World* (Oxford University Press, 2018), pp. 151–76.
35. The Journal of the House of Lords records that 'None of the Decrees of the said Court are to be found'; 'As to the Bills, Answers, &c. of the Star Chamber; they have lain many Years in a very great Heap, undigested, without any Covering from Dust, or Security from Rats and Mice' (Journal of House of Lords Volume 21: April 1719 (11–20), https://www.british-history.ac.uk/lords-jrnl/vol21/pp125-152. Accessed 4 August 2020. See also E. M. Hallam, 'Problems with Record Keeping in Early Eighteenth Century London: Some Pictorial Representations of the State Paper Office, 1705–1706', *Journal of Society of Archivists*, 6 (1979): 219–26, at 221.
36. Eamon Duffy, *Fires of Faith: Catholic England Under Mary Tudor* (Yale University Press, 2010), pp. 102–3.
37. Ruth Ahnert, 'Imitating Inquisition: Dialectical Bias in Protestant Prison Writings', in Mary C. Flannery and Katie L. Walter (eds), *The Culture of Inquisition in Medieval England* (D. S. Brewer, 2013), pp. 146–63, at 149. See also: Duffy, *Fires of Faith*. Duffy warns that although the defendant's own accounts are 'rich in circumstantial detail and reported speech', as opposed to the official records which are 'characteristically terse and uninformative', 'we need to bear constantly in mind that we see that campaign and its personnel almost entirely through the eyes of its victims and opponents' (pp. 102–3).
38. Mush, 'True Report', p. 375.
39. Genelle Gertz, *Heresy Trials and English Women Writers, 1400–1670* (Cambridge University Press, 2012), p. 128. For more on conventions of saints' lives and how Clitherow's biography adheres to these, see: Anne Dillon, *The Construction of Martyrdom in the English Catholic Community, 1535–1603* (Ashgate, 2002).
40. Gertz, *Heresy Trials*, p. 141; Peter Lake and Michael Questier, *The Trials of Margaret Clitherow: Persecution, Martyrdom and the Politics of Sanctity in Elizabethan England* (Continuum, 2011), p. 207, note 1; Dillon, *The Construction*, p. 280; Lake and Questier, *The Trials*, p. 101; Katherine M. Longley, *Saint Margaret Clitherow* (Anthony Clarke, 1986), p. 191.

These critics have remarked on the notable stylistic and linguistic differences between chapters eighteen to twenty, on the one hand, and the rest of *A True Report* on the other. In the first section, for example, the subject of the text is indicated by her name, in the latter, she is only referred to as 'the martyr'.

41. Hutton's 'Notes by a Prisoner' certainly demonstrates that he had knowledge of her incarceration and the time leading up to her death, see William Hutton, 'Notes by a Prisoner in Ousebridge Kidcote', in John Morris (ed.), *The Troubles of our Catholic Forefathers Related by Themselves*, Vol. 3 (Burns and Oates, 1877), pp. 233–330, at 308–10.
42. Dillon, *The Construction*, p. 249.
43. Gertz, *Heresy Trials*, p. 129.
44. Ibid., p. 128.
45. Carole Levin and Patricia A. Sullivan, 'Politics, Women's Voices, and the Renaissance: Questions and Context', in Carole Levin and Patricia A. Sullivan (eds), *Political Rhetoric, Power and Renaissance Women* (State University of New York Press, 1995), pp. 1–14, at 10.
46. Anne Askew, *The First Examination of the Worthy Seruant of God, Maistres Anne Askew* (1560), STC (2nd ed.) / 853, sig. B1r.
47. Gertz, *Heresy Trials*, p. 122.
48. Mush, 'True Report', p. 425.
49. Gertz, *Heresy Trials*, p. 129.
50. Dillon, *The Construction*, p. 298.
51. Christine Peters takes the opposite stance, emphasising the differences between the trial narratives of Clitherow and Askew in particular, arguing that those differences make it difficult to fruitfully compare the two texts (Peters, *Patterns of Piety: Women, Gender and Relation in Late Medieval and Reformation England* (Cambridge University Press, 2003), p. 287).
52. Mush, 'True Report', p. 419.
53. Ibid., p. 374.
54. Christina Luckyj, *'A Moving Rhetoricke', Gender and Silence in Early Modern England* (Manchester University Press, 2002), p. 60.
55. Suzanne Trill, 'Religion and the Construction of Femininity', in Helen Wilcox (ed.), *Women and Literature in Britain, 1500–1700* (Cambridge University Press, 1996), pp. 30–55, at 41.
56. Indeed, some 400 years later the account of Mrs Clitherow's life still divides public opinion, witness the debate between Longley and Juliana Wadham (Longley, 'The "Trial"'; Juliana Wadham, 'Saint Margaret Clitherow: Her Trial on Trial: The Case against Her by Juliana Wadham', *Ampleforth Journal*, 76 (1971): 9–22. See also pp. 7–11 of Lake and Questier's introduction for a more extensive analysis of the debate between Longley and Wadham.
57. Ford, Dekker and Rowley are the only named playwrights; the text itself indicates that the three dramatists collaborated with (unnamed) others as well. All references to the play are taken from Thomas Dekker, John Ford and William Rowley, *The Witch of Edmonton*, ed. by Lucy Munro

(The Arden Shakespeare, 2019); Pauline Rubery-Blanc, '*The Witch of Edmonton*: The Witch next Door or Faustian Anti-Heroine?', in Richard Hillman and Pauline Rubery-Blanc (eds), *Female Transgression in Early Modern Britain: Literary and Historical Explorations* (Ashgate, 2014), pp. 51–69, at 51.

58. Orna Alyagon Darr, *Marks of an Absolute Witch: Evidentiary Dilemmas in Early Modern England* (Ashgate, 2011), p. 7.
59. For more on this public debate, involving lawyers, doctors, villagers and royals, see Darr, *Marks*, pp. 7–8.
60. Henry Goodcole, *The Wonderfull Discouerie of Elizabeth Sawyer a Witch, Late of Edmonton, her Conuiction and Condemnation and Death. Together with the Relation of the Diuels Accesse to Her, and Their Conference Together* (London, 1621), STC 12014, sig. B3v.
61. Thomas counted seven men out of a total of 109 of those executed for witchcraft: Keith Thomas, *Religion and the Decline of Magic: Studies in Popular Beliefs in Sixteenth and Seventeenth Century England* (1971; Weidenfeld and Nicolson, 1980), p. 520; C. L'Estrange Ewen (ed.), *Witch Hunting and Witch Trials: the Indictments for Witchcraft from the Records of 1373 Assizes held for the Home Circuit AD 1559–1736* (Kegan Paul, Trench, Trubner & Co., 1929), pp. 102–8.
62. Dekker, *The Witch*, 2.1.133–4.
63. 1542: 33 Hen. VIII, cap. 8; 1563: 5 Eliz., cap. 16.
64. 1604: 1 Jac. I, c. 12. This statute endured until 1736. Only then did witchcraft cease to be a statutory offence. For a more elaborate discussion of these statutes, see Thomas, *Decline of Magic*, pp. 442–3.
65. Goodcole, *Discouerie*, sig. A4.
66. Randall Martin, *Women, Murder, and Equity in Early Modern England* (Routledge, 2008), p. 24. Angela McShane warns us that we must not overstress the idea of the ballad as 'vehicle of information': although ballads contained information, they were primarily used as examples of wider truths, she argues (Angela McShane, '*The Gazet in Meter; or the Rhyming Newsmonger*. The English Broadside Ballad as Intelligencer. A New Narrative', in Joop W. Koopmans (ed.), *News and Politics in Early Modern Europe* (Peeters, 2005), pp. 131–46.
67. Kirilka Stavreva, *Words Like Daggers: Violent Female Speech in Early Modern England* (University of Nebraska Press, 2015), p. 84, note 38. See also Peter Haining, *The Witchcraft Papers: Contemporary Records of the Witchcraft Hysteria in Essex, 1560–1700* (Robert Hale & Company, 1974), p. 72. The ballad is not on the *English Broadside Ballad Archive*.
68. The text is taken from Peter Haining's *Witchcraft Papers*, pp. 73–5. Haining has selected only a few of all of the verses from the manuscript version (which was in his personal possession at the time), as the manuscript 'is so faded and torn as to make its reproduction in full impossible'. He also notes that he has added 'a few words to complete them, retaining as best as possible the style and intention of the original' (p. 72).

69. Sarah F. Williams, *Damnable Practises: Witches, Dangerous Women, and Music in Seventeenth-Century English Broadside Ballads* (Ashgate, 2015), p. 75.
70. Mary E. Trull, *Performing Privacy and Gender in Early Modern Literature* (Palgrave Macmillan, 2013), p. 85.
71. Goodcole, *Discouerie*, sig. A3v.
72. Christopher Chapman, 'Goodcole, Henry (bap. 1586, d. 1641)', *Oxford Dictionary of National Biography*, Oxford University Press (23 September 2004). Accessed 18 March 2024.
73. Goodcole, *Discouerie*, sig. A3v.
74. See also Todd Butler, 'Swearing Justice in Henry Goodcole and The Witch of Edmonton', *Studies in English Literature 1500–1900*, 50(1) (2010): 127–45, at 130.
75. Goodcole, *Discouerie*, sig. A4v-B1.
76. Ibid., sig. B.
77. Ibid., sig. B.
78. Ibid., sig. D1v.
79. Ibid., sig. D3.
80. Ibid., sig. D2.
81. Ibid., sig. A4, C1.
82. Frances E. Dolan, *True Relations: Reading, Literature, and Evidence in Seventeenth-Century England* (University of Pennsylvania Press, 2013), p. 3. Alex MacConochie suggests that the base facts of Goodcole's account of Sawyer's trial, at least, must be true, as the pamphlet competed with other texts whose 'saleable commodity' was truth (MacConochie, 'Touching on the Margins: Elizabeth Sawyer's Body in Performance and Print', Lisa Hopkins and Aidan Norrie (eds), *Women on the Edge in Early Modern Europe* (Amsterdam University Press, 2019), pp. 93–112, at 95. See also Una McIlvenna, *Singing the New of Death: Execution Ballads in Europe 1500–1900* (Oxford University Press, 2022), particularly chapter 3.
83. Goodcole, *Discouerie*, sig. C1.
84. Ibid., sig. A2.
85. Marion Gibson, *Early Modern Witches: Witchcraft Cases in Contemporary Writing* (Routledge, 2000), p. 299.
86. Arthur F. Kinney, 'Introduction', in Thomas Dekker, John Ford and William Rowley, *The Witch of Edmonton*, ed. by Arthur F. Kinney (1998; A&C Black, 2005), pp. ix–xlii, at xvi.
87. See also Peter Lake, 'Cheap Print, Protestantism and Murder', in Kevin Sharpe and Peter Lake (eds), *Culture and Politics in Early Stuart England* (Macmillan, 1994), pp. 257–83, at 260.
88. Goodcole, *Discouerie*, sig. B3v.
89. Ibid., sig. C2v.
90. Ibid., sig. C3–C3v.
91. Ibid., sig. B4.
92. Kinney, 'Introduction', p. xvi.

93. Ibid., p. xiii.
94. Peter Corbin and Douglas Sedge, 'Introduction', in Peter Corbin and Douglas Sedge (eds), *Three Jacobean Witchcraft Plays: The Tragedy of Sophonisba, The Witch, The Witch of Edmonton* (Manchester University Press: 1986), pp. 1–32, at 21–2.
95. In the play the dog says 'Ho! Have I found thee cursing? Now thou art mine own' (2.1.120); according to Goodcole the dog said '*Oh! haue I now found you cursing, swearing, and blaspheming? now you are mine*' (Goodcole, *Discouerie*, sig. C1v).
96. Goodcole, *Discouerie*, sig. C4v; Dekker, *The Witch*, 2.1.194.
97. Goodcole, *Discouerie*, sig. A4–A4v; Dekker, *The Witch*, 4.1.22–4; 32–3.
98. Corbin and Sedge, 'Introduction', p. 22.
99. Dekker, *The Witch*, 2.1.8–10.
100. Goodcole mentions Sawyer's husband testified during her trial (sig. C4). The qualification of 'Spinster' presumably refers to other work she did alongside selling brooms (Goodcole, *Discouerie*, sig. A4).
101. Helen Vella Bonavita, 'Maids, Wives and Widows: Multiple Meaning and Marriage in The Witch of Edmonton', *Parergon*, 23(2) (2006): 73–95, at 74.
102. Dekker, *The Witch*, 4.1.139–41.
103. Ibid., 2.1.3.
104. Ibid., 4.1.93–5, 4.1.84.
105. Ibid., 2.1.6–8.
106. Goodcole, *Discouerie*, sig. D2v.
107. Dekker, *The Witch*, 5.2.46.
108. Ibid., 5.2.70.
109. Ibid., 4.1.51–3.
110. Margaret Cavendish, 'A True Relation of My Birth, Breeding, and Life', in Sylvia Bowerbank and Sara Mendelson (eds), *Paper Bodies: A Margaret Cavendish Reader* (Broadview Press, 2000), pp. 41–63, at 63.

Conclusion: Shared Strategies in Women's Self-Representation

In 1664 Margaret Fell (1614–1702) appeared before judge Thomas Twisden (1602–1683) of the Lancaster Assizes to answer the charge of holding Quaker meetings. A pamphlet co-authored with George Fox (1624–91),[1] a founder of the Quaker movement who had been imprisoned on similar charges, gave the following account of part of Fell's trial:

> M.F. What law have I broken for worshipping God in my own house?
>
> Judge. What law?
>
> M.F. What law have I broken for worshipping God in my own house?
>
> Judge. The Common Law.
>
> M.F. I thought you had proceeded by a statute. Then the sheriff whispered to him, and mentioned the statute of the 35th of Elizabeth.
>
> Judge. I could tell you of a law, but it is too penal for you, for it might cost you your life.
>
> M.F. I must offer and tender my life and all for my testimony if it be required of me.
>
> Then the latter part of the statute was read to the jury for the Oath of Obedience, and the judge informed the jury and the prisoner concerning the penalty of the statute upon refusal, for it would be to the forfeiture of all her estate real and personal, and imprisonment during life.
>
> M.F. I am a widow and my estate is a dowry, and I have five children unpreferred, and if the King's pleasure be to take my estate from me upon the account of my conscience, and not for any evil or wrong one; let him do as he pleases, and further I desire that I may speak to the jury of the occasion of my being here.
>
> Judge. The jury is to hear nothing, but me to tender you the Oath, and you to refuse it, or take it.[2]

In line with Quaker practice, however, Fell both refused to swear the required Oath of Allegiance and refused to refrain from holding meetings. As a result, the court passed a sentence of *praemunire* against her, which caused all her property to become forfeit to the Crown (though it was never actually confiscated) and ensured her imprisonment till mid-1668.

Upholding her religious beliefs may have cost Fell much in personal terms, but the situation also had its advantages: it allowed Fell and Fox to turn their trial into a public spectacle with which they might gain sympathy and, ultimately, followers for their cause. Richard Bauman has deemed it a 'social drama' – sharing as it does many features with theatrical drama – in which both Fell and Fox 'played strongly to the public and defied the judges in highlighting the agonistic focus of the confrontation'.[3] Fell's legal knowledge, flippant responses to the judge, combative nature and refusal to sacrifice her beliefs all helped to ensure that an audience might feel sympathetic towards her. Just like the women whose legal activities have been the focus of this book, Fell and Fox utilised specific rhetorical and narrative strategies to manipulate their audience. Their account differs from the legal records left by our early modern women in an important way, however: *The examination and tryall of Margaret Fell and George Fox* was published in print. The Quaker community expended no little effort into the publishing and publicising of such trial narratives. By the mid- to late seventeenth century, then, trial narratives were beginning to be seen as a powerful weapon in the constant battle to promote the cause of Quakerism, amongst other things. And the primary thrust of these narratives was the presentation of the lives of the accused as a lesson to posterity.

Fell was not the only Quaker woman who recounted her troubles with the law and law enforcement in printed form, as the medium quickly found favour among women who felt themselves to be persecuted by the courts. Priscilla Cotton and Mary Cole (fl. 1650s/60s) were imprisoned for promoting their Quaker beliefs in public. During their stay in Exeter prison, they co-authored their joint tract *To the Priests and People of England, we discharge our consciences and give them warning* (1655). This tract contains the only detailed biographical information available for these two women.[4] In this piece, Cotton and Cole make a case for women's preaching – the very offence that landed them in prison – arguing that the prohibition against women's public speech is not directed at *all* women, but only the weak: 'Here mayest thou see from the Scriptures, that the woman or weakness, whether male or female, is forbidden to speak in the church'.[5] To their eyes weakness can occur in either sex, as can the strength to preach in church:

> Indeed, you yourselves are the women that are forbidden to speak in the church, that are become women; for two of your priests came to speak with us, and when they could not bear sound reproof and wholesome doctrine that did concern them, they railed on us with filthy speeches, as no other they can give to us, that deal plainly and singly with them, and so ran from us.

In this re-assignment of gender roles, Cotton and Cole stake out their own position and redefine the rules of public speech and authority in the scriptures and word of God. In their closing remarks, the two Quaker women ask that their audience be allowed 'in all your consciences to judge of what we have writ', feeling confident that they have been persuasive. Their status as 'prisoners' may appear to have rendered them passive, but their respect 'for the word of God' sees them taking control of their defence. As Caroline Baker has explained, 'Quakerism allowed women to express their experiences, assessing and recording in detail their own lives',[6] and because as much as 45 per cent of all writings published by women in the 1650s was from the pens of Quaker women, it appears that very many of them made full use of their opportunity.[7] It was as a result of the opposition these women faced, the efforts that were made to ensure their silence, as well as, of course, the falling away of censorship, that they found the means to defend themselves in the most public and persistent of media: print.

In the printed accounts of these women's trial narratives and accounts of their imprisonment, we can trace some of the rhetorical and narrative strategies used by earlier litigants. These include the *ad hominem* attack, strategies of elision and alignment with the biblical widow. These strategies were so successful – or perhaps so intuitive to women as members of society used to negotiating their passage around certain expectations – that later seventeenth-century life-writers adopted these techniques in their own texts, both in manuscript and in printed form. While the legal and societal restrictions on women limited their room to manoeuvre, both in terms of their activities and speech within society and their self-representation in the courts of law, they also forced them to find a way to represent themselves and their life experiences. By navigating their way through a society dominated by male cultural and literary norms, women came to express themselves in the courtroom. By the later seventeenth century, the Quakers had come to appreciate the opportunities legal accounts could offer, inspired, no doubt, by the accounts of Marian Protestants in Foxe's *Book of Martyrs* roughly a century earlier. The mode of self-representation available to women, in particular, held so much promise that Quaker women started to use it in print, and with not only men's approval, but even their encouragement.[8]

The aim of this book has been to show that early modern English women left traces of their lives in legal documents – records not normally included within the critical framework of 'life-writing'. What is more, the courts could, in certain cases, offer women *more* freedom to account for themselves than traditional forms of life-writing could. Restrictions of a medium like the spiritual diary ensured that victims of domestic abuse, for instance, were more or less forced to explore their own sins, while the courts and the antagonistic nature of legal procedures gave those women a voice with which they could counter their abusers. As such, the courts had their own ways of allowing women to speak for themselves, making it necessary to place their records beside other forms of life-writing when trying to trace women's life stories. This also serves to remind us that each genre has its own conventions and that fiction plays a role in the life-writing found in legal records as well as that in autobiographies and diaries: none of these forms of self-accounting is free of mediation or conformation to their generic or institutional form.

Following the lead of life-writers such as Anne, Lady Halkett, who adjusted her self-portrayals to take her changing marital status into account, this book has focused on the differing modes of self-portrayal employed by women as they negotiated their ways through the three main stages in their life: maids, wives and widows. These three parts of the life-cycle were supplemented with accounts related to women's sexual reputations and their afterlives. What we have seen allows us to draw the following conclusions about women's legal status during these different life stages and how particular features of these stages necessarily shaped the way they could, and would, present themselves in the legal context.

The claim in *The Lawes Resolution of Womens Rights* (1632), that women were understood either as 'married or to be married', emphasises just how important marriage was in understanding how a woman was viewed in the early modern period, whether by herself, by her peers or by society at large.[9] Finding a suitable partner was therefore a key occupation of single women. Should a courtship fail, however, the behaviour of the woman during the romance's downfall was heavily scrutinised: too vile a treatment of the ex-suitor could prevent others from courting the jilted or jilting woman. With an eye to protecting themselves for future matches, women suing and being sued over courtship cases sought to only subtly discredit their male opponents while carefully defending their own reputations. This careful rhetorical balancing act stood in stark contrast with the more aggressive and malicious attacks made by women suing for alimony or separation. Occasion thus shaped a woman's self-portrayal. Rather than letting the legal system restrain them, maids and wives knew how to work it to their advantage by creating records that allowed them to vindicate their choices in crucial matters surrounding marriage.

Whether they were maids or wives or even widows, a woman's sexual reputation always had to be safeguarded. Although women did not refrain from talking about sex, this was usually done in relation to others. Talking about one's own sexual activities was done with more reluctance and embarrassment. It is absent from autobiographical texts, and when insisted upon in court, it is only mentioned in an evasive manner: by leaving gaps in the story and by blaming others. Using language free of sexual references allowed women accused of fornication to hope that reputations could be saved and punishment avoided. Their full understanding of the severity of sexual impropriety taught women to diminish their own part in sexual activities when talking about it: a chaste tongue begat a chaste soul, just as an immoderate tongue merely attracted accusations and approbation.

The legal shackles that governed the life of a married woman fell away on the death of her spouse. Although this could lead to a newfound sense of legal freedom, societal pressure still abounded and encouraged women to portray themselves in relation to their late husbands. Widows could model themselves as biblical widow, eternal wife, *feme sole* or, if they had children, mother. The choice of model would depend on the task at hand, and widows could invoke a different model in each individual situation, even to the point of invoking a plurality of selves. Where legal records left no space for widows to explore the different aspects of their identity, forcing them to choose between the various options, diaries and autobiographies allowed women to shift between their different personas within the same text, or across their various texts, foregrounding the idea that a widow's identity was multifold.

Upon their deathbeds, many women instructed their family members or the executors of their last will and testament to destroy their autobiographical traces after their deaths. Legal records, by contrast, are not as vulnerable to such whims: once part of the public record, such records would remain in the archive for perpetuity unless some accident or the vicissitudes of time intervened. On the one hand this allows modern-day scholars to work with such sources, but it also means these documents are open to interpretation and appropriation by others. If the original legal documentation is no longer extant, any new version of events can come to obliterate the 'true' story, especially if it bears the specious authority of contemporaneity. It can even bring into existence yet another alternative version of events. Such a proliferation of 'truths' often marks a shift from the legal domain to the literary sphere: what was once an autobiographical story can be eclipsed and replaced by alternative realities. When a woman's story does move out of the court and into the public sphere, control was often asserted over it by a man. In the courtroom, conversely, women were able to remain, at least partly, in control of their story, despite the mediation of lawyers or clerks. As such, the courts of law were particularly fertile grounds for the sowing and production of women's stories.

Regardless of life stage, women's modes of self-representation in the legal archives are united by some general strategies, strategies notably distinct from the kinds of 'self-fashioning' employed by canonical male writers as discussed by Georges Gusdorf and Stephen Greenblatt. This unity of strategy allows us to use legal records to study the lives of hitherto marginalised (poor and illiterate) women, and thus we are bound to include such records in the critical framework that is 'life-writing'. The relative paucity of female-authored texts can even be supplemented with many more documents, if we accept that the idea of a single author in the early modern period is more often than not mere fiction. Reading legal records as an arena in which women could, and did, assert themselves as individuals allows us to better understand the subtle but influential ways in which women shaped the early modern literary sphere.

Notes

1. See David Booy's *Autobiographical Writings by Early Quaker Women* (Ashgate, 2004) for more on the exact attribution of authorship of this pamphlet (p. 155, footnote 26).
2. Booy, *Autobiographical Writings*, p. 156.
3. Richard Bauman, *Let Your Words Be Few: Symbolism of Speaking and Silence among Seventeenth-Century Quakers* (Cambridge University Press, 1983), pp. 104; 114.
4. Paul Salzman, 'Introduction', in Paul Salzman (ed.), *Early Modern Women's Writing: An Anthology, 1560–1700* (Oxford University Press, 2000), pp. ix–xxxi, at xxii.
5. All quotes from Priscilla Cotton and Mary Cole, *To the Priests and People of England, we discharge our consciences and give them warning*, in Salzman (ed.), *Anthology*, pp. 142–7, at 147.
6. Caroline Baker, 'An Exploration of Quaker Women's Writing Between 1650 and 1700', *Journal of International Women's Studies*, Vol. 5, No. 2 March 2004, pp. 8–20.
7. Richard Bell and Patricia Crawford, 'Appendix 2: Statistical Analysis of Women's Printed Writings 1600–1700', in Mary Prior (ed.), *Women in English Society, 1500–1800* (Methuen, 1985), pp. 265–74, Table 7.3 at 269.
8. Phyllis Mack suggests that the Quakers were the religious society 'most receptive to the spiritual authority of women' of all the religious groups appearing between 1640–1660 (*Visionary Women: Ecstatic Prophecy in Seventeenth-Century England* (University of California Press, 1992), p.1).
9. T. E., *The Lawes Resolutions of Womens Rights* (London, 1632), STC 7437, p. 6.

Bibliography

Manuscript Sources

Cheshire Record Office
CR 63/2/19, Commonplace book of W. Davenport

Chichester, West Sussex Record Office
Diocese and Archdeaconry of EP/ Court Records
EP/I/11, Deposition Books, 1557–1694

Edinburgh, Scotland, National Library of Scotland
MS 6489–6502, Meditations of Anne, Lady Halkett

Kew, The National Archives
Court of Chancery
C 5, Six Clerks Office Pleadings, 1613–1714

Court of Requests
Req 1, Books, 1492–1643
Req 2, Pleadings, 1485–1649

Court of Star Chamber
STAC 7, Proceedings, 1558–1603
STAC 8, Proceedings, 1558–1649

Prerogative Court of Canterbury and related Probate Jurisdictions
PROB 11, Will Registers, 1384–1858

London, British Library
Add MS 4454, Diary of Katherine Austen
Add MS 47608, Papers relating to Mary Fenwick
Add MS 32376, Diary of Anne Halkett

London, Bethlem Hospital Royal Archives
Court of Governors
BCB, Minutes of the Court of Governors, 1559–1658

London, Lambeth Palace Library
Court of Arches
Arches A, Acts Books, 1635–1773
Arches E, Pleas, 1660–1799
Arches Eee, Depositions, 1661–1855

London, London Metropolitan Archives
Diocese of London Consistory Court
DL/C, Court Records, 1467–1972

Perdita Online Database
Sarah Cowper, *Diary*
Anne, Lady Halkett, *Meditations*

Printed Primary Sources

Askew, Anne, *The First Examination of the Worthy Seruant of God, Maistres Anne Askew* (1560), STC (2nd ed.) / 853

Austen, Katherine, 'Book M', in Pamela S. Hammons (ed.), *Book M: A London Widow's Life Writings* (Iter Inc., 2013)

Austen, Katherine, *Book M: British Library, Additional Manuscript 4454*, ed. by Sarah C. E. Ross (ACMRS, 2011)

Beadle, John, *The Journal or Diary of a Thankful Christian* (London, 1656), archive.org/details/journalor00bead

Bruce, Thomas, *Memoirs of Thomas, Earl of Ailesbury*, ed. by W. E. Buckley, Vol. 2, Roxburghe Club 122 (Nichols and Sons, 1890)

Bruto, Giovanni Michele, *The Necessarie, Fit, and Convenient Education of a Young Gentlewoman* (London: 1598), STC 3947

Caesar, Julius, *The Ancient State, Authoritie, and Proceedings of the Court* (1596), STC (2nd ed.) / 4341

Cavendish, Margaret, 'A True Relation of My Birth, Breeding, and Life', in Sylvia Bowerbank and Sara Mendelson (eds), *Paper Bodies: A Margaret Cavendish Reader* (Broadview Press, 2000), pp. 41–63

Chamberlain, John, *The Letters of John Chamberlain*, ed. by Norman Egbert McClure, Vol. 2 (The American Philosophical Society, 1939)

Chapman, George, *The Widow's Tears*, ed. by Akihiro Yamada (Methuen, 1975)

Clifford, Anne, *Anne Clifford's Autobiographical Writing, 1590–1676*, ed. by Jessica L. Malay (Manchester University Press, 2018)

Clifford, Anne, *The Diaries of Lady Anne Clifford*, ed. by D. J. H. Clifford (The History Press, 2005)

Clifford, Anne, *The Diary of Anne Clifford, 1616–1619*, ed. by Katherine Acheson (Garland Publishing, 1995)

Coke, Sir Edward, *The First Part of the Institutes of the Lawes of England* (1628; London, 1629), STC (2nd ed.) / 15785

Cotton, Priscilla and Mary Cole, *To the Priests and People of England, we discharge our consciences and give them warning*, in Paul Salzman (ed.), *Early Modern Women's Writing: An Anthology, 1560–1700* (Oxford University Press, 2000), pp. 142–7

Culpeper, Nicholas, *A Directory for Midwives: or, a Guide for Women, in Their Conception, Bearing, and Suckling Their Children, etc.* (1651; London, 1693), C7495

Cunningham, Margaret, *A Pairt of the Life of Lady Margaret Cuninghame that She Had with her First Husband, the Master of Evandale, as it Was at First Written with Her Own Hand*, ed. by C. K. Sharpe (James Ballantque and Co., 1824)

Cutpurse, Moll, 'The Life and Death of Mal Cutpurse', in Janet Todd and Elizabeth Spearing (eds), *Counterfeit Ladies* (William Pickering, 1994), pp. 1–73

Dekker, Thomas, John Ford, and William Rowley, *The Witch of Edmonton*, ed. by Lucy Munro (The Arden Shakespeare, 2019)

Delaval, Elizabeth, *The Meditations of Lady Elizabeth Delaval, Written Between 1662 and 1671*, ed. by Douglas G. Green (Northumberland Press Limited, 1978)

Donne, John, *Letters to Severall* Persons *of Honour* (London, 1651), Wing D1864

E., T., *The Lawes Resolution of Womens Rights* (London: 1632), STC 7437

Fanshawe, Ann, 'The Memoirs of Ann, Lady Fanshawe', in John Loftis (ed.), *The Memoirs of Anne, Lady Halkett and Ann, Lady Fanshaw* (Clarendon Press, 1979)

Finch, Anne, *The Poems of Anne Finch, Countess of Winchelsea*, ed. by Myra Reynolds (University of Chicago Press, 1903)

Goodcole, Henry, *The Wonderfull Discouerie of Elizabeth Sawyer a Witch, Late of Edmonton, her Conuiction and Condemnation and Death. Together with the Relation of the Diuels Accesse to Her, and Their Conference Together* (London, 1621), STC 12014

Gouge, William, *Of Domesticall Duties* (London, 1622), STC 12119

Gouge, William, *Of Domesticall Duties* (London, 1622), facsimile reproduction in *The English Experience*, Number 803 (Walter J. Johnson, Inc., 1976)

Halkett, Anne, *The Autobiography of Anne Lady Halkett*, ed. by John Gough Nichols (Camden Society, 1875)

Halkett, Anne, 'Memoirs', in John Loftis (ed.), *The Memoirs of Anne, Lady Halkett and Ann, Lady Fanshawe* (Clarendon Press, 1979)

Halkett, Anne, 'Ocational Meditations and Select Contemplations, 1668–1670/1', in Suzanne Trill (ed.), *Lady Anne Halkett: Selected Self-Writings* (Ashgate, 2007)

Halkett, Anne, 'Occationall Meditations, 1660–63', in Trill (ed.), *Lady Anne Halkett*

Halkett, Anne, 'The Autobiography of Anne, Lady Halkett, 1677–78', in Trill (ed.), *Lady Anne Halkett*

Halkett, Anne, 'The Widows Mite, & Occationall Meditations, 1673–41', in Trill (ed.), *Lady Anne Halkett*

Hudson, William, *A Treatise of the Court of Star Chamber* (Legal Classics Library, 1986)

Hutchinson, Lucy, 'Life of Mrs. Hutchinson', in Lucy Hutchinson, *Memoirs of the Life of Colonel Hutchinson, Written by his Widow Lucy*, ed. by Harold Child (Kegan Paul Trench Trubner, 1904, pp. 17–34)

Hutchinson, Lucy, *Memoirs of the Life of Colonel Hutchinson, Written by his Widow Lucy*, ed. by Harold Child (Kegan Paul Trench Trubner, 1904)

Hutton, William, 'Notes by a Prisoner in Ousebridge Kidcote', in John Morris (ed.), *The Troubles of our Catholic Forefathers Related by Themselves*, Vol. 3 (Burns and Oates, 1877), pp. 233–330

Jonson, Ben, *The Staple of News*, ed. by Anthony Parr (Manchester University Press, 1999)

Kempe, Margery, *The Book of Margery Kempe: An Abridged Translation*, ed. by Liz Herbert McAvoy (D. S. Brewer, 2003)

Middleton, Thomas, 'The Widow', in Gary Taylor and John Lavagnino (eds), *Thomas Middleton: The Collected Works* (Clarendon Press, 2010)

Mush, John, 'A True Report of the Life and Martyrdom of Mrs. Margaret Clitherow', in John Morris (ed.), *The Troubles of Our Catholic Forefathers, Related by Themselves*, Vol. 3 (Burns and Oates, 1877), pp. 360–440

Pepys, Samuel, *The Diary of Samuel Pepys: A New and Complete Transcription,* Vol. V, ed. by Robert Latham and William Matthews (G. Bell and Sons Ltd, 1971)

Pepys, Samuel, *The Diary of Samuel Pepys: A New and Complete Transcription*, Vol. IX, ed. by Robert Latham and William Matthews (Bell and Hyman, 1986)

Primaudaye, Peter de la, *The French Academie* (London, 1586), STC 15233

Rich, Barnabe, *The Excellency of Good Women* (London, 1613), STC 20982

Shakespeare, William, *All's Well that Ends Well*, in John Jowett, William Montgomery, Gary Taylor and Stanley Wells (eds), *The Oxford Shakespeare: The Complete Works*, 2nd ed. (Oxford University Press, 2005)

Shakespeare, William, *Measure for Measure*, in John Jowett, William Montgomery, Gary Taylor and Stanley Wells (eds), *The Oxford Shakespeare: The Complete Works*, 2nd ed. (Oxford University Press, 2005)

Smith, Henry, *A Preparative to Marriage* (London, 1591), STC 22686
Thornton, Alice Wandesford, *The Autobiography of Alice Thornton: Of East Newton, County, York* (Andrews and Co., 1875)
Verstegan, Richard, *Theatrum Crudelitatum Haereticorum Nostri Temporis* (Antwerp, 1587)
Webster, John, *The Duchess of Malfi*, ed. by Leah S. Marcus (The Arden Shakespeare, 2009)
West, William, *Of Symboleography the Second Part* (London, 1597), STC (2nd ed.) / 25277
Wilson, Thomas, *Arte of Rhetorique*, ed. by Thomas J. Derrick (Garland Publishing, Inc., 1982)

Secondary Sources

Ahnert, Ruth, 'Imitating Inquisition: Dialectical Bias in Protestant Prison Writings', in Mary C. Flannery and Katie L. Walter (eds), *The Culture of Inquisition in Medieval England* (D. S. Brewer, 2013), pp. 146–63
Akkerman, Nadine, *Invisible Agents: Women and Espionage in Seventeenth-Century Britain* (Oxford University Press, 2018)
Alfar, Cristina León, *Women and Shakespeare's Cuckoldry Plays: Shifting Narratives of Marital Betrayal* (Routledge, 2017)
Almasy, Rudolph P., 'Anne Askew Constructing Her Text, Constructing Her Self', *Reformation*, 10(1) (2005): 1–20
Amussen, Susan, '"Being Stirred to Much Unquietness": Violence and Domestic Violence in Early Modern England', *Journal of Women's History*, 6(2) (1994): 70–89
Amussen, Susan D. and David E. Underdown, *Gender, Culture and Politics in England, 1560–1640: Turning the World Upside Down* (Bloomsbury, 2017)
Anselment, Raymond A., 'Feminine Self-Reflection and the Seventeenth-Century Occasional Meditation', *Seventeenth Century*, 26(1) (2011): 69–93
Anselment, Raymond A., 'Katherine Austen and the Widow's Might', *Journal of Early Modern Cultural Studies*, 5(1) (2005): 5–25
Anselment, Raymond A., '"My first Booke of my Life:" The Apology of a Seventeenth-Century Gentry Woman', *Prose Studies*, 24(2) (2001): 1–14
Anselment, Raymond A., 'Seventeenth-Century Manuscript Sources of Alice Thornton's Life', *Studies in English Literature*, 45(1) (2005): 135–55
Arnold, John H., *Inquisition and Power: Catharism and the Confessing Subject in Medieval Languedoc* (University of Pennsylvania Press, 2001)
Avery, Margaret Elizabeth, 'Proceedings in the Court of Chancery up to *c.*1460' (PhD dissertation, University of London, 1958)
Bailey, Joanne, *Unquiet Lives: Marriage and Marriage Breakdown in England, 1660–1800* (Cambridge University Press, 2003)

Bailey, Joanne, 'Voices in Court: Lawyers' or Litigants'?', *Historical Research*, 74 (2001): 392–408

Baker, Caroline, 'An Exploration of Quaker Women's Writing Between 1650 and 1700', *Journal of International Women's Studies*, 5(2) (2004): 8–20

Baker, J. H., *An Introduction to English Legal History*, 4th ed. (Oxford University Press, 2007)

Bal, Mieke, *Narratology: An Introduction to the Theory of Narrative*, 4th ed. (1985; University of Toronto Press, 2017)

Ball, R. M., 'The King's Remembrancer's Office in the Eighteenth Century', *Journal of Legal History*, 11 (1990): 90–113

Barahona, Renato, *Sex Crimes, Honour, and the Law in Early Modern Spain: Vizcaya, 1528–1735* (University of Toronto Press, 2003)

Barclay, Katie, *Love, Intimacy and Power: Marriage and Patriarchy in Scotland, 1650–1850* (Manchester University Press, 2011)

Bauman, Richard, *Let Your Words Be Few: Symbolism of Speaking and Silence among Seventeenth-Century Quakers* (Cambridge University Press, 1983)

Beal, Peter, *A Dictionary of English Manuscript Terminology, 1450–2000* (Oxford University Press, 2008)

Beattie, Cordelia, 'Choosing Chancery? Women's Petitions to the Late Medieval Court of Chancery', in Teresa Phipps and Deborah Youngs (eds), *Litigating Women: Gender and Justice in Europe, c.1300–c.1800* (Routledge, 2021), pp. 99–115

Beattie, Cordelia, '"Living as a Single Person": Marital Status, Performance and the Law in Late Medieval England', *Women's History Review*, 17(3) (2008): 327–40

Beattie, Cordelia, 'Single Women, Work, and Family: The Chancery Dispute of Jane Wynde and Margaret Clerk', in Michael Goodich (ed.), *Voices From the Bench: The Narratives of Lesser Folk in Medieval Trials* (Palgrave Macmillan, 2006), pp. 177–202

Beattie, Cordelia, 'Your Oratrice: Women's Petitions to the Late Medieval Court of Chancery', in Bronach Kane and Fiona Williamson (eds), *Women, Agency and the Law, 1300–1700* (Pickering & Chatto, 2013), pp. 17–30

Beattie, Cordelia, Suzanne Trill, Joanne Edge, and Sharon Howard, 'Alice Thornton's Books: Remembrances of a Woman's Life in the Seventeenth Century', *Alice Thornton's Books*. https://thornton.kdl.kcl.ac.uk/

Beilin, Elaine V., 'A Woman of All Seasons: The Reinvention of Anne Askew', in Pamela Joseph Benson and Victoria Kirkham (eds), *Strong Voices, Weak History: Early Women Writers and Canons in England, France, and Italy* (University of Michigan Press, 2005), pp. 341–64

Bell, H. E., *An Introduction to the History and Records of the Court of Wards and Liveries* (Cambridge University Press, 1953)

Bell, Richard and Patricia Crawford, 'Appendix 2: Statistical Analysis of Women's Printed Writings 1600–1700', in Mary Prior (ed.), *Women in English Society, 1500–1800* (Methuen, 1985), pp. 265–74

Bellany, Alastair, 'Cecil, Anne, Lady Ros', *ODNB*

Bellany, Alastair, *The Politics of Court Scandal in Early Modern England: News Culture and the Overbury Affair, 1603–1660* (Cambridge University Press, 2002)

Bellany, Alastair and Andrew McRae (eds), 'Early Stuart Libels: An Edition of Poetry from Manuscript Sources', *Early Modern Literary Sources Text Series I* (2005), http://purl.oclc.org/emls/texts/libels/

Benstock, Shari, 'Authorizing the Autobiographical', in Shari Benstock (ed.), *The Private Self: Theory and Practice of Women's Autobiographical Writings* (Routledge, 1988), pp. 10–33

Birch, Dominic, 'Legal Pluralism in Early Modern England and Colonial Virginia', *Journal of Institutional Studies*, 5(2) (2019): 717–46

Bonavita, Helen Vella, 'Maids, Wives and Widows: Multiple Meaning and Marriage in The Witch of Edmonton', *Parergon*, 23(2) (2006): 73–95

Booy, David, *Autobiographical Writings by Early Quaker Women* (Ashgate, 2004)

Botonaki, Effie, *Seventeenth-Century English Women's Autobiographical Writings, Disclosing Enclosures* (The Edwin Mellen Press, 2004)

Botonaki, Effie, 'Seventeenth-Century Englishwomen's Spiritual Diaries: Self-Examination, Covenanting, and Account Keeping', *The Sixteenth-Century Journal*, 30(1) (1999): 3–21

Bowen, Lloyd, 'Genre, Authorship and Authenticity in the Petitions of Civil War Veterans and Widows from North Wales and the Marches', in Waddell and Peacey (eds), *The Power of Petitioning*, pp. 33–60

Brayman Hackel, Heidi, *Reading Material in Early Modern England: Print, Gender, and Literacy* (Cambridge University Press, 2005)

Brayman Hackel, Heidi and Catherine E. Kelly, 'Introduction', in Heidi Brayman Hackel and Catherine E. Kelly (eds), *Literacy, Authorship, and Culture in the Atlantic World, 1500–1800* (University of Pennsylvania Press, 2008), pp. 1–10

Brodsky, Vivien, 'Widows in Late Elizabethan London: Remarriage, Economic Opportunity and Family Orientations', in Lloyd Bonfield, Richard M. Smith and Keith Wrightson (eds), *The World We Have Gained: Histories of Population and Social Structure* (Basil Blackwell, 1986), pp. 122–54

Brodzki, Bella, 'Gender and Life Writing', in Margaretta Jolly (ed.), *Encyclopedia of Life Writing: Autobiographical and Biographical Forms*, Vol. 1 (Fitzroy Dearborn Publishers, 2001), p. 870

Brodzki, Bella, 'Testimony', in Margaretta Jolly (ed.), *Encyclopedia of Life Writing: Autobiographical and Biographical Forms*, Vol. 2 (Fitzroy Dearborn Publishers, 2001), pp. 870–1

Brodzki, Bella and Celeste Schenck, 'Introduction', in Bella Brodzki and Celeste Schenck (eds), *Life/Lines: Theorizing Women's Autobiography* (Cornell University Press, 1988), pp. 1–15

Brooks, C. W., *Pettyfoggers and Vipers of the Commonwealth: the 'Lower Branch' of the Legal Profession in Early Modern England* (Cambridge University Press, 1986)

Bunker, Nancy Mohrlock, *Marriage and Land Law in Shakespeare and Middleton* (Fairleigh Dickinson University Press, 2014)
Burke, Victoria E., 'Manuscript Miscellanies', in Laura Knoppers (ed.), *Cambridge Companion to Early Modern Women's Writing* (Cambridge University Press, 2009), pp. 54–67
Burton, Gideon O., 'synonymia', *Silva Rhetoricae*, http://rhetoric.byu.edu
Butler, Todd, 'Swearing Justice in Henry Goodcole and The Witch of Edmonton', *Studies in English Literature 1500–1900*, 50(1) (2010): 127–45
Campbell, Kenneth L., *Windows into Men's Souls: Religious Nonconformity in Tudor and Early Stuart England* (Lexington Books, 2012)
'Canons (1604), Section C', www.anglican.net/doctrines/1604-canon-law
Capp, Bernard, 'The Double Standard Revisited: Plebeian Women and Male Sexual Reputation in Early Modern England', *Past & Present*, 162 (1999): 70–100
Capp, Bernard, *When Gossips Meet: Women, Family, and Neighbourhood in Early Modern England* (Oxford University Press, 2003)
Chadwick, Mary, Daniel Patterson and Jessica Malay, 'Autobiographical Acts in Seventeenth-Century English Petitioning', *Journal for Early Modern Cultural Studies*, 22(1) (2022): 84–106
Chandler, Abby, *Law and Sexual Misconduct in New England, 1650–1750: Steering Toward England* (Routledge, 2015)
Chapman, Christopher, 'Goodcole, Henry', *ODNB*
Cioni, Maria L., *Women and Law in Elizabethan England with Particular Reference to the Court of Chancery* (Garland Publishing, 1985)
Clarke, Danielle, 'Producing Gender: Mary Sidney Herbert and Her Early Editors', in Sarah C. E. Ross and Paul Salzman (eds), *Editing Early Modern Women* (Cambridge University Press, 2016), pp. 40–59
Clarke, Helen I., *Social Legislation* (Appleton-Century-Crofts, 1957)
Cockburn, J. S., *A History of English Assizes, 1558–1714* (Cambridge University Press, 1972)
Coolahan, Marie-Louise, 'Redeeming Parcels of Time: Aesthetics and Practice of Occasional Meditation', *The Seventeenth Century*, 22(1) (2007): 124–43
Corbin, Peter and Douglas Sedge, 'Introduction', in Peter Corbin and Douglas Sedge (eds), *Three Jacobean Witchcraft Plays: The Tragedy of Sophonisba, The Witch, The Witch of Edmonton* (Manchester University Press, 1986), pp. 1–32
Corbin, Peter and Douglas Sedge (eds), *Three Jacobean Witchcraft Plays: The Tragedy of Sophonisba, The Witch, The Witch of Edmonton* (Manchester University Press, 1986)
Cormack, Bradin, *A Power to Do Justice: Jurisdiction, English Literature, and the Rise of Common Law, 1509–1625* (Chicago University Press, 2007)
Costley King'oo, Clare, 'Authenticity and Excess in The Examinations of Anne Askew', *Reformation*, 19(1) (2014): 21–39

Crawford, Patricia, 'Women's Published Writings 1600–1700', in Mary Prior (ed.), *Women in English Society 1500–1800* (Routledge, 1985), pp. 211–82

Cressy, David, *Birth, Marriage, and Death: Ritual, Religion, and the Life-Cycle in Tudor and Stuart England* (1997; Oxford University Press, 2002)

Cressy, David, *Dangerous Talk: Scandalous, Seditious, and Treasonable Speech in Pre-Modern England* (Oxford University Press, 2010)

Cressy, David, *Literacy and the Social Order: Reading and Writing in Tudor and Stuart England* (Cambridge University Press, 1980)

Crick, Julia and Alexandra Walsham, 'Introduction', in Julia Crick and Alexandra Walsham (eds), *The Uses of Script and Print, 1300–1700* (Cambridge University Press, 2004), pp. 1–28

Cross, Claire, 'An Elizabethan Martyrologist and his Martyr: John Mush and Margaret Clitherow', in Diana Wood (ed.), *Martyrs and Martyrologies* (Blackwell Publishers, 1993), pp. 271–81

Cusack, Bridget (ed.), *Everyday English 1500–1700: A Reader* (Edinburgh University Press, 2006)

Dabhoiwala, Faramerz, *The Origins of Sex: A History of the First Sexual Revolution* (Oxford University Press, 2012)

Darr, Orna Alyagon, *Marks of an Absolute Witch: Evidentiary Dilemmas in Early Modern England* (Ashgate, 2011)

Davis, Natalie Zemon, 'Boundaries and the Sense of Self in Sixteenth-Century France', in Thomas C. Heller, Morton Sosna and David E. Wellbery (eds), *Reconstructing Individualism: Autonomy, Individuality, and the Self in Western Thought* (Stanford University Press, 1988), pp. 53–63

Davis, Natalie Zemon, *Fiction in the Archives* (Stanford University Press, 1987)

Daybell, James, *Women Letter-Writers in Tudor England* (Oxford University Press, 2006)

Delany, Paul, *British Autobiography in the Seventeenth Century* (Routledge & Kegan Paul, 1969)

Dillon, Anne, *The Construction of Martyrdom in the English Catholic Community, 1535–1603* (Ashgate, 2002)

Dixon, Peter (ed.), *The Country Wife and Other Plays* (Oxford University Press, 1996)

Dodd, Gwilym, 'Writing Wrongs: The Drafting of Supplications to the Crown in Later Fourteenth-Century England', *Medium Aevum*, 80(2) (2011): 217–46

Dolan, Frances E., *Dangerous Familiars: Representations of Domestic Crime in England, 1550–1700* (Cornell University Press, 1994)

Dolan, Frances E., *True Relations: Reading, Literature, and Evidence in Seventeenth-Century England* (University of Pennsylvania Press, 2013)

Doll, Dan and Jessica Munns, 'Introduction', in Dan Doll and Jessica Munns (eds), *Recording and Reordering: Essays on the Seventeenth- and Eighteenth-Century Diary and Journal* (Rosemont Publishing & Printing Corp., 2006), pp. 9–21

Dowd, Michelle M. and Julie A. Eckerle, 'Introduction', in Michelle M. Dowd and Julie A. Eckerle (eds), *Genre and Women's Life Writing in Early Modern England* (Ashgate, 2007), pp. 1–13

Dowd, Michelle M. and Julie A. Eckerle, 'Recent Studies in Early Modern English Life Writing', *English Literary Renaissance*, 40(1) (2010): 132–62

Duffy, Eamon, *Fires of Faith: Catholic England Under Mary Tudor* (Yale University Press, 2010)

Dunn, Caroline, *Stolen Women in Medieval England: Rape, Abduction, and Adultery, 1100–1500* (Cambridge University Press, 2013)

Eckerle, Julie A., *Romancing the Self in Early Modern Englishwomen's Life Writing* (Ashgate Publishing Limited, 2013)

Egan, Clare, 'Women and the Performance of Libel in Early-Modern Devon', *Medieval English Theatre*, 38 (2017): 145--62

Elk, Martine van, 'The Counterfeit Vagrant: The Dynamics of Deviance in the Bridewell Court Records and the Literature of Roguery', in Craig Donne and Steve Mentz (eds), *Rogues and Early Modern English Culture* (University of Michigan Press, 2004), pp. 120–39

Erickson, Amy Louise, 'Property and Widowhood in England 1660–1840', in Sandra Cavallo and Lyndan Warner (eds), *Widowhood in Medieval and Early Modern Europe* (Pearson Education Limited, 1999), pp. 145–63

Erickson, Amy Louise, *Women and Property in Early Modern England* (Routledge, 1993)

Ewen, C. L'Estrange (ed.), *Witch Hunting and Witch Trials: the Indictments for Witchcraft from the Records of 1373 Assizes held for the Home Circuit AD 1559–1736* (Kegan Paul, Trench, Trubner & Co., 1929)

Ezell, Margaret J. M., 'Elizabeth Delaval's Spiritual Heroine: Thoughts on Redefining Manuscript Texts by Early Women Writers', in Peter Beal and Jeremy Griffiths (eds), *English Manuscript Studies 1100–1700*, Volume 3 (University of Toronto Press, 1992), pp. 216–37

Ezell, Margaret J. M., *Social Authorship and the Advent of Print* (Johns Hopkins University Press, 1999)

Ezell, Margaret J. M., 'The Posthumous Publication of Women's Manuscripts and the History of Authorship', in George L. Justice and Nathan Tinker (eds), *Women's Writing and the Circulation of Ideas: Manuscript Publication in England, 1550–1800* (Cambridge University Press, 2002), pp. 121–36

Ezell, Margaret J. M., '"To Be Your Daughter in Your Pen": The Social Functions of Literature in the Writings of Lady Elizabeth Brackley and Lady Jane Cavendish', *Huntington Library Quarterly*, 51(4) (1988): 281–96

Farge, Arlette, *The Allure of the Archives*, trans. by Thomas Scott-Railton (Yale University Press, 2013)

Ferguson, Margaret W. and Mihoko Suzuki, 'Women's Literacies and Social Hierarchy in Early Modern England', *Literature Compass*, 12(11) (2015): 575–90

Fikkers, Lotte, 'Early Modern Women in the English Courts of Law', *Literature Compass*, 15(12) (2018): doi.org/10.1111/lic3.12499

Firth, C. H. and R. S. Rait (eds), *Acts and Ordinances of the Interregnum, 1642–1660* (HMSO, 1911)

Flannigan, Laura, 'Litigants in the English "Court of Poor Men's Causes," or Court of Requests, 1515–25', *Law and History Review*, 38(2) (2020): 303–37

Fletcher, Anthony, *Gender, Sex and Subordination in England 1500–1800* (Yale University Press, 1995)

Fouassier-Tate, Frédérique, 'Fact versus Fiction: The Construction of the Figure of the Prostitute in Early Modern England, Official and Popular Discourses', in Richard Hillman and Pauline Ruberry-Blanc (eds), *Female Transgression in Early Modern Britain: Literary and Historical Explorations* (Ashgate, 2014), pp. 71–89

Fox, Adam, *Oral and Literate Culture in England, 1500–1700* (Oxford University Press, 2000)

Fox, Adam, 'Popular Verses and Their Readership in the Early Seventeenth Century', in James Raven, Helen Small and Naomi Tadmor (eds), *The Practice and Representation of Reading in England* (Cambridge University Press, 1996), pp. 125–37

Foyster, Elizabeth, 'Male Honour, Social Control and Wife Beating in Late Stuart England', *Transactions of the Royal Historical Society*, 6 (1996): 215–24

Foyster, Elizabeth, *Marital Violence: An English Family History, 1660–1875* (2005; Cambridge University Press, 2009)

Foyster, Elizabeth, 'Marrying the Experienced Widow in Early Modern England: The Male Perspective', in Sandra Cavallo and Lyndan Warner (eds), *Widowhood in Medieval and Early Modern Europe* (Longman, 1999), pp. 108–24

Freeman, Thomas S., '"Imitatio Christi with a Vengeance": The Politicisation of Martyrdom in Early-Modern England', in Thomas S. Freeman and Thomas F. Mayer (eds), *Martyrs and Martyrdom in England c.1400–1700* (The Boydell Press, 2007), pp. 35–69

Freeman, Thomas S., 'The Scribal Culture of the Marian Martyrs', in Julia Crick and Alexandra Walsham (eds), *The Uses of Script and Print, 1300–1700* (Cambridge University Press, 2004), pp. 235–54

Freeman, Thomas S. and Sarah Elizabeth Wall, 'Racking the Body, Shaping the Text: The Account of Anne Askew in Foxe's "Book of Martyrs"', *Renaissance Quarterly*, 54(4) (2001): 1,165–96

French, Henry, 'Legal and Judicial Sources', in Laura Sangha and Jonathan Willis (eds), *Understanding Early Modern Primary Sources* (Routledge, 2016), pp. 35–57

Gaskill, Malcolm, *Crime and Mentalities in Early Modern England* (Cambridge University Press, 2000)

Gaskill, Malcolm, 'Reporting Murder: Fiction in the Archives in Early Modern England', *Social History*, 23(1) (1998): 1–30

Geng, Penelope, *Communal Justice in Shakespeare's England: Drama, Law, and Emotion* (University of Toronto Press, 2021)

Gertz, Genelle, *Heresy Trials and English Women Writers, 1400–1670* (Cambridge University Press, 2012)

Gibson, Marion, *Early Modern Witches: Witchcraft Cases in Contemporary Writing* (Routledge, 2000)

Gibson, Marion, *Reading Witchcraft: Stories of Early English Witches* (Routledge, 1999)

Glaser, Brigitte, *The Creation of the Self in Autobiographical Forms of Writing in Seventeenth-Century England: Subjectivity and Self-Fashioning in Memoirs, Diaries, and Letters* (C. Winter, 2001)

Goldberg, Jeremy, 'Echoes, Whispers, Ventriloquisms', in Bronach Kane and Fiona Williamson (eds) *Women, Agency and the Law, 1300–1700* (Pickering & Chatto, 2013), pp. 31–41

Gowing, Laura, *Common Bodies: Women, Touch and Power in Seventeenth-Century England* (Yale University Press, 2003)

Gowing, Laura, *Domestic Dangers: Women, Words, and Sex in Early Modern London* (Oxford University Press, 1996)

Gowing, Laura, 'Gender and the Language of Insult in Early Modern London', *History Workshop Journal*, 35 (1993): 1–21

Gowing, Laura, *Gender Relations in Early Modern England* (Routledge, 2014)

Gowing, Laura, *Ingenious Trade: Women and Work in Seventeenth-Century London* (Cambridge University Press, 2021)

Gowing, Laura, 'Secret Births and Infanticide in Seventeenth-Century England', *Past & Present*, 156 (1997): 87–115

Graham, Elspeth, 'Women's Writing and the Self', in Helen Wilcox (ed.), *Women and Literature in Britain 1500–1700* (Cambridge University Press, 1996), pp. 209–33

Graham, Elspeth, Hilary Hinds, Elaine Hobby and Helen Wilcox, 'Introduction', in Elspeth Graham, Hilary Hinds, Elaine Hobby and Helen Wilcox (eds), *Her Own Life: Autobiographical Writings by Seventeenth-Century Englishwomen* (1989; Routledge, 2005), pp. 1–25

Gray, Martin, *A Dictionary of Literary Terms* (Longman York Press, 1992)

Grazia, Margreta de and Stanley Wells (eds), *The New Cambridge Companion to Shakespeare* (Cambridge University Press, 2011)

Greenblatt, Stephen, *Renaissance Self-Fashioning: From More to Shakespeare* (University of Chicago Press, 1980)

Griffiths, Paul, *Lost Londons: Change, Crime, and Control in the Capital City, 1550–1660* (Cambridge University Press, 2008)

Griffiths, Paul, 'Punishing Words: Insults and Injuries, 1525–1700', in Angela McShane and Garthine Walker (eds), *The Extraordinary and the Everyday in Early Modern England: Essays in Celebration of the Work of Bernard Capp* (Palgrave Macmillan, 2010), pp. 66–85

Gusdorf, Georges, 'Conditions and Limits of Autobiography', trans. by James Olney, in James Olney (ed.), *Autobiography: Essays Theoretical and Critical* (Princeton University Press, 1980), pp. 28–48

Guy, J. A., *The Court of Star Chamber and Its Records of the Reign of Elizabeth I*, Public Record Office Handbooks, No. 21 (H. M. Stationery Office, 1985)

Habermann, Ina, *Staging Slander and Gender in Early Modern England* (Ashgate, 2003)

Haining, Peter, *The Witchcraft Papers: Contemporary Records of the Witchcraft Hysteria in Essex, 1560–1700* (Robert Hale & Company, 1974)

Hammons, Pamela S., *Gender, Sexuality, and Material Objects in English Renaissance Verse* (Ashgate, 2010)

Hammons, Pamela S., 'Introduction', in Katherine Austen, 'Book M', in Pamela S. Hammons (ed.), *Book M: A London Widow's Life Writings, Katherine Austen* (Iter, 2013), pp. 1–37

Hawkes, Emma, '"[S]he Wil . . . Protect and Defend Her Rights Boldly by Law and Reason . . .": Women's Knowledge of Common Law and Equity Courts in Late-Medieval England', in Noël James Menuge (ed.), *Medieval Women and the Law* (The Boydell Press, 2000), pp. 145–61

Hayes, Patrick, 'Human 2.0? Life-Writing in the Digital Age', in Zachary Leader (ed.), *On Life-Writing* (Oxford University Press, 2015), pp. 233–56

Heinzelman, Susan Sage and Zipporah Batshaw Wiseman, 'Preface', in Susan Sage Heinzelman and Zipporah Batshaw Wiseman (eds), *Representing Women: Law, Literature, and Feminism* (Duke University Press, 1994), pp. vii–ix

Helmholz, R. H., *The Profession of Ecclesiastical Lawyers: An Historical Introduction* (Cambridge University Press, 2019)

Herbert McAvoy, Liz, '"Wonderfully Turnyng & Wrestyng Hir Body": Agonies, Ecstasies, and Gendered Performances in *The Book of Margery Kempe*', in Margery Kempe, *The Book of Margery Kempe: An Abridged Translation*, ed. by Liz Herbert McAvoy (D. S. Brewer, 2003)

Hill, Lamar M., '"Extreame Detriment": Failed Credit and the Narration of Indebtedness in the Jacobean Court of Requests', in Buchanan Sharp and Mark Charles Fissel (eds), *Law and Authority in Early Modern England* (Rosemont Publishing, 2007), pp. 136–57

Hindle, Steve, *The State and Social Change in Early Modern England, 1550–1640* (Palgrave Macmillan, 2000)

Holdsworth, William, *A History of English Law*, Vol. IX (Methuen & Company, 1976)

Holmes, Rachel E., 'A Widow's Will: Adapting the Duchess of Amalfi in Early Modern England and Spain', *Studies in Philology*, 116(4) (2019): 728–57

Hopkins, Paul, 'Sir John Fenwick', *ODNB*

Houlbrooke, Ralph, *Church Courts and the People during the English Reformation, 1520–1570* (Oxford University Press, 1979)

Houlbrooke, Ralph, *The English Family 1450–1700* (Longman, 1984)

Howell, Martha, 'The Problem of Women's Agency in Medieval and Early Modern Europe', in Sarah Joan Moran and Amanda Pipkin (eds), *Women and Gender in the Early Modern Low Countries* (Brill, 2019), pp. 21–31

Hubbard, Eleanor, *City Women: Money, Sex, and the Social Order in Early Modern London* (Oxford University Press, 2012)

Hubbard, Eleanor, 'Reading, Writing, and Initialing: Female Literacy in Early Modern London', *Journal of British Studies*, 54 (2015): 553–77

Hudson, Judith, *Crime and Consequence in Early Modern Literature and Law* (Edinburgh University Press, 2021)

Hughes, Paul L. and James F. Larkin (eds), *Tudor Royal Proclamations*, Vol. 1 (Yale University Press, 1964)

Hurstfield, Joel, *The Queen's Wards: Wardship and Marriage under Elizabeth I*, 2nd ed. (1953; Frank Cass, 1973)

Hutson, Lorna, *The Invention of Suspicion. Law and Mimesis in Shakespeare and Renaissance Drama* (Oxford University Press, 2007)

Ingram, Martin, *Church Courts, Sex and Marriage in England, 1570–1640* (Cambridge University Press, 1987)

Ingram, Martin, 'Ridings, Rough Music and the "Reform of Popular Culture" in Early Modern England', *Past & Present*, 105 (1984): 79–113

Jackson, Charles, 'The Preface', Alice Wandesford Thornton, *The Autobiography of Alice Thornton: of East Newton, County, York* (Andrews and Co., 1875), pp. v–xv

Jackson, Mark, *New-Born Child Murder: Women, Illegitimacy and the Courts in Eighteenth-Century England* (Manchester University Press, 1996)

James, Susan E., *Women's Voices in Tudor Wills, 1485–1603* (Routledge, 2016)

Jardine, Lisa, '"Why Should He Call Her Whore?": Defamation and Desdemona's Case', in Margaret Tudeau-Clayton and Martin Warner (eds), *Addressing Frank Kermode: Essays in Criticism and Interpretation* (Macmillan, 1991), pp. 124–53

Jenkinson, Hilary, 'Elizabethan Handwritings: A Preliminary Sketch', *The Library*, 3(1) (1922): 1–50

Jones, W. J., *The Elizabethan Court of Chancery* (Clarendon Press, 1967)

Jordan, Jennifer, 'Her-story Untold: The Absence of Women's Agency in Constructing Concepts of Early Modern Manhood', *Cultural and Social History*, 4 (2007): 575–83

Juneja, Renu, 'The Widow as Paradox and Paradigm in Middleton's Plays', *The Journal of General Education*, 34(1) (1982): 3–19

Kane, Bronach C., *Popular Memory and Gender in Medieval England: Men, Women, and Testimony in the Church Courts, c.1200–1500* (The Boydell Press, 2019)

Kaplan, M. Lindsay, *The Culture of Slander in Early Modern England* (Cambridge University Press, 1997)

Kearns, Judith, 'Fashioning Innocence: Rhetorical Construction of Character in the Memoirs of Anne, Lady Halkett', *Texas Studies in Literature and Language*, 26(3) (2004): 340–62

Kelly, Philippa, Lloyd Davis, and Ronald Bedford, 'Introduction', in Ronald Bedford, Lloyd Davis, and Philippa Kelly (eds), *Early Modern Autobiography: Theories, Genres, Practices* (University of Michigan Press, 2006), pp. 1–16

Kermode, Jenny and Garthine Walker, 'Introduction', in Jenny Kermode and Garthine Walker (eds), *Women, Crime and the Courts in Early Modern England* (UCL Press, 1994), pp. 1–15

Kermode, Jenny and Garthine Walker (eds), *Women, Crime and the Courts in Early Modern England* (UCL Press, 1994)

Kesselring, K. J. and Tim Stretton, *Marriage, Separation, and Divorce in England, 1500–1700* (Oxford University Press, 2022)

Kestemont, Mike, Folgert Karsdorp, Elisabeth de Bruijn, Matthew Driscoll, Katarzyna A. Kapitan, Pádraig Ó Macháin, Daniel Sawyer, Remco Sleiderink and Anne Chao, 'Forgotten Books: The Application of Unseen Species Models to the Survival of Culture', *Science,* 375 (2022): 765–9

Kimura, Asuka, 'The Representation of Widows and Widowhood in English Drama, 1576–1642' (PhD dissertation, UCL, 2016)

Kinney, Arthur F., 'Introduction', in Thomas Dekker, John Ford and William Rowley, *The Witch of Edmonton*, ed. by Arthur F. Kinney (1998; A&C Black, 2005), pp. ix–xlii

Kugler, Anne, *Errant Plagiary: The Life and Writing of Lady Sarah Cowper, 1644–1720* (Stanford University Press, 2002)

Lake, Peter, 'Cheap Print, Protestantism and Murder', in Kevin Sharpe and Peter Lake (eds), *Culture and Politics in Early Stuart England* (Macmillan, 1994), pp. 257–83

Lake, Peter and Michael Questier, 'Agency, Appropriation and Rhetoric under the Gallows: Puritans, Romanists and the State in Early Modern England', *Past & Present,* 153 (1996): 64–107

Lake, Peter and Michael Questier, *The Trials of Margaret Clitherow: Persecution, Martyrdom and the Politics of Sanctity in Elizabethan England* (Continuum, 2011)

Lanum, Faith, 'Biography of Margaret Cunningham', *Perdita* online database

Lassiter, J. C., 'Defamation of Peers: The Rise and Decline of the Action for Scandalum Magnatum', 1497–1773', *American Journal of Legal History*, 22 (1978): 216–36

Leader, Zachary (ed.), *On Life-Writing* (Oxford University Press, 2015)

Levin, Carole and Patricia A. Sullivan (eds), *Political Rhetoric, Power and Renaissance Women* (State University of New York Press, 1995)

Levin, Carole and Patricia A. Sullivan, 'Politics, Women's Voices, and the Renaissance: Questions and Context', in Carole Levin and Patricia A. Sullivan (eds), *Political Rhetoric, Power and Renaissance Women* (State University of New York Press, 1995), pp. 1–14

Lewis, Katherine J., 'Women, Testamentary Discourse and Life-Writing in Later Medieval England', in Noël James Menuge (ed.), *Medieval Women and the Law* (The Boydell Press, 2000), pp. 57–76

Lipscomb, Suzannah, *The Voices of Nîmes: Women, Sex, and Marriage in Reformation Languedoc* (Oxford University Press, 2019)

Loftis, John (ed.), *The Memoirs of Anne, Lady Halkett and Ann, Lady Fanshawe* (Clarendon Press, 1979)

Longley, Katherine M., *Saint Margaret Clitherow* (Anthony Clarke, 1986)

Longley, Katherine M., 'The "Trial" of Margaret Clitherow', *Ampleforth Journal*, 75 (1970): 335–64

Luckyj, Christina, *'A Moving Rhetoricke', Gender and Silence in Early Modern England* (Manchester University Press, 2002)

Luckyj, Christina (ed.), *The Duchess of Malfi: A Critical Guide* (Continuum, 2011)

MacConochie, Alex, 'Touching on the Margins: Elizabeth Sawyer's Body in Performance and Print', Lisa Hopkins and Aidan Norrie (eds), *Women on the Edge in Early Modern Europe* (Amsterdam University Press, 2019), pp. 93–112

Macfarlane, Alan, *The Family Life of Ralph Josselin, a Seventeenth-Century Clergyman* (Cambridge University Press, 1970)

Mack, Phyllis, *Visionary Women: Ecstatic Prophecy in Seventeenth-Century England* (University of California Press, 1992)

Macnair, Michael R. T., *The Law of Proof in Early Modern Equity* (Duncker und Humblot, 1999)

Magnusson, Lynne, 'A Rhetoric of Requests: Genre and Linguistic Scripts in Elizabethan Women's Suitors' Letters', in James Daybell (ed.), *Women and Politics in Early Modern England, 1450–1700* (Ashgate, 2004)

Malay, Jessica L., 'Constructing a Narrative of Time and Place: Anne Clifford's *Great Books of Record*', *The Review of English Studies*, 66(277) (2015): 859–75

Malay, Jessica L., 'Introduction', in Anne Clifford, *Anne Clifford's Autobiographical Writing, 1590–1676*, ed. by Jessica L. Malay (Manchester University Press, 2018), pp. 1–14

Marcus, Leah S., 'The Duchess's Marriage in Contemporary Contexts', in Christina Luckyj (ed.), *The Duchess of Malfi: A Critical Guide* (Continuum, 2011), pp. 106–18

Martin, A. Lynn, *Alcohol, Sex, and Gender in Late Medieval and Early Modern Europe* (Palgrave Macmillan, 2001)

Martin, Randall, *Women, Murder, and Equity in Early Modern England* (Routledge, 2008)

Mason, Mary G., 'The Other Voice: Autobiographies of Women Writers', in James Olney (ed.), *Autobiography: Essays Theoretical and Critical* (Princeton University Press, 1980), pp. 207–35

Mason, Rebecca, 'Women, Marital Status, and Law: The Marital Spectrum in Seventeenth-Century Glasgow', *Journal of British Studies*, 58 (2019): 787–804

Matchinske, Megan, 'Serial Identity: History, Gender, and Form in the Diary Writing of Lady Anne Clifford', in Michelle M. Dowd and Julie A. Eckerle (eds), *Genre and Women's Life Writing in Early Modern England* (Ashgate, 2007), pp. 65–80

Matthews, William, *British Diaries: An Annotated Bibliography of British Diaries Written between 1442 and 1942* (Cambridge University Press, 1950)

May, Steven W. and Heather Wolfe, 'Manuscripts in Tudor England', in Kent Cartwright (ed.), *A Companion to Tudor Literature* (Wiley-Blackwell, 2010), pp. 125–39

McIlvenna, Una, *Singing the New of Death: Execution Ballads in Europe 1500–1900* (Oxford University Press, 2022)

McRae, Andrew, 'Reading Libels: An Introduction', *Huntington Library Quarterly*, 69(1) (2006): 1–14

McShane, Angela, '*The Gazet in Meter; or the Rhyming Newsmonger*. The English Broadside Ballad as Intelligencer. A New Narrative', in Joop W. Koopmans (ed.), *News and Politics in Early Modern Europe* (Peeters, 2005), pp. 131–46

McShane, Angela and Garthine Walker, 'Introduction: The Extraordinary and the Everyday in Early Modern England', in Angela McShane and Garthine Walker (eds), *The Extraordinary and the Everyday in Early Modern England: Essays in Celebration of the Work of Bernard Capp* (Palgrave Macmillan, 2010), pp. 1–5

Mendelson, Sara Heller, 'Stuart Women's Diaries and Occasional Memoirs', in Mary Prior (ed.), *Women in English Society 1500–1800* (Routledge, 1985), pp. 181–210

Meyer, Liam. J., '"Humblewise": Deference and Complaint in the Court of Requests', *Journal of Early Modern Studies*, 4 (2015): 261–85

Mirabella, Bella, 'Feminist Self-Fashioning: Christine de Pizan and *The Treasure of the City of Ladies*', *The European Journal of Women's Studies*, 6 (1999): 9–20

Molekamp, Femke, *Women and the Bible in Early Modern England: Religious Reading and Writing* (Oxford University Press, 2013)

Moore, Lindsay R., *Women before the Court: Law and Patriarchy in the Anglo-American World, 1600–1800* (Manchester University Press, 2019)

Morris, John (ed.), *The Troubles of Our Catholic Forefathers, Related by Themselves*, Vol. 3 (Burns and Oates, 1877)

Muir, Edward and Guido Ruggiero, 'Afterword: Crime and the Writing of History', in Edward Muir and Guido Ruggiero (eds), *History from Crime*, trans. by Corrada Biazzo Curry, Margaret A. Gallucci and Mary M. Gallucci (Johns Hopkins University Press, 1994), pp. 226–36

Mukherji, Subha, *Law and Representation in Early Modern Drama* (Cambridge University Press, 2006)

Muldrew, Craig, *The Economy of Obligation: The Culture of Credit and Social Relations in Early Modern England* (Macmillan, 1998)

Murphy, Jeffrie G., *Punishment and the Moral Emotions: Essays in Law, Morality, and Religion* (Oxford University Press, 2012)

Nandi, Miriam, *Reading the Early Modern English Diary* (Palgrave Macmillan, 2021)

Norbrook, David, 'Lucy Hutchinson's "Elegies" and the Situation of the Republican Woman Writer', *English Literary Renaissance*, 27(3) (1993): 468–521

Nussbaum, Felicity A., *The Autobiographical Subject: Gender and Ideology in Eighteenth-Century England* (Johns Hopkins University Press, 1989)

Nuttall, A. D., '"Measure for Measure": The Bed-Trick', *Shakespeare Survey*, 28 (1975): 51–6

O'Hara, Diana, '"Ruled by my Friends": Aspects of Marriage in the Diocese of Canterbury, *c.* 1540–1570', *Continuity and Change*, 6(1) (1991): 9–41

Olney, James (ed.), *Autobiography: Essays Theoretical and Critical* (Princeton University Press, 1980)

Olson, Rebecca, 'The Continuing Adventures of Blanchardyn and Eglantine: Responsible Speculation about Early Modern Fan Fiction', *PMLA*, 134(2) (2019): 298–315

Ottway, Sheila, 'They Only Lived Twice: Public and Private Selfhood in the Autobiographies of Anne, Lady Halkett and Colonel Joseph Bampfield', in Henk Dragstra, Sheila Ottway and Helen Wilcox (eds), *Betraying Our Selves: Forms of Self-Representation in Early Modern English Texts* (Palgrave, 2000), pp. 136–47.

Outhwaite, R. B., *Clandestine Marriage in England, 1500–1850* (The Hambledon Press, 1995)

Panek, Jennifer, '"This Base Stallion Trade": He-Whores and Male Sexuality on the Early Modern Stage', *English Literary Renaissance*, 40(3) (2010): 357–92

Pearsall Smith, Logan (ed.), *The Life and Letters of Sir Henry Wotton*, Vol. 2 (Clarendon Press, 1907)

Peck, Imogen, '"For the dead Fathers sake"? Orphans, Petitions and the British Civil Wars, 1647–1679', in Waddell and Peacey (eds), *The Power of Petitioning*, pp. 143–68

Pender, Patricia, 'Reading Bale Reading Anne Askew: Contested Collaboration in The Examinations', *Huntington Library Quarterly*, 73(3) (2010): 507–22

Peters, Christine, *Patterns of Piety: Women, Gender and Relation in Late Medieval and Reformation England* (Cambridge University Press, 2003)

Peters, Kate, '"Friction in the Archives": Access and the Politics of Record-Keeping in Revolutionary England', in Kate Peters, Alexandra Walsham and Liesbeth Corens (eds), *Archives and Information in the Early Modern World* (Oxford University Press, 2018), pp. 151–76

Phipps, Teresa and Deborah Youngs (eds), *Litigating Women: Gender and Justice in Europe, c.1300–c.1800* (Routledge, 2021)

Pohlig, Veronika Christine, 'Adultery in Early Stuart England' (PhD dissertation, Freie Universität Berlin, 2009)

Pomerleau, Cynthia S., 'The Emergence of Women's Autobiography in England', in Estelle Jelinek (ed.), *Women's Autobiography: Essays in Criticism* (Indiana University Press, 1980), pp. 21–38

Powell, Jonathan, '"Scarce expressible in English": Theatre and the Common Law, c.1597–1624', (PhD dissertation, King's College London, 2022)

Prest, Wilfrid P., *The Rise of the Barristers: A Social History of the English Bar 1590–1640* (Clarendon Press, 1986)

Price, Vicki Kay, '"Twoo Muche Vayne and Idle Chardge": The Precision of Inheritance in the 1601 Will of Bess of Hardwick', *Law & Literature*, (2021): doi.org/10.1080/1535685X.2021.1902639

Probert, Rebecca, *Marriage Law and Practice in the Long Eighteenth Century: A Reassessment* (Cambridge University Press, 2009)

Pryor, Felix, *Elizabeth I: Her Life in Letters* (University of California Press, 2003)

Purkiss, Diane, *The English Civil War: A People's History* (Harper Perennial, 2007)

Purkiss, Diane, *The Witch in History: Early Modern and Twentieth-Century Representations* (Routledge, 1996)

Quaife, G. R., *Wanton Wenches and Wayward Wives: Peasants and Illicit Sex in Early Seventeenth Century England* (Croom Helm, 1979)

Quintrell, Brian, 'Montagu, Henry, first earl of Manchester', *ODNB*

Raymond, Joad, *Pamphlets and Pamphleteering in Early Modern Britain* (Cambridge University Press, 2003)

Reichardt, Dosia, 'The Constitution of Narrative Identity in Seventeenth-Century Prison Writing', in Ronald Bedford, Lloyd Davis and Philippa Kelly (eds), *Early Modern Autobiography: Theories, Genres, Practices* (University of Michigan Press, 2006), pp. 115–30

Richards, Jennifer, 'The Voice of Anne Askew', *Journal of the Northern Renaissance*, 9 (2017)

Richardson, Catherine, *Domestic Life and Domestic Tragedy in Early Modern England: The Material Life of the Household* (Manchester University Press, 2006)

Rickman, Johanna, *Love, Lust, and License in Early Modern England: Illicit Sex and the Nobility* (Ashgate, 2008)

Rogers, D. M. (ed.), *English Recusant Literature, 1558–1640*, Vol. 393 (Scolar Press, 1979)

Roper, Lyndal, *Oedipus & the Devil: Witchcraft, Sexuality and Religion in Early Modern Europe* (Routledge, 1994)

Ross, Sarah C. E., 'Introduction', in Katherine Austen, *Book M: British Library, Additional Manuscript 4454*, ed. by Sarah C. E. Ross (ACMRS, 2011), pp. 1–47

Ross, Sarah C. E., '"Like Penelope, Always Employed": Reading, Life-Writing, and the Early Modern Female Self in Katherine Austen's Book M', *Literature Compass*, 9(4) (2012): 306–16

Rubery-Blanc, Pauline, '*The Witch of Edmonton*: The Witch next Door or Faustian Anti-Heroine?', in Richard Hillman and Pauline Rubery-Blanc (eds), *Female Transgression in Early Modern Britain: Literary and Historical Explorations* (Ashgate, 2014), pp. 51–69

Sale, Carolyn, 'Contested Acts: Legal Performances and Literary Authority in Early Modern England' (PhD dissertation, Stanford University, 2002)

Sale, Carolyn, 'The "Roman Hand": Women, Writing and the Law in the *Att.-Gen. V. Chatterton* and the Letters of the Lady Arbella Stuart', *English Literary History*, 70(4) (2003): 929–61

Salter, Elisabeth, 'Women's Last Wills and Testaments in Hull, England (c.1450–1550)', *Early Modern Women*, 12(2) (2018): 33–53

Salzman, Paul, 'Introduction', in Paul Salzman (ed.), *Early Modern Women's Writing: An Anthology, 1560–1700* (Oxford University Press, 2000), pp. ix–xxxi

Shapin, Steven, *A Social History of Truth: Civility and Science in Seventeenth-Century England* (University of Chicago Press, 1994)

Shapin, Steven and Simon Schaffer, *Leviathan and the Air-Pump: Hobbes, Boyle, and the Experimental Life* (Princeton University Press, 1985)

Shapiro, Barbara J., *A Culture of Fact: England, 1550–1720* (Cornell University Press, 2000)

Shapiro, Barbara J., 'Oaths, Credibility and the Legal Process in Early Modern England: Part One', *Law and Humanities*, 6 (2012): 145–68

Sharp, Buchanan and Mark Charles Fissel (eds), *Law and Authority in Early Modern England* (Rosemont Publishing, 2007)

Sharpe, J. A., *Defamation and Sexual Slander in Early Modern England: The Church Courts at York*, Borthwick Papers no. 58 (Borthwick Publications, 1980)

Sharpe, James, *Instruments of Darkness: Witchcraft in Early Modern England* (University of Pennsylvania Press, 1996)

Sharpe, James, 'The People and the Law', in Barry Reay (ed.), *Popular Culture in Seventeenth-Century England* (Croon Helm, 1985), pp. 244–70

Sharpe, Kevin and Peter Lake (eds), *Culture and Politics in Early Stuart England* (Macmillan, 1994)

Shepard, Alexandra, *Accounting for Oneself: Worth, Status, and the Social Order in Early Modern England* (Oxford University Press, 2015)

Shepard, Alexandra, *Meanings of Manhood in Early Modern England* (Oxford University Press, 2003)

Sherlock, Peter, 'Monuments and Memory', in Patricia Phillippy (ed.), *A History of Early Modern Women's Writing* (Cambridge University Press, 2018), pp. 292–311

Shugg, Wallace, 'Prostitution in Shakespeare's London', *Shakespeare Studies*, 10 (1997): 291–313

Simonton, Deborah, 'Community of Goods, Coverture and Capability in Britain: Scotland versus England', in Anna Bellavitis and Beatrice Zucca Micheletto (eds), *Gender, Law and Economic Well-Being in Europe from the Fifteenth to the Nineteenth Century: North versus South?* (Routledge, 2019), pp. 31–46

Skinner, Quentin, *Forensic Shakespeare* (Oxford University Press, 2014)

Skura, Meredith Anne, *Tudor Autobiography: Listening for Inwardness* (University of Chicago Press, 2008)

Smith, Helen, *'Grossly Material Things': Women and Book Production in Early Modern England* (Oxford University Press, 2012)

Smith, Sidonie, *A Poetics of Women's Autobiography: Marginality and the Fictions of Self-Representation* (Indiana University Press, 1987)

Smith, Sidonie and Julia Watson, *Reading Autobiography: A Guide for Interpreting Life Narratives*, 2nd ed. (University of Minnesota Press, 2010)

Smyth, Adam, *Autobiography in Early Modern England* (Cambridge University Press, 2010)

Smyth, Adam, 'Introduction: The Range, Limits, and Potentials of the Form', in Adam Smyth (ed.), *A History of English Autobiography* (Cambridge University Press, 2016), pp. 1–10

Sokol, B. J. and Mary Sokol, *Shakespeare, Law, and Marriage* (Cambridge University Press, 2003)

Spence, Cathryn, '"For his interest"? Women, Debt and Coverture in Early Modern Scotland', in Cordelia Beattie and Matthew Frank Stevens (eds), *Married Women and the Law in Premodern Northwest Europe* (The Boydell Press, 2013), pp. 173–90

Spence, Richard T., 'Clifford, Anne', *ODNB*

Spence, Richard T., *Lady Anne Clifford, Countess of Pembroke, Dorset and Montgomery (1590–1676)* (Sutton Publishing, 1997)

Spring, Eileen, *Law, Land, & Family: Aristocratic Inheritance in England, 1300 to 1800* (University of North Carolina Press, 1993)

Stanford Friedman, Susan, 'Women's Autobiographical Selves: Theory and Practice', in Sidonie Smith and Julia Watson (eds), *Women, Autobiography, Theory: a Reader* (University of Wisconsin Press, 1998), pp. 72–82

Stavreva, Kirilka, *Words Like Daggers: Violent Female Speech in Early Modern England* (University of Nebraska Press, 2015)

Stewart, Alan, *The Oxford History of Life-Writing*, Vol. 2 Early Modern (Oxford University Press, 2018)

Stokes, Charity Scott, 'Last Years, Re-drafting of Liber I, Writing of Liber II', *Mystics Quarterly*, 25 (1999): 45–6

Stoler, Ann, *Along the Archival Grain: Epistemic Anxieties and Colonial Common Sense* (Princeton University Press, 2008)

Stone, Lawrence, *Road to Divorce: England 1530–1987* (Oxford University Press, 1990)

Stretton, Tim, *Marital Litigation in the Court of Requests, 1542–1642* (Cambridge University Press, 2008)

Stretton, Tim, 'Women, Legal Records, and the Problem of the Lawyer's Hand', *Journal of British Studies*, 58 (2019): 684–700

Stretton, Tim, 'Women, Property and Law', in Anita Pacheco (ed.), *Early Modern Women's Writing* (Blackwell, 2002), pp. 40–57

Stretton, Tim, *Women Waging Law in Elizabethan England* (Cambridge University Press, 1998)

Stretton, Tim and Krista J. Kesselring, 'Introduction: Coverture and Continuity', in Tim Stretton and Krista J. Kesselring (eds), *Married Women and the Law: Coverture in England and the Common Law World* (McGill-Queen's University Press, 2013), pp. 3–23

Strohm, Paul, *The Poet's Tale: Chaucer and the Year that Made the Canterbury Tales* (Profile Books, 2014)

Suzuki, Mihoko, 'Daughters of Coke: Women's Legal Discourse in England, 1642–1689', in Sigrun Haude and Melinda S. Zook (eds), *Challenging Orthodoxies: The Social and Cultural Worlds of Early Modern Women* (Ashgate, 2014), pp. 165–92

Syme, Holger Schott, *Theatre and Testimony in Shakespeare's England* (Cambridge University Press, 2012)

Taylor, Gary and John Lavagnino (eds), *Thomas Middleton: The Collected Works* (Clarendon Press, 2010)

Taylor, Hillary, 'The Price of the Poor's Words: Social Relations and the Economics of Deposing for One's "Betters" in Early Modern England', *Economic History Review*, 72(3) (2019): 828–47

Thomas, Keith, *Religion and the Decline of Magic: Studies in Popular Beliefs in Sixteenth and Seventeenth Century England* (1971; Weidenfeld and Nicolson, 1980)

Thomas, Keith, 'The Double Standard', *Journal of the History of Ideas*, 20 (1959): 195–216

Thomas, Keith, 'The Puritans and Adultery: The Act of 1650 Reconsidered', in Donald Pennington and Keith Thomas (eds), *Puritans and Revolutionaries: Essays in Seventeenth-Century History Presented to Christopher Hill* (Clarendon Press, 1978), pp. 257–82

Thompson, Anne, *Parish Clergy Wives in Elizabethan England* (Brill, 2019)

Todd, Barbara J., 'The Remarrying Widow: A Stereotype Reconsidered', in Mary Prior (ed.), *Women in English Society 1500–1800* (Routledge, 1985), pp. 54–92

Todd, Barbara J., 'The Virtuous Widow in Protestant England', in Sandra Cavallo and Lyndan Warner (eds), *Widowhood in Medieval and Early Modern Europe* (Longman, 1999), pp. 66–83

Traub, Valerie, *Thinking Sex with the Early Moderns* (University of Pennsylvania Press, 2016)

Trill, Suzanne, 'Beyond Romance? Re-Reading the "Lives" of Anne, Lady Halkett (1621/2?–1699)', *Literature Compass*, 6(2) (2009): 446–59

Trill, Suzanne, 'Introduction', in Suzanne Trill (ed.), *Lady Anne Halkett: Selected Self-Writings* (Ashgate, 2007), pp. xvii–xlii

Trill, Suzanne, 'Religion and the Construction of Femininity', in Helen Wilcox (ed.), *Women and Literature in Britain, 1500–1700* (Cambridge University Press, 1996), pp. 30–55

Trill, Suzanne, '"We Thy Sydnean Psalmes Shall Celebrate": Collaborative Authorship, Sidney's Sister and the English Devotional Lyric', in Susan Wiseman (ed.), *Early Modern Women and the Poem* (Manchester University Press, 2013), pp. 97–116

Trill, Suzanne (ed.), *Lady Anne Halkett: Selected Self-Writings* (Ashgate, 2007)

Truelove, Alison, 'Commanding Communications: The Fifteenth-Century Letters of the Stonor Women', in James Daybell (ed.), *Early Modern Women's Letter Writing, 1450–1700* (Palgrave, 2001), pp. 42–58

Trull, Mary E., *Performing Privacy and Gender in Early Modern Literature* (Palgrave Macmillan, 2013)
Tudeau-Clayton, Margaret and Martin Warner (eds), *Addressing Frank Kermode: Essays in Criticism and Interpretation* (Macmillan, 1991)
Turner, David M., *Fashioning Adultery: Gender, Sex and Civility in England, 1600–1740* (Cambridge University Press, 2002)
Veerapen, Steven, 'Slander and Sedition in Elizabethan Law, Speech and Writing' (PhD dissertation, University of Strathclyde, 2014)
Waddell, Brodie and Jason Peacey (eds), *The Power of Petitioning in Early Modern Britain* (UCL Press, 2024)
Wadham, Juliana, 'Saint Margaret Clitherow: Her Trial on Trial: The Case against Her by Juliana Wadham', *Ampleforth Journal*, 76 (1971): 9–22
Walker, Garthine, *Crime, Gender and Social Order in Early Modern England* (Cambridge University Press, 2003)
Walker, Garthine, 'Just Stories: Telling Tales of Infant Death in Early Modern England', in Margaret Mikesell and Adele Seeff (eds), *Culture and Change: Attending to Early Modern Women* (Associated University Presses, 2003), pp. 98–115
Walker, Garthine, '"Strange Kind of Stealing": Abduction in Early Modern Wales', in Michael Roberts and Simone Clark (eds), *Women and Gender in Early Modern Wales* (University of Wales Press, 2000), pp. 50–74
Walker, Garthine, 'The Strangeness of the Familiar: Witchcraft and the Law in Early Modern England', in Angela McShane and Garthine Walker (eds), *The Extraordinary and the Everyday in Early Modern England: Essays in Celebration of the Work of Bernard Capp* (Palgrave Macmillan, 2010), pp. 105–24
Walker, Sue Sheridan, 'Widow and Ward: The Feudal Law of Child Custody in Medieval England', in Susan Mosher Stuard (ed.), *Women in Medieval Society* (University of Pennsylvania Press, 1976), pp. 159–72
Wall, Alison D. (ed.), *Two Elizabethan Women: Correspondence of Joan and Maria Thynne, 1575–1611* (Wiltshire Record Society, 1983)
Wall, Wendy, *The Imprint of Gender: Authorship and Publication in the English Renaissance* (Cornell University Press, 1993)
Walsham, Alexandra, 'The Social History of the Archive: Record-Keeping in Early Modern Europe', *Past & Present*, Supplement 11 (2016): 9–48
Walter, John, '"Law-Mindedness": Crowds, Courts and Popular Knowledge of the Law in Early Modern England', in Michael Lobban, Joanne Begatio and Adrian Green (eds), *Law, Lawyers and Litigants in Early Modern England: Essays in Memory of Christopher W. Brooks* (Cambridge University Press, 2019), pp. 164–84
Walton, Douglas, *One-Sided Arguments, a Dialectical Analysis of Bias* (State University of New York, 1999)
Walton, Douglas, *Witness Testimony Evidence: Argumentation, Artificial Intelligence, and Law* (Cambridge University Press, 2008)

Wayne, Valerie, 'Introduction', in Valerie Wayne (ed.), *Women's Labour and the History of the Book in Early Modern England* (The Arden Shakespeare, 2020), pp. 1–26

Wayne, Valerie (ed.), *Women's Labour and the History of the Book in Early Modern England* (The Arden Shakespeare, 2020)

Wiesner, Merry E., *Women and Gender in Early Modern Europe* (Cambridge University Press, 2000)

Wilcox, Helen, '"Free and Easy as Ones Discourse"?: Genre and Self-Expression in the Poems and Letters of Early Modern Englishwomen', in Michelle M. Dowd and Julie A. Eckerle (eds), *Genre and Women's Life Writing in Early Modern England* (Ashgate, 2007), pp. 15–32

Williams, Sarah F., *Damnable Practises: Witches, Dangerous Women, and Music in Seventeenth-Century English Broadside Ballads* (Ashgate, 2015)

Windeatt, Barry, 'Medieval Life-Writing: Types, Encomia, Exemplars, Patterns', in Adam Smyth (ed.), *A History of English Autobiography* (Cambridge University Press, 2016), pp. 13–26

Wiseman, Susan, *Conspiracy and Virtue: Women, Writing, and Politics in Seventeenth-Century England* (Oxford University Press, 2006)

Wiseman, Susan, 'The Contemplative Woman's Recreation? Katherine Austen and the Estate Poem', in Susan Wiseman (ed.), *Early Modern Women and the Poem* (Manchester University Press, 2013), pp. 220–43

Wiseman, Susan, 'Elizabeth Delaval's *Memoirs and Meditations*: Textual Transmission and Jacobite Context', *Early Modern Women: An Interdisciplinary Journal*, 10(1) (2015): 68–92

Wiseman, Susan, '"The Most Considerable of My Troubles": Anne Halkett and the Writing of Civil War Conspiracy', in Jo Wallwork and Paul Salzman (eds), *Women Writing, 1550–1750* (Meridian, 2001), pp. 25–45

Worthen, Hannah, 'The Process and Practice of Petitioning in Early Modern England', in Waddell and Peacey (eds), *The Power of Petitioning*, pp. 61–82

Woudhuysen, H. R., 'Shakespeare's Writing: From Manuscript to Print', in Margreta de Grazia and Stanley Wells (eds), *The New Cambridge Companion to Shakespeare* (Cambridge University Press, 2011), pp. 31–44

Wray, Ramona, 'Autobiography', in Laura Knoppers (ed.), *The Cambridge Companion to Early Modern Women's Writing* (Cambridge University Press, 2009), pp. 194–207

Wright, Nancy E., 'Accounting for a Life: The Household Accounts of Lady Anne Clifford', in Ronald Bedford, Lloyd Davis and Philippa Kelly, *Early Modern Autobiography: Theories, Genres, Practices* (University of Michigan Press, 2006), pp. 234–51

Youngs, Deborah, '"A Besy Woman . . . and Full of Lawe": Female Litigants in Early Stuart Star Chamber', *Journal of British Studies*, 58(4) (2019): 735–50

Zimmermann, T. C. Price, 'Confession and Autobiography in the Early Renaissance', in Anthony Molho and John A. Tedeschi (eds), *Renaissance Studies in Honor of Hans Baron* (Northern Illinois University Press, 1971), pp. 119–40

Index

EU Authorised Representative:
Easy Access System Europe Mustamäe tee 50, 10621 Tallinn, Estonia
gpsr.requests@easproject.com

Printed and bound by CPI Group (UK) Ltd, Croydon, CR0 4YY
29/09/2026
02224981-0009